D1428888

The Chap-Book

**A Journal of
American Intellectual Life
in the 1890s**

Studies in
American History and Culture, No. 35

Robert Berkhofer, Series Editor

Director of American Culture Programs
and Richard Hudson Research Professor of History
The University of Michigan

Other Titles in This Series

The Chap-Book
A Journal of
American Intellectual Life
in the 1890s

by
Wendy Clauson Schlereth

UMI RESEARCH PRESS
Ann Arbor, Michigan

Copyright © 1980, 1982
Wendy Clauson Schlereth
All rights reserved

Produced and distributed by
UMI Research Press
an imprint of
University Microfilms International
Ann Arbor, Michigan 48106

Library of Congress Cataloging in Publication Data

Schlereth, Wendy Clauson.
The Chap-book.

(Studies in American history and culture ; no. 35)
Revision of thesis (Ph.D.)—University of Iowa, 1980.
Bibliography: p.
Includes index.
1. Chap-book. 2. United States—Intellectual life—
1865-1918.   I. Title. II. Series.
PN4900.C49S3 1982   051   81-16337
ISBN 0-8357-1278-8   AACR2

For my father

[Frank Hazenplug,] / Untitled illustration for W. B. Yeats, "S. Patrick and the Pedants," *The Chap-Book,* vol. V, no. 2 (June 1, 1896), 50.

Contents

Acknowledgments

Many years accumulated many debts in the researching and writing of this study. Professor Stow Persons, of the University of Iowa, was constant in his support of my work, even when other responsibilities delayed its completion; and Professor Sherman Paul read this manuscript with the same care which he took with all my other work. From both these men—from their teaching, scholarship and personal examples—I learned a great deal.

I also benefited from the sources and support of a number of institutions and individuals. The University of Iowa was generous in supplying me with all the necessary resources to pursue my studies. The Harvard University Archives held particular treasures necessary for the completion of this research, and I am grateful for their permission to use these materials. The Newberry Library offered me its books, periodicals, manuscripts, a research fellowship, and the much appreciated help of John Aubrey and Diana Haskell. The University of Notre Dame granted me special privileges regarding the use of its copies of *The Chap-Book*, and I am especially grateful to Anton Masin, Curator of Rare Books, for these favors. Notre Dame not only put the magazine at my disposal, it gave me the time I needed to pursue my research and writing: I am especially grateful to Rev. Thomas E. Blantz, C.S.C., Rev. Theodore M. Hesburgh, C.S.C., Professor Timothy O'Meara, and Rev. Ferdinand Brown, C.S.C. for their support. My secretary, Teresa A. Tincher, deserves many thanks for protecting me from intrusions that could have wrecked my leave of absence, and also for typing the final copy of my manuscript.

My other debts are personal. I trust that friends and family know how much a part they were of the process of writing this piece, just as they are of most everything I do. But one among them deserves special credit for his support and encouragement of my work. If during the past several years it has seemed as if I've eaten and slept with *The Chap-Book*, so has he. To my husband, Thomas J. Schlereth, I owe my greatest thanks.

1

Misconceptions of a Mind
and a Magazine

A little magazine has come to represent for modern readers, seemingly by self-definition, a curious experiment in providing something different from what is available and deemed acceptable in established periodical literature. *The Chap-Book*, published successively by the young firms of Stone & Kimball and Herbert S. Stone & Co., 1894–1898, has often been heralded as the progenitor of this literary tradition in America. It was new, it looked different, and it was almost instantaneously hailed by numerous imitators as their inspiration for deviation from traditional literary conventions.

This "first" of America's little magazines, upon its own self-reflection and as seen by later scholars, was not, however, nearly so experimental as first appearances seemed to indicate. It was, in fact, very much a product of what detractors came to call the establishment culture. It was begun by two young Harvard undergraduates, neither decadents nor aesthetes, and found its initial support from among the members of the larger Cambridge intellectual community. Within six-months' time it was removed to Stone's and Kimball's hometown of Chicago and came to play an important part in "The Upward Movement" of Chicago's cultural elite.

As a journal that enjoyed the somewhat paradoxical distinction of operating as both a literary rebel and a respected member of the intellectual establishment, *The Chap-Book* provides us now with something more significant than simply its debatable role as a periodical promulgator of the avant-garde. Precisely because it was neither exclusively advanced nor conforming, its pages served as a proving ground for new ideas, testing them against firmly established and acceptable norms. The following examination of the intellectual context of this journal, the individuals associated with it, and especially the content of its pages, provides the historian with a perspective on American intellectual life at the turn of the last century.

An end of a century, much like the culmination of some cataclysmic event, easily lends itself to generalizations regarding the periodization of history: one specific time period is ending, another is beginning. Contemporaries in the 1890s, accustomed to the organic rhetoric of the nineteenth century, quite naturally fell into a pattern of defining their era through the use of terms associated with natural life cycles. As the century drew to a close, its life was ending. "Fin de siècle," a seemingly impartial description of a chronological sequence, was used then as now to connote more than the mere passage of time. It became an opprobrious epithet, a synonym for "decadence" describing the effects of old age. The cultural life that the nineteenth century had nurtured was now in an advanced state of decay.

One of the most popular treatises of the day was Max Nordau's inflammatory study *Degeneration*, which purported to analyze scientifically the state of mind known as "fin de siècle." Nordau claimed its victims, divorced from any vital contact with reality, had succumbed to "the disposition of the mystically degenerate mind, with its shifting nebulous ideas, its fleeting formless shadowy thought, its perversions and aberrations, its tribulations and impulsions." While it had first manifested itself in France, by the time of his writing in 1895 it was "everywhere to be met with." For expression, it was forced to create its own language to describe a reality which, in Nordau's mind, did not exist. "This debauch in pathological and nauseous ideas of a deranged mind with gustatory perversion is a delirium, and has no foundation whatever in philological facts."[1]

Nordau and many of his contemporaries believed that this "fin de siècle" malaise was the particular property of those writers, artists and intellectuals who had deviated from the healthy and natural cultural norms of the nineteenth century. The Symbolists, otherwise known as the Decadents, bore the brunt of these attacks, as they experimented with language's conscious and unconscious symbolistic values, espoused mysticism, and annihilated traditional forms of truth and beauty. But while Nordau saw these "fin de siècle" writers as evolutionary freaks or misfits doomed to extinction, literary criticism in the twentieth century has tended to view them as the logical heirs of the transcendental Romantic tradition which had dominated a large part of the nineteenth century's intellectual life.[2] Their ideas, at the century's end, marked the culmination of one strain of thought that was to have no animate role in the new century.[3] It was not only the Decadents and their "fin de siècle" notions that were doomed, but also many of the most cherished ideals of a moribund literary establishment. What was passed was finished, dead; what was to come would be new and different.

A new world was seemingly waiting to be born with the advent of a new century. Henry Adams claimed that in 1900 "the continuity" of history "snapped." All children born after that "cataclysmic" date would have to grow and be educated to live in a new world.[4] This modern era was to be characterized by a pragmatic devotion to science, and its literary practitioners would probe life's meaning by exploring reality purged of all spiritual fantasies. Transcendental values were meaningless in a world seeking to affirm existence's realities in what was tangible, verifiable and immanently knowable.

If 1900 was to mark the birth of a new and different intellectual life, the 1890s might have been its period of gestation. Grant Knight has termed the decade "critical" in determining the future growth of this country's literary production; and his language emphasizes the distinct differences that separated the old century's state of mind from modern life: "in those years the makers of our literature, standing at a point of decision, had to choose whether to perpetuate the old romanticism through practice and censorship, the experiment with decadence and symbolism, which were the newer European fashions, or to adopt a realism which had made little headway in this country during the nineteenth century."[5] Particular note should be taken of the fact that Knight stresses the existence of "a point of decision" when Americans "had to choose" between the literature of the nineteenth century and that which was to become the literature of the twentieth century, literature which the older tradition had refused to foster while it remained in control. Like Adams, he sees the continuity of the past snapped with the new imperative to choose a different direction.

This fascination with marking the end of the century as an identifiable turning point in American life has continued among scholars, playing an important role in determining their interpretations of our intellectual life. Henry Commager, in his 1950 exposition of the American mind, called the nineties a "watershed," and more recently John Higham identified the decade as a period of "cultural reorientation" that amounted to an actual "revolution" for American intellectuals.[6] Though really only a highly artificial boundary of time, the end of one century has come to delineate an important intellectual division in our collective consciousness. The twentieth century was a "new" time and called for new ideas.

Changing critical assessments of the nature of one magazine of the period, *The Chap-Book*, and of its role in determining (or, more modestly, reflecting) the future direction of American literary thought, fall into a predictable pattern of judgments on both sides of the old versus new life controversy. When *The Chap-Book* first appeared it was hailed by contemporaries as something daring, modern and different. It was to be the spokesman of the new order. On its own pages it trumpeted its early press notices: "a little Jack-the-Giant-Killer in literature" (*The Boston Transcript*); "the most unique of all the magazines ever published" (*The Boston Times*); "the medium of communicating to the public all that is most modern and aggressive in the Young Man's literature" (*The New York Tribune*); and "an entertaining and frankly modern assemblage of the fads and fashions in ideas today" (*The Portland Oregonion*).[7] This magazine was distinctly not the same old thing in periodical literature, and the editors used public recognition of this fact as a means of advertising their publication.

One reason why *The Chap-Book* struck contemporaries as so new and so modern undoubtedly was its appearance. It looked different. At a time when most journals conformed to a size of roughly 12" × 8", *The Chap-Book* attracted attention by the fact that it was a mere 7½" × 4½". Printed with bold black and red ink in Janson type on heavy, uncut paper, and illustrated largely by specially designed woodcuts in black and white, it did present a striking and handsome appearance (and does to this day). A contemporary, reminiscing about the art of printing in the nineties and *The Chap-Book* in particular, writes: "No younger man can fully appreciate the impact of that simple and casual little magazine on a world of stodgy and commonplace printing. It turned attention toward the relation of type to the things printed with it."[8] What looked new to the eye was thought to be new to the mind as well.

This supposed integral relation between content and aesthetic form has played a large part in determining *The Chap-Book*'s critical reputation over the years. Writing about the early numbers of *The Chap-Book*, Frank L. Mott, historian of American magazines, noted: "the liveliness and sharp originality of its contents and the distinction of its format and typography made the little magazine immediately popular among the elite, and it was soon an important undertaking itself."[9] A detailed examination of the nature of *The Chap-Book*'s contents follows later in this study, but for the moment it is important to note that Mott's assessment regarding both form and content of the early numbers of this magazine is one that has been generally supported by other scholars, who have taken their cue from contemporary readers.

Leader of the pack in acknowledging the impact of *The Chap-Book*'s appearance on periodical literature of the 1890s was a rival publisher, Gelett Burgess. Editor of San Francisco's avowedly rebellious and short-lived (May 1, 1895–May 1, 1897) little magazine, *The Lark*, Burgess credited *The Chap-Book* with being the inspiration for his own publication and numerous others. In his mind, deviation from accepted forms went hand-in-glove with radical content.

The success of the 'Chap Book' incited the little riot of Decadence, and there was a craze for odd sizes and shapes, freak illustrations, wide margins, uncut pages, Janson types, scurrilous abuse and petty jealousies, impossible prose and doggerel rhyme. The movement asserted itself as a revolt against the commonplace; it aimed to over-throw the staid respectability of the larger magazines and to open to younger writers opportunites to be heard before they had obtained recognition from the autocratic editors [of the standard journals].[10]

Complaints had become frequent that the standard journals of the day, wedded to canons of literary conformity, were not living up to their true function of being, in Hamlin Garland's words, "the greatest outlet for distinctive American art."[11] Frank Munsey later noted, to the staff of *Munsey's Magazine*, that by 1891 American magazines "seemed made for anaemics and their editors editing for themselves and not their sub-scribers."[12] This judgment that the leading journals of the day lacked essential qualities of vitality has been corroborated by recent scholarship: "The irregularities of personal feeling had been pumice-stoned to a dismal level. Individuality and private opinion had disappeared in favor of a ho-mogenized pap which offended none, but which also enlightened and enriched none."[13]

Whatever were the causes for such complaints, or even their justifi-cation, *The Chap-Book*'s reputation was enhanced because of them. For those who felt the want of something different in their magazines, of personality and individual distinctiveness, *The Chap-Book* filled their needs. In the words of Percival Pollard, a contemporary journalist, this magazine was "the first efflorescence of the New in American periodical litera-ture."[14] Its tone was personal, especially in its "Notes" section which was originally entitled as remarks by "The Egoist." Chatty in style, often witty in critique, it appeared to be a refreshingly open forum for a dis-cussion of current ideas concerning art and literature. Welcoming new authors as contributors was as much a matter of necessity for a fledgling periodical as a decision of editorial policy. Interesting copy, regardless of the reputation of its source, was accepted if it met the editorial standards of the young publishers.

Succinctly spelled out in their closing statement, these standards had simply been "to give their public what seemed to them the best writing they could procure." And this provides a crucial clue to *The Chap-Book*'s identity. No revolt was ever intended, only an attempt to set a higher standard of critical appraisal than what the editors found in other peri-odicals.[15] Success in finding an audience that wanted what *The Chap-Book* offered was evidenced by a rapid rise in the magazine's circulation and the numerous offspring that it spawned. While it redounds to *The Chap-Book*'s credit that subsequent scholarship has borne out judgments that this journal served as a widely imitated archetype for the perhaps more important little magazines of the twentieth century,[16] its successful reputation as a "little magazine" has seriously affected its reputation *in toto*.

For *The Chap-Book* "grew up," in terms of both longevity and size, and its reputation changed. In January 1897, it abandoned its small size and came to resemble in physical appearance the standard journals of the day. This coming of age marked the definite end of its newness; and the ideas that had seemed so modern and radical on its little pages now appeared staid and respectably mature. Writing in the *New York Journal*, James L. Ford noted:

> *The Chap-Book* has been cured of its radicalism by the same process that has been employed with so much success and skill in English politics, and is now a staid and respectable member of the literary House of Lords, and presents, I am bound to say, a most dignified appearance wrapped in its ermine of publishers' advertising.[17]

Advertising had certainly been a consideration in enlarging the size of the magazine,[18] but so had the desire to appear dignified apart from the advertising. In a letter requesting his brother's opinion of the new *Chap-Book*, Herbert Stone explained: "We are trying to make it dignified and important without being stupid."[19]

While this attempt was a very conscious effort on the part of its publishers to make *The Chap-Book* resemble its British literary cousins,[20] to some this change in appearance marked the abandonment not merely of its diminutive size, but also of a rather decadent influence, always seen as "foreign." Henry Blake Fuller observed in *The Atlantic Monthly*, October 1897, that *The Chap-Book* had "lately enlarged itself and subdued the intensity of a yellow tone reflected from London," and could "now be fully accepted" as Chicago's contribution to periodical literature.[21] Aping the *Athenaeum* seemed to have definitively removed it from association with foreign vice and the international little magazine movement, and British respectability was an acceptable quality in an American magazine wishing to make an important contribution to periodical literature. If *The Chap-Book* was now respectable, in an acceptable American sense, it seemed to matter little that its influence was foreign.

Scholarly opinion has continued in the critical tradition established by contemporaries of dividing *The Chap-Book* into two periods, and remains preoccupied with establishing which side of the conservative-avant-garde, genteel-decadent, romantic-modern, nineteenth-twentieth century chasm it lay. In its smallness and youth, most maintain that it attempted to lead its readers into the modern era, introducing them to new and foreign trends in literature and art. If not all saw foreign decadence, or even American decadence, as the wave of the literary future, they at least applauded *The Chap-Book*'s openness to experiment with a new option. But when it grew up, its critics aver that it turned its back on all new options and swung back into the nineteenth century, becoming a mere period piece of respectability and conformity.

With the advantage of hindsight, former contemporaries writing after the cataclysmic turning point of 1900 lamented *The Chap-Book*'s failure to remain forever young, and consequently modern. One booster of what he saw as the innovative early *Chap-Book* claimed that its enlarged size marked the final stage of an aging process which brought about the magazine's demise.[22] Another, Percival Pollard, noted: "eventually this *enfant terrible* began to give pink teas, to make much of Great Personages, and curb its bold impertinence; the novelty was exhausted; the old audacity gone; and before its pale insipidity public interest flagged and died. So eventually, did the 'Chap-Book.' "[23] In their opinion a transformation had occurred in the very nature of the magazine with its maturity and physical growth. It was only a matter of time before this aged publication would die a natural death.

Historians, whom one naively might assume to be sympathetic to things of a certain vintage, have followed suit in lauding what seemed new and ahead of its time and decrying what seemed old (that is, predictably nineteenth-century) and of the period. Sidney Kramer, historian and apologist of the two publishing companies that produced *The Chap-Book*, claimed that with the passage of time, as the magazine grew older and grew up, it became more conservative, "developed its own taboos, calling attention to hidden perversities," and suffered a sharp drop in both circulation and advertising when it adopted the "full-size" format.[24] Even in the most recent critical reassessment that the magazine has received, Jack Patnode concludes: "it did not pursue its original aim of using the best of the old and the new. Especially in its later years it allowed the tried and respectable to thrust the new from its pages. Its critics and editors became increasingly conservative, and its commercial motivations turned *The Chap-Book* into something not much different from its competitors among the big literary magazines."[25] *The Chap-Book* had come into existence looking like something different. When it abandoned this difference, it failed both commercially and in the eyes of those latter-day critics who favored what they considered to be the original, "new", and distinctly different *Chap-Book*.

Hidden within all the judgments that *The Chap-Book* underwent a metamorphosis which significantly altered its character as well as its appearance, are some contradictory and incorrect assumptions. For those establishment critics of the 1890s who welcomed *The Chap-Book*'s changed facade (contemporaries like Ford and Fuller) it was assumed that now the magazine had "made it." Advertising had never appeared more substantial, the magazine's contents were thought to be respectably mature, and support from an admiring public which appeared to be getting what it wanted ostensibly looked assured. If *The Chap-Book* had been forced to alter its ways because of commercial exigencies, the success of its early days was obviously not as great as proponents of the little magazine would like to maintain.

Conversely, critics who favor the young *Chap-Book* have seen the magazine's change as the reason for its failure. In its youth, they maintain, it had been successful; when it abandoned the new, which they identify in its littleness, it failed. The curious paradox in this argument is that when *The Chap-Book* was giving the nineteenth century a product that was judged to be ahead of its time—more modern than contemporaries were willing to be—then and only then was it popularly received. When it conformed to contemporary standards, it failed in a material sense. This might be explained by assuming that the journal's initial audience was distinctly different from the audiences of the standard journals. When the magazine ceased to appeal to these radicals it lost them as readers, and simply failed to attract the presumably already satisfied readers of the older, established journals.

Both scenarios on *The Chap-Book*'s reception by its largely American readership share one very important characteristic. They are almost pure speculation, based largely on each author's intellectual predisposition regarding the nature of good periodical literature in the 1890s. Neither scenario can be substantiated in any significant way by available facts.[26] Indeed, both are vitiated by the facts.

During its period of littleness, *The Chap-Book* was successful in the sense that it did experience a rapidly rising circulation. But this success was not translated into financial gain for its publishers. Throughout this period *The Chap-Book*, as a business venture, required subsidization from other resources of Stone & Kimball and later from Herbert S. Stone & Co. Ironically, the only reference in extant evidence suggesting that the magazine ever, during its entire life, broke into the profit column dates from the autumn immediately preceding its change in size. On October 10, 1896, Herbert Stone wrote: "The Chap Book has taken a new boom and is making money—not much—but some."[27] This pleasing state of affairs was not a stable one, however. More characteristic of the actual situation was Stone's earlier reflection: " 'The Chap-Book' . . . is really meeting with great success. The papers are speaking beautifully of it and we are not losing much money."[28] By December 1896 Stone had become convinced that they would never be able to attract the advertisers they needed to underwrite the magazine's publication costs as long as they adhered to their original small format.[29]

While commercial motivations had dictated the changed format of *The Chap-Book*, and the change met a generally favorable critical reception and increased advertising prospects,[30] receipts were slow to increase. In April, 1897 Stone was writing that he hoped "before the year is out, the CB will be making several dollars. The moment that happens we are all fixed for good and all."[31] But that moment never arrived. And the reason it never arrived appears to have had more to do with the business ineptitude of the publishers than with any intrinsic qualities of the magazine.

Initially begun as the first periodical offering of two young Harvard undergraduate publishers, Herbert Stuart Stone and Hannibal Ingalls Kimball, *The Chap-Book* represented a learn-as-you-go course in magazine production for its owners and creators. Neither man had any real experience in the field, but each had a wealth of ambition, and together they received substantial financial support from Herbert Stone's father, Melville E. Stone, the founder of the Chicago *Daily News* and the Associated Press. Young Stone had grown up in the Chicago world of journalism, and the literary connections of his father were of considerable importance in launching Herbert's publishing career. Kimball, the son of a prominent Southern manufacturer who had moved to Chicago at the time of the World's Columbian Exposition in 1893, was eager to find an outlet for his entrepreneurial ambitions.

Given their respective backgrounds, it was not surprising that Stone became the real moving force behind the literary aspects of the publishing company of Stone & Kimball, while Kimball functioned as its business manager. Although both men had taken courses together from the time they entered Harvard as freshmen in the fall of 1890, it was only midway through their junior year, in the beginning of 1893, that their partnership was formed. At that time Stone had already put together a guide to the Columbian Exposition, which he was having difficulty marketing, and was well into a second project of bringing out a collectors' guide to first editions of American authors. Kimball impressed Stone with his ideas for promoting and distributing the Exposition guide, and a partnership was formed hopefully to reap windfall profits from Stone's work.[32]

Fate was not so beneficent to this endeavor as the two young men had wished, but they attributed their difficulties to a number of extenuating circumstances. They were, after all, both full-time students and could not devote their total energies to promoting their publishing interests. It was also understandably difficult to arrange for and handle the distribution of Chicago-based publications while having to maintain residence in Cambridge. Ultimately these two factors played an important part in the young partners' decisions to abandon their college work before the completion of their degrees, and to consolidate their offices (which had been in both Cambridge and Chicago) exclusively on the shores of Lake Michigan.

Even before their college work was abandoned, however, during those early months of *The Chap-Book*'s publication, Stone should have had some inkling that the business procedures and acumen of his partner were not all that could be desired. Stone had been a frequent contributor to Harvard's daily newspaper, the *Crimson*, and was elected to its editorial board a year before he and Kimball formed their partnership. Later in the same month that Stone took on Kimball as the business manager of his publishing interests, January 1893, the *Crimson* editorial board elected Kimball as its assistant business manager. Later that same year he succeeded to the position of manager. But Kimball's tenure in this office was not altogether successful. Indeed, by the spring of 1894 the board had authorized an audit of their accounts, which revealed unauthorized payments by Kimball to himself and an unauthorized loan of *Crimson* funds in the amount of $500 to an H.I. Kimball of 80 Broadway, New York. In May of that year, just weeks after *The Chap-Book* first appeared, the *Crimson* board voted to require Kimball to make good these sums, and in June his resignation was offered and accepted.[33]

While there is no evidence that Stone's faith in Kimball's business abilities was shaken at this point, the latter's slipshod methods of handling Stone & Kimball's affairs after they moved to Chicago caused Stone and his father considerable distress. At the time they moved their offices in August, 1894, Stone was hopeful that all they needed was a good bookkeeper in order to show company profits.[34] As it turned out, they needed considerably more help than that, and the company was forced to rely heavily on financial support provided by young Stone's father to keep them afloat. Relations between the two partners steadily deteriorated and by June, 1895 Stone was forced to admit: "Some change will have to take place before long." The change he envisioned was to have the business a strictly family affair.[35] Later that summer, while Stone was in Europe negotiating with the British publisher, John Lane, over a possible English edition of *The Chap-Book*, his father cabled him proposing a sale of one third of the magazine as a means of alleviating their financial difficulties,[36] but further action was forestalled until April 1896 when Stone and Kimball severed their relationship.

The original arrangement was for Kimball to buy out Stone, and take control of all the assets and debts, including *The Chap-Book*, of Stone

& Kimball. Of this Stone wrote to his brother: "Of course, I was not anxious to go. I really wanted to buy up the business for us both but the present scheme is very much better than going on with him and as we all think I shall probably be able to buy back the business at a lower figure in six months." He had no confidence left in Kimball as a business manager: "Kim can never run it: he is too short sighted and the thing will surely fail." Not only did Kimball lack the financial acumen to run the business, he also now lacked Stone's contacts with contemporary writers ("I know the authors and Kim has never met them. . . ."), as well as the funding which Stone's father had provided. "Kim is going to have a hard time. He can't get any credit and he has no one to do the work for him. We all think his career will be a short one."[37] And short it was, at least as far as the publications of Stone & Kimball were concerned. *The Chap-Book* never left Herbert Stone's hands, and in October 1897, Stone was able to buy back all the imprints he wanted at Kimball's liquidation sale, for what Kimball himself called "absurdedly [sic] low" prices.[38]

Unfortunately, while Stone may have come to realize the weaknesses of his partner, his own naivete in financial matters and seemingly total unfamiliarity with sound business procedures were to prove equally disastrous for the success of *The Chap-Book* once he took it over with the May 1, 1896 issue as a publication of his new firm, Herbert S. Stone & Co. Repeatedly there were complaints from authors after receiving no payment for their contributions, or worse, no word even that their contributions had been accepted, used and payment was due. On August 15, 1897 Ellen Glasgow wrote: "I see to my amazement a poem of mine in the issue of *The Chap-Book* for this week. This poem was sent to you by my friend Clarence Wellford, but we had neither of us received any acknowledgement of it what-so-ever. It seems to me at least a lack of courtesy to put a thing into print without consulting me as to the value I set upon it. . . ."[39] Nor was Glasgow's a unique case. It unfortunately represented a pattern established when Kimball was still the magazine's business manager,[40] a pattern which Stone was never able to break. And always there were other creditors waiting for payments, creditors such as their printers who could not be put off so easily as their sometime contributors.

Sloppy operating procedures and a lack of financial accountability were not limited merely to this magazine, but its publishers' growing reputation in these regards was to seriously affect the magazine's ability to attract contributors. By May 1898, when Stone was in London trying to secure new material (primarily book-length manuscripts, but also materials for *The Chap-Book*), it was finally impressed upon him just how bad his reputation was and how unwilling British authors and literary agents had become to market their wares with Herbert S. Stone & Co. Writing back to his Chicago office, Stone begged them to somehow find money to pay their English debts, perhaps by putting off some local people. "You can deal with the people at home for they know us and know father but these creditors 3000 miles away don't know the family and don't like the slow pay."[41]

Advertising and advertising rates had certainly increased from the magazine's early days, as had its circulation,[42] but not enough to counteract the debilitating effects of a very poorly run business operation. On July 15, 1898 *The Chap-Book* succumbed to the inevitable fate of all unprofitable business ventures. After four years of trying to make it a financial success, its heavily indebted publisher saw the demise of the magazine as one way to cut losses. Stone was in England when his family pressed him for a decision regarding discontinuing *The Chap-Book*, and he responded: "I'm ready to consent to its being stopped. There is no sense in our going on forever losing money over it. . . ."[43]

The Chap-Book was not the only reason Herbert S. Stone & Co. was in debt, but the hope was that once the company was relieved of this heavy burden (in terms of money, time and effort), the publishers would be able to increase the financial returns from their book publishing. Herbert Stone was to find this dream, like so many of his optimistic goals, as illusive as financial success for *The Chap-Book*. Since no intrinsic faults had occasioned the failure of the magazine, neither could its cessation cure the monetary ills that plagued its publishers. At the century's end, Stone was still relying on his father's help in borrowing funds to keep his business going, and still optimistic that soon he would finally be out of debt.[44] Instead, the first years of the twentieth century saw the slow, and seemingly inevitable, deterioration of his publishing company.[45]

Since both Kimball and then Stone were unable to translate popular into financial success, *The Chap-Book*'s critical reputation should not have to rest on their failures as businessmen. For too long historians have been content to base their judgments of this magazine on readily perceived external realities. There was most certainly a distinct change in *The Chap-Book*'s appearance midway in its life, but contrary to the opinions expressed earlier, this change did not alter in any significant way the intellectual content of its pages. There were not two *Chap-Books*, as the following pages will show. It was not successively modern then conservative, advanced then moribund. It was consistently a magazine that gave space to ideas that were both old and new, respectable and suspect, tried and tentative. Working its way toward a new century, it reflects no either/or decisions, no critical junctures. Rather it portrays a mind trying to accommodate intellectual changes in terms of an inherited, and respected, intellectual tradition. Never was it the radical proponent of the avant-garde that some critics would like to make it out to be in its early days. Neither was it an anachronistic throwback to mid-nineteenth-century conventions. A journal of the 1890s, it reflects a link in our intellectual lives, not a break.

Given our scholarly predisposition to look for a radical change in intellectual directions at the changing of the centuries, *The Chap-Book* has not fared well at the hands of those historians seeking to identify a clear fissure between what went before and what was to come. It has been variously described as the abortive beginning of an "amoral revolt" from conventional society that really did not take hold until later in the twentieth century;[46] as part of a brief flirtation with decadence that was a mild precursor to twentieth-century bohemianism;[47] or as an ineffectual, because only half-hearted, attempt to break out of nineteenth-century literary conventions, particularly those of Romantic idealism.[48] *The Chap-Book* was certainly never amoral, nor really very decadent (although it printed the works of the Symbolists and some American and English "Decadents"), and consistently avowed the value of romance and idealism, yet these categorizations persist.

Problems of intellectual identification have been compounded by the fact that certain of *The Chap-Book*'s contributors have earned the dubious notoriety of being classified by labels, supposedly unerring signs pointing out the intellectual bents of their owners. It is hypothesized that the presence of certain "modern" or "advanced" thinkers on the pages of this magazine indicate a radically changed intellectual perspective. But then there are also those others with different labels, the "genteel custodians" of old ideas. Thus the final verdict on *The Chap-Book*'s mental state must be "debilitating schizophrenia." It couldn't, or wouldn't, choose which century in which it wanted to live. At that critical point of decision, it failed to decide.

Perhaps the reason this occurred was because no decision was necessary. Recent scholarship has begun to show that this hypothesized break between the dominant intellectual tradition of the nineteenth century and modern twentieth-century intellectual life was not nearly so decisive as previously thought. George Bornstein, in bringing together a collection of essays which explore the similarities of Romanticism and Modernism, asserts "the positive centrality of Romanticism for measuring and understanding the Modern achievement." Once this centrality has been recognized, he maintains, scholars will have to admit that twentieth-century literary thought is post-Romantic (perhaps even late-Romantic), rather than anti-Romantic.[49] Intellectual life, as examined by exponents of this approach, is not one living reality that existed in the nineteenth century and died at its conclusion, being replaced by a new, young life of twentieth-century modernism. Rather it is an evolving creation that moves in time, growing and changing instead of dying and being replaced by something new and different.

The following detailed internal examination of the ideas presented on the pages of *The Chap-Book*, seen in the context of the intellectual environment which first nurtured them, attempts to restore some integrity to the charge that this magazine was a period piece by establishing the integrity of the period. It was not merely a harbinger of what was to come, nor a holdover of what had been. It was, like all historical periods, a combination of both. In the process of elucidating the intellectual composition of life in the 1890s, this study will further assert the positive importance of an intellectual tradition open to change and accommodation. The period neither marked a termination nor a new beginning, but rather a point in the time of a continuing tradition. As *The Chap-Book* editors reflected: "A true child of the age is caught in the swirl of each new eddy and feels cresting behind him the wave of each new movement. I do not claim to be, in the full meaning of the term, a prophet of the advanced, but I am that rather than the tail of the kite."[50] They believed that they were responding to the ebb and flow of the intellectual currents of their day, as did their readers, and that for the moment they were helping to chart the future course of American literary thought. But the vessel which was carrying them into uncharted waters was equipped with well-used riggings from an earlier day. How they responded to new situations was determined in part by the craft which they cherished, and in part by their vision of what lay ahead.

2

A Harvard Education, 1890–1894

Harvard, as Stone and his classmates found it in the autumn of 1890, was a place rich with tradition, cherished ideals, and youthful opportunities. To be a Harvard man was to be a part of it all: its history, its standards, its expectations. No neutral environment, this was the self-conscious school of formation for the next generation of American leaders. As Charles Eliot Norton, intellectual godfather of countless Harvard youths, asserted, Harvard was a leader among the country's "superior institutions of learning," helping to form "the head-waters of the stream of education by which the general intellectual and moral life of the community is in large measure supplied and sustained."[1] To be at Harvard was to be at the beginnings of one's career in future American leadership. It was also to be at the place where the nation's intellectual and moral consciousness was, in part, formed.

It was not without some awareness of all this that Herbert Stone arrived in Cambridge in the summer of 1890 to study for Harvard's entrance examinations. After a two-year stay in Europe doing preparatory work at a private school near Geneva (following his father's retirement from the Chicago *Daily News*), Stone slogged through a summer of intensive study, hoping for at least admission to the university as a special student.[2] With some admitted conceit, he rejoiced over his success in gaining regular student status that September, gleeful over the jealousy he anticipated his friends would feel when they heard that he had entered Harvard.[3] Truly, he felt he had arrived.

Writing of Harvard in 1890, Norton noted: "No one denies that their surroundings have a subtle and strong, though perhaps unconsciously received, influence upon the disposition of men."[4] The influences of Harvard's surroundings were many: its buildings celebrating "lofty virtues"; on these facades the images of past scholars, poets and heroes who had served either the cause of learning or the state; and the overarching presence of generations of Harvard men who had lived in this environment before.

He must be of a dull spirit . . . who at times does not feel his heart glow and quicken with the thought that, as a member of the university, he is an associate with men in whose characters and lives the worth of its teachings and influence has been expressed, and that he is surrounded by a cloud of witnesses who claim of him that he show himself worthy to belong to their company.[5]

Virtue, duty and pride were all inextricably linked to the obligations of a Harvard education, as they had been for centuries. One not only learned one's lessons, one went out and lived them in order to educate the larger community. As Harvard's buildings gave physical testimony to the virtues and aspirations which the university cherished, so its graduates were charged to embody what their education taught them.

A crucial component of Harvard's education was its history. Tracing its "evolution" as parallel to that of the nation, Norton praised "those fundamental principles of the commonwealth" of Massachusetts upon which Harvard was founded, principles "which have so largely contributed to the shaping of the character of the United States." Far from being static, Harvard's charter, like its Puritan legacy, was "so constructed as to admit of extension without essential change of plan;" and had "been adapted and enlarged to answer to the new and increasing needs of new times."[6] History, directed toward a purpose, open to the demands of changing circumstances, permeated the atmosphere of Harvard and left an imprint on its young men. For Herbert Stone it was an imprint all the more impressive because he traced his own New England ancestry back to 1635, one year before the founding of his college.[7]

In a curious way, the sense of history which was verbalized, and in some concrete instances visualized, by and for the undergraduates was not didactically ethnocentric. Yet it was totally consistent with their Puritan forebearers' insistence on the positive value of education. Knowledge was not to be feared, nor its perimeters circumscribed, but was rather to be sought as a means of comprehending the nature and duties of human existence. In history, one found the record of past insights, achievements and failures—lessons of instruction to aid the attentive student in his own task of living a meaningful and purposeful life. And, as will be demonstrated, the primary goal of this life-long task was the achievement of intellectual freedom and spiritual unity.

When Rev. Newman Smyth, in the autumn of 1890, told the congregation assembled at morning prayer in Harvard's Appleton Chapel that their lives should be composed of "manly virtue, spiritual aspiration, a looking up to some ideal and a religious decision; which is the mastery of life by the spirit that is in man,"[8] he was not some lone voice crying in a materialistic wilderness. Harvard was a place dedicated to the enrichment of the mind, which also meant the spirit. As President Charles

Eliot put it, a university should not only seek out truth, but should also stand "for intellectual and spiritual forces against materialism and luxury."[9] In good New England fashion, Harvard was still committed to promoting an education, as defined by the original charter of 1650, composed of both "knowledge and godliness."[10] Materialism and luxury were not only conditions that could govern one's physical existence, but they could also usurp the place of more essential concerns in one's life as an intellectual and moral being. A Harvard education was meant to counteract this tendency; and its students were meant to go out from Harvard and to counteract this tendency in the general populace.

It is appropriate that at the school where Henry Adams played a key role in creating the academic profession of history,[11] one of the historical periods most attractive to students of the early 1890s was the Middle Ages. The medieval period, marked by its fusion of intellectual and spiritual concerns, was a natural historical haunt for those seeking a place where the highest pursuits of the mind and spirit were successfully integrated into actual life. Young assistant professor Edward Channing taught the history department's introductory course during the 1890–1891 academic year, "History 1. Mediaeval and Modern European History," and among his students was the freshman Herbert Stone. After taking Professor Norton's "Fine Arts 4. Roman and Mediaeval Art, with special study of the Development of Gothic Architecture, and of the Revival of Art in Italy in the 13-th-C." the following year, Stone had been exposed to a historical period that was to strongly influence his intellectual expression in the coming years.

As Norton lectured in his course that year, he explained that his specific interest in the architectural achievements of the Middle Ages stemmed from the fact that they were: "the only beautiful buildings which moderns have erected out of their own consciousness." The Middle Ages were not merely time past, but the beginning of modern time present. With its monuments immortalizing the real presence of spiritual concerns, Gothic architecture was a "genuine expression" of its builders' "religious life which was the greater part of their intellectual life"[12] according to Norton. It marked a positive evolution of man's intellectual life from the simplicities of classical antiquity, for these buildings—more than those of any other architectural mode—revealed man's essential quest: that of "poetic aspiration."[13]

This intellectual movement unfortunately did not, in Norton's view, enjoy an uninterrupted development. When Western civilization passed out of the Middle Ages into the Renaissance era, it passed out of a period when ideals were accepted in confidence as part of human life. Like childhood, the Middle Ages had an aura of happy innocence, confidence and dependence. With the beginning of the Renaissance, man moved into a period of increased intellectual maturity, but holistic acceptance of life (including its intangible spiritual dimensions) gave way to sceptical questioning and loss of confidence, with a consequent loss of a sense of well-being.[14] An essential dimension of life had been cast aside. Man in the Middle Ages was advanced enough to recognize the presence of spiritual ideals in life, but not so advanced as to question their reality. Norton, unlike others who were to champion the Gothic Revival, did not advocate a resurgence of this architectural style in contemporary America. That would be anachronistic.[15] He did, however, advocate a resurgence of the spiritual ideals which had, at one time, inspired this mode of artistic expression.

Outside of the classroom, concern for these ideals was as real to the men of Stone's circle as it was to Norton behind his lectern. One contemporary of Stone, a member of his literary group and later contributor to *The Chap-Book*, was soon to become America's foremost architect of the Gothic Revival. Ralph Adams Cram described what life was like around Harvard during these years: "the varied personalities, their visions and ambitions, the tentative motions made toward creative action, and the workings of that spiritual influence that seemed implicit in the air we breathed."[16] Noting the "real appeal" of religion to them, he recalled: "Those of us who recognized religion as a part of the general scheme of things were *very* High Church."[17] High Church was the church of the Middle Ages, and it followed logically that those artists and intellectuals who felt some kinship with that period would also be drawn to its most important cultural institution. After tracing his own conversion from Unitarianism to "the Anglican Communion of the Catholic Church," Cram described his decision to design buildings in the Gothic mode as an attempt to pick up the threads of a broken tradition, threads "most untimely cut off by the synchronizing of the Classical Renaissance and the Protestant Revolution."[18]

Cram's conversion came on the heels of a European excursion, during which he was exposed to the art of pre-Renaissance Europe in the churches of England, France and Italy rather than in the classrooms of Harvard. He recounted: "all the art of a thousand years, in which I was fast becoming immersed, was getting in its deadly work, and I was beginning to realize that if it had validity, if it related itself to life, it was not the life of rationalism and physical science and liberal Unitarianism, but very specifically the life of the Catholic Church." Eschewing Western civilization's intellectual tradition that progressively moved further and further away from animate contact with the spirit, Cram gloried in the revelation he experienced when he first attended Mass at the Church of

San Luigi dei Francesi. "I did not understand all of this with my mind, but I *understood*."[19]

Tracing the odyssey of both Stone's and Kimball's religious lives while at Harvard corroborates the strength of the attraction which drew Cram into the Anglican fold. Stone, whose family line was sprinkled with Methodist ministers, stated in 1894 that he was a member of a Congregational church, but his religious preference was "Catholic."[20] Kimball, who had entered Harvard as a Methodist and joined the evangelically oriented Young Men's Christian Association during the first month of his freshman year,[21] listed his church membership and religious preference in 1894 as "Episcopal."[22] Stone's best friend, by the autumn of 1892, had "about decided to take English university orders and to enter the Church of England" once he graduated from Harvard. Stone, remarking over the change in his friend, noted that he was "much more serious and has really begun to think." On the whole, Stone was "rather pleased" with the decision.[23]

Few of Stone's acquaintances, not even Stone himself, were able to go so far as to embrace institutional Catholicism, or its Anglo-Catholicism variant, as a desirable means of expressing their spiritual concerns, but Catholicism was a force which penetrated their consciousness both inside and outside their classroom experiences. One example of the hospitality which Harvard extended to these ideas occurred in the fall of Stone's freshman year. The Rt. Rev. Bishop John J. Keane, rector of The Catholic University, was the first Catholic ever invited to give the Dudleian lecture at Harvard. Following his address on "Christ as God's Revelation," *The Daily Crimson* (Harvard's student newspaper) issued an editorial call for the addition of a Catholic to the preachers of the university, arguing that it would be a means of strengthening Harvard's effort to induce freedom of thought in its students.[24] More important sources of influence on Herbert Stone, however, came through his personal relationship with Louise Imogen Guiney and in the lessons he learned in Lewis E. Gates's English classes during his sophomore and junior years.

As Cram described Guiney, she was "the most vital and creative personal influence in the lives of all of us who gathered together at this time." She was "a good Catholic, a theoretical Jacobite and monarchist, a poet and essayist of singular charm and distinction, and, withal, the best of good fellows." Postmistress of the small town of Auburndale just outside Boston, her Catholicism precipitated an active movement in the early 1890s by the Protestants in that postal district to remove her from her official duties. Harvard students, learning of this bigoted persecution, were instrumental in subverting the attempt to deprive Guiney of her livelihood. Combined with a love of fantasy and an "exquisite sense of humor,"[25] Guiney's Catholicism and romantic attachment to various lost causes of times past, were inextricable components of a highly religious woman's intellectual makeup. Later they were to find numerous opportunities for expression on the pages of *The Chap-Book* and were highly influential in determining the tone of its crucial editorial "Notes" section.

Helping to set the stage for Harvard students' appreciation of an essentially "Romantic" Catholicism, were the courses taught by Lewis Gates. When Stone was enrolled in his "English Literature of the Eighteenth Century," Gates began by describing the "positive mind" of that century which could only create prose, not poetry. "This coldness & materialness & lack of enthusiasm & passion is a prosaic mood. If you check the emotions of the heart you will never have any poetry of the highest kind." And the eighteenth century had no good poetry. Their "rationalizing tendency, [&] critical mood" eventually proved self-destructive when criticism was turned on reason itself. The natural reaction to this situation was Romanticism, with its emphases on feelings, Nature "as an Objective Fact, and as a Spiritual power," an "awakening interest in the past," and a recognition that classical literature had grown tiresome. "There was a desire for something mysterious & less conventional."[26] The prosaic mood was too limited, and the Romantics of the nineteenth century wanted to explore more than these limitations would allow.

After breaking the bonds which had restricted the literature of the eighteenth century, Gates argued that even the prose writers of the nineteenth century were free to express the spirit exhilarating their times. In his course given in 1891–1892 on this facet of English literature, Gates outlined for Stone and his fellow students three main areas of concern: romance, realism and idealism. One writer in particular who reflected these concerns, and whose works Gates analyzed, was Cardinal Newman. Leader of the Oxford Movement, tenacious opponent of the tendency toward rationalism in the church, and the most famous convert to Catholicism in the nineteenth century, Gates saw Newman's writing as exemplifying the major tenets of romanticism. Indeed, he went so far as to say that Coleridge, acknowledged "father of romanticism," had "prepared the way for Cardinal Newman."[27] The thread that Cram picked up in architecture had already been picked up in literature by one of the most lucid prose writers of the nineteenth century.

Later in the nineties, Gates published his thoughts on Newman's kinship with the Romantics, and listed this identification as recognizable: "in his imaginative sympathy with the past, in the range and perspective of his historical consciousness, and in his devotion to an ideal framed largely in accordance with a loving reverence for mediaeval life." Detailing traits that were still respected among Gate's Harvard contemporaries, he went on to describe Newman's "vein of mysticism, his imaginative sympathy with Nature as symbolic of spiritual truth, his rejection of reason as the guide of life, and his recognition of the inadequacy of generalizations and formulas to the wealth of actual life and to the intensity and variety of personal experience." These were the characteristics, expressed in a prose style which impressed Gates with its "glowing beauty," "picture-making power," "occasional imaginative splendour," and "elaborate swelling music" that earned Newman's writing a place among "the best and most vital literature of his day and generation."[28]

Perhaps it was testimony to Gates's effectiveness as a teacher, or perhaps it was the result of accumulated similar interests that were widespread around Harvard at this time, but romanticism was not a moribund intellectual movement for the men of Stone's generation. Although a distinctive hallmark of romanticism was its fascination with the past, its intent was not retreat into a simpler world but advancement beyond the limits of the Enlightenment's rationalism. Earlier ages had recognized these other realms of human experience, forgotten or shunned for the past several centuries. And when Gates described the Romantics' desire to recapture these lost insights he was not describing an escape from reality, rather an attempt to move beyond rational limits of apprehension. As Gates explained: "The Romanticists sought to enrich life with new emotions, to conquer new fields of experience, to come into imaginative touch with far distant times, to give its due to the encompassing world of darkness and mystery, and even to pierce through the darkness in the hope of finding, at the heart of the mystery, a transcendental world of infinite beauty and eternal truth."[29]

From the Renaissance on, the great thrust of rationalism, with its ever increasing scientific knowledge and technological advancement, had continued to gain momentum. Even at the height of what the Romantics considered their revolt from this myopic world view, the progress of the Age of Reason and its growing materialistic preoccupation continued unchecked. The task of convincing contemporaries that the progress of mere rationalism was no meaningful progress at all had not been completed by the Romantics' own greatest sectaries. At Harvard in the 1890s there were some latter-day Romantics convinced of the continuing relevancy of the Romantic quest. And they assumed the burden of applying to life in their own time the major concepts of the Romantics' pursuit of knowledge.

Complaints were still rampant in the last decade of the century against reliance on science and reason as the primary modes of trying to comprehend the varying dimensions of human life, and Newman's writings continued to play an active role in precipitating staunch assertions re-, garding the limitations of the rational mind. Gates led the field and his students followed. In 1891, E.A. Abbott issued a new attack on Newman and the young Harvard professor labelled these charges "the result of prejudice and temperamental hostility" to a way of thinking that went beyond the critic's own limitations. "Mr. Abbott is a bit of a formalist, a Caledonian intellect, a thoroughgoing positivist, a thinker for whom the only truth that exists is truth that can be scientifically verified." The truth that Newman sought was "a much subtler matter, a much more elusive substance, than it is to the positivist, to the mere intellectual dealer in facts and in figures."[30]

When Leslie Stephen published in *The Fortnightly* a criticism of Newman's theory of belief as elaborated in *The Grammar of Assent*, it drew the same kind of reaction from within the Harvard student body as Abbott's criticism had from the faculty. Robert Morss Lovett, an under- graduate writer from whom Stone & Kimball would later attempt to solicit manuscripts,[31] used the pages of *The Harvard Monthly*, January 1893, to reiterate the limitations of reason as set forth by Newman.[32] Newman did not hold that reason was false, merely that it was "inadequate;" and it was this contention that Stephen failed to allow in his critique. Stephen's unwillingless to admit the possibility of truth lying outside the realm of reason brought forth Lovett's spirited defense of Newman's position, just as Abbott's similar reluctance had called forth Gates's response.[33]

Neither Gates nor Lovett were arguing for Newman's theological position or spiritual system, however, As Lovett put it, "the age has moved far from the pillars of Newman's faith. We can no longer cry *Credo in Newmanum*. We cannot take his words as an Evangel. In theology and in philosophy we must account him a reactionary force." What they did support was his firm belief in spiritual realities. "In that world, where, to quote Professor Royce, 'the intelligent man of today is praying hourly for proof that there are spiritual chains worthy enough and holy enough to bind his will and his reason'—there he [Newman] may be a saviour if we will let him."[34] Similarly, undergraduate Norman Hapgood (later a *Chap-Book* contributor) had earlier in *The Harvard Monthly* (November, 1890) published a review of another Catholic writer, supporting the thrust of his argument without endorsing its (to Hapgood's mind) parochial goal. Mallock's *Is Life Worth Living?* had proved conclusively for Hapgood "that the claim of the positivist to build a life upon exact knowledge is the tamest of superstitions," and that "the real point at issue" in the query Mallock raised in his title, was "beyond the criticism of the finite mind."[35] Science, to these men, was a closed system of knowledge, even a primitive one, and they had no wish for its limitations, nor those of any other system.

Even as science stood on the brink of redefining its own intellectual framework, particularly in the areas of psychology and physics, young artists at Harvard recognized that science alone could not provide all the answers to life's most important questions. Philip Savage, a young Harvard poet who would later publish in *The Chap-Book*, lamented in verse the fact that Western civilization, really the Northern European mind, had concentrated all of its efforts on the essentially materialistic endeavor of accumulating scientific and factual data. The church had been replaced by a temple of science, now complete but ultimately useless.

"The Builder—Science"

I saw in outline on the northern skies
   A fair-haired giant, building, with his hands,
   And lifting rock on rock; and now expands
The growing structure; skillful, ay, and wise,
He shapes and plans, and wearies as he tries
   To fit the mighty work to those demands
   His laboring brain requires; till now there stands
A towered temple complete before his eyes,
   He rests, and lies beside a running brook,
And in its voice grows thoughtful; then in pain
   He starts, and knows the birth of the divine.
Touched with the dreadful question of that look
   I turned away, but saw him once again
Dead, lying where he should have built his shrine.[36]

Science had been allowed to move into areas where it had no legitimacy, and in the process had either destroyed that which it was examining or distracted its practitioners from more important concerns. Even literature, complained Harvard student Robert Herrick (later an important Chicago writer, published by Herbert S. Stone & Co.), was now being subjected to the laboratory method "where each element of a work of art is resolved into its constituents." Citing L.A. Sherman in his recently published *The Analytics of Literature* as fallaciously applying the scientific method to literature, Herrick particularly lamented the effects of such a procedure on the fine arts. Even if one could skillfully classify and analyse the act of artistic creation, the results would be depressing. For "one might say that the eternal charm of fine art is that, like the ultimate mystery of life, the secret remains unsolved; that as soon as man finds out why a certain combination of colors, or lines, or movements, or sounds, or ideas, rouses his deepest emotions, his toy will be forever broken, and his existence a dreary monotony of the known."[37]

Not all Harvard men were so critical of the advancement of science and reason, and this was particularly true of Josiah Royce, the university's preeminent philosopher. The autumn that Herbert Stone entered Harvard, Royce gave a series of public lectures that were subsequently published as *The Spirit of Modern Philosophy*. Attendance at the lectures was overwhelming; and *The Daily Crimson*, which before each lecture published an outline of topics to be discussed and afterwards printed a summary of the presentation (both often front page news items), led a movement to find a larger auditorium to accommodate adequately the crowds that came to hear Royce explain the relationship between "modern thinkers" and "certain significant spiritual problems of our day."[38] Royce did not reject science or rational empiricism as modes of knowing, he merely believed them to be limited in their apprehension of reality.

After dividing the modern era into three different and chronologically sequential periods (I. Seventeenth century naturalism; II. Eighteenth century humanism, or the "Study of the Inner Life" of man's mind; and III. Kant to the present),[39] Royce concentrated his attention on recent attempts, undertaken in the third and present stage, to synthesize previous philosophic insights into a more comprehensive whole. "Man we once more see to be, not merely the sentimental rebel and creative hero of Rousseau and the romantics, not merely the organ of the world-forming reason of the Kantian schools, but also, and just as truly, the mechanism which the seventeenth century declared him to be." The question to be solved by the modern era was still one of "the ancient paradox of the double nature of man." That is: "How can he be both these things, that is, both natural and spiritual? How can he have sprung from an animal ancestry, yes, ultimately from dead matter, and yet be the embodiment, the organ of the absolute reason? How can he at once be part of the spirit whose live thinking dreams out this whole frame of things, and yet be himself the slave of the very order of nature which this dream creates?"[40] Rather than choosing one side of an either/or alternative, Royce believed that previous eras had given partial answers, each containing some relevant insights. The truth would be found by examining "their conflict and variety" and drawing their "fragmentary" expressions of reality into a larger picture.[41]

Modern philosophy, in its current stage, could embark on a post-scientific synthesis of knowledge because Kant's theory of the subjectivity of time and space had located the limits of science. The world outside of man's mind was neither spatial nor temporal, hence "utterly unknowable." Man could "never know things in themselves" precisely because they were not of himself and only perceived through his own illusory sense impressions.[42] Kant's solution was for modern man to build his world based on the dictates of a moral law inherent in his better nature. As Royce interpreted him, it was a dictate to "Serve the unseen God as if he were present with you."[43] And upon this premise Royce based his theory "that the whole universe, including the physical world also, is essentially one live thing, a mind, one great Spirit."[44] That "Spirit" was alive in each individual, its presence giving meaning to Kant's moral imperative.

Speculative idealism may have been Royce's solution for rebuilding a "lost spiritual world, which skepticism shattered,"[45] but for most of the men of Stone's circle it was too abstract. If there was a wider realm of experience waiting to be explored, a reality other than that of sensory perceptions or rational deductions, there had to be a way of discovering and apprehending it in a more vital manner than that of metaphysical speculation. They needed some more tangible evidence of life's spiritual dimensions manifest in contemporary life, and they found it in artistic expression. It was not the power of Kant's moral law and will or Royce's world spirit, but the functioning of the imaginative faculty.

Students of Norton rather than disciples of Royce, the aspiring literary men of Harvard found in the arts man's realization of visions of the ideal.[46] As Norton told Stone's class in the fall of 1891: "All arts rest finally in the effort of the imagination to realize in visible or audible form some ideal of the mind."[47] These ideals of the mind were not rational constructions, however, but visionary images emanating from the spirit within man, that is, his "soul." Neither sense nor reason were sufficient guides to undertake alone the exploration of ideal reality. Only the cultured imagination, which lifted man's concerns above limited materialistic considerations, was capable of taking what man learned through his other faculties and using that knowledge to express a more perfect vision of ultimate reality. It was the imagination which Norton sought to educate in his Fine Arts course, and he lamented the fact that "This course is almost the only one [at Harvard] intended to cultivate the imagination, the most important faculty of the soul."[48]

Even at Harvard Norton felt there was too much concern for that which could be dissected, plotted, and physiologically and psychologically probed. It was easier to concentrate on those aspects of life which could be apprehended and analyzed by the thinking mind or perceiving senses. But in Norton's view, this left another dimension of life ignored. Instead of exploring the realm of the imagination, contemporary man now studied psychology, and the two were not the same. The imagination, that "faculty which most elevates man," had been "singularly neglected ever since psychology began to be studied."[49] Norton's intention to help his students cultivate their imaginations was part of a deliberate attempt to free them from the restraints of circumscribing systems. He wanted them to be cultured men, to see that culture was not simply an acquisition, but a process, "the process by which a man is made master of his own faculties. This implies the attainment of intellectual freedom."[50] Science was "useless" in this process[51] because it did not free man's intellect, it restricted it.

Acknowledging that the scientific age had driven out of men's minds thoughts regarding the existence and needs of the soul, Norton was not arguing for a revived metaphysic to supersede belief in natural causation. If studying the arts as revelations of the functioning imagination was to aid man in his quest for wider knowledge and intellectual freedom, that study had to be pursued in freedom from external or arbitrary restraints. He warned his students to be wary of systems, especially those imposed on them from outside their own individual experiences. "Avoid universally treatises on aesthetics, which are based universally on preconceived ideas, none of them are free from the curse of metaphysical speculation."[52] What he was arguing for was the cultivation of each individual's innate imaginative faculty—distinct from both his rational mind and perceiving senses, yet inextricably linked to them.

Integration of all of man's faculties was Norton's aim, rather than the mere development of isolated parts of them. Yet there existed within his scheme a definite hierarchy of perceptions and expressions, and the expression of the soul's life was at its pinnacle. "The human soul is a unity—not divided into cupboards of imagination, memory etc. All faculties play together . . . & the expression of the soul is the expression of the whole."[53] Man's sense-abilities were not denigrated, but neither were they deified. They were useful only so long as they contributed to an awareness of something beyond their limitations. "Sense and soul interact all the time: sense has no other end than as [an] instrument of the soul.—cultivated the instrument can serve to reveal the beauties of the world. Train yourself both ways from sense up to soul & from soul down to sense."[54]

Through one's sense one could learn the beauty of the spirit as revealed in natural reality, but this was only man's penultimate achievement. "Visionary imaginary appearances are nobler & more true than any real appearances"[55] because they reflect the play of man's imagination in contact with his environment, not the mere passive reception of sense data. Norton's aesthetic was a refinement of the Romantic's glorification of the spirit made manifest in nature, in that he was primarily concerned with a reality which existed beyond the realm of nature's tangible evidence. Imagination functioned in both life and art as "the endeavor to form and shape the external world, nature, to the desires of the mind; to produce a higher perfection than exists in nature." True beauty, true harmony found its closest approximation only where the imagination was allowed to rearrange the facts of nature into a representation of spiritual ideality. Evidence of this phenomenon could be seen in the great Romantic landscape painters themselves, particularly Turner who lifted his pictures "out of the prose of actuality into the poetry of the ideal."[56]

There was nothing novel in Norton's beliefs. Even the notion that nature could be perfected by an act of creative imagination was a well-known, and accepted, intellectual maxim. Norton himself cited Shelley as an adherent of such a position,[57] and Royce's lectures on Kant's theory of the "constructive imagination" were of similar focus. Royce was persuaded of the veracity of Kant's theory that a sane man created his own knowledge of the world and his place in it through the use of his imaginative faculty, connecting sense impressions of the "outer world" into a unified apperception of transcendental reality. Noting a key facet of the imagination, Royce affirmed its largely unconscious nature: "this process of constructively making my world coherent, is, on its theoretical side indeed unconscious, just as the inventions of an artistic mind are often unconsciously made." Continuing, he reiterated that the constructive imagination, which the scientists also relied on to formulate their "sublimest constructions," was that power which "builds our world as a great genius makes a poem, how, he knows not; it is involuntary, hidden away in the mind, the servant of our understanding, the minister of the forms of thought."[58] Imagination was a creative power which intrigued art critic and philosopher alike. Both Norton and Royce would have understood the impetus behind the theologian Newman's desire that the epitaph on his tomb read: "ex umbris et imaginibus in veritatem," for the truth to which they all sought to give expression was not that of the material world or the exclusively rational mind.

Freedom from the materialism, both of thought and of living, that dominated so much of nineteenth-century existence, was of crucial importance to these men and their like-minded contemporaries. With the self-confidence of an elite, they disdained the "Philistinism" of their age with its materialistic preoccupations. The essence of Philistinism, as defined in 1892 by George Santayana (then a young instructor of philosophy at Harvard and soon to be one of Stone & Kimball's first procured authors), was to adhere to an "unquestioning subordination of mind to matter and of ends to means." Against these traits of conventionality, the "lovers of decaying arts"—musicians, painters and poets—continued to assert their "spiritual freedom." The true artist, devoted to "aesthetic and unutilitarian" concerns, was guided "if not by ideas, at least by emotions, and in his enthusiasm for beauty, in his capacity for rapture, in his unfettered life, he shows the blithe spirit of an angel." Santayana the idealist was afraid of an idealism that was strictly rational because he saw its dangers evidenced by the Philistines. A Philistine not only "muffled" his senses with his intellect, but coupled this tendency with a general indifference to "the supreme and ultimate." Scorning the rational materialism of the mind as well as the materialism of matter, Santayana's idealism was a truly religious devotion to a spiritual life which acknowledged "the supreme and ultimate," what traditional religions called God.[59]

Santayana was no traditionalist, however, and conformity to established religious systems was no guarantee that the practitioner was spiritually alive. Systems might govern outward behavior but they could not insure an indwelling, active spirit. The Philistine could conform to the outward forms of religious orthodoxy, but "he would cease to be a Philistine if he had instinctive piety and an inward, imaginative appreciation of his faith. For these things require a certain wealth of emotion and scope of imagination; they involve what we call unworldliness." Santayana's unworldliness, living "in the sight of the ideal," was vital only when the imagination made an individual aware of life's passionate spiritual dimensions. Rejecting specific forms or systems, he maintained: "It matters not what the sacred passion or what the work of love may be: the infinite surrounds us in every direction, and all who at any time have caught a glimpse of it have something in common. They have for a moment escaped convention and felt the relativity and possible indifference of all earthly goods."[60]

What was true regarding religion was equally true regarding art. The Philistine was both a materialist and a realist, only capable of purchasing art not producing it. Place him in front of a painting and his perceptions would only be concerned with its accuracy of representation. "But how the image of a face can represent anything besides, or the copy of a landscape be more beautiful than the original, he can never conceive." He lacked an inner comprehension "that depends on the awakening of many dim and profound suggestions, on the creation in the beholder's mind of some ideal of beauty or of happiness, on the quick passing of some infinitely tragic and lovely vision."[61]

Echoing thoughts that were common around Cambridge during these days, writers inevitably described the imagination in terminology more familiar to religious topics than profane aesthetics. One contributor to *The Harvard Monthly* exclaimed: "Divine imagination! source of power and progress—lust of the soul!" Nearly overcome with rapture, he elaborated: "To thee man is indebted for such ideas as he has of perfection, which is no affair of his world. . . . He who bows before the real is an idolater, bound to the earth, in whom can rise no thought of beauty, in

whom works the leaven of death: man's one rational devotion is to phantoms of the imagination." For this young man, "the phantom world is
after all the real world." In explaining his position, however, he quite
explicitly repudiated any attempt to define the workings of the imagination
synonymously with mere flights of fancy. Fancy was "a quality of the
mind" which "hovers over the real," camouflaging physical reality. Imagination was "of the soul," quite often seeking "refuge in religion." Rising
"into the firmament of the unknown," imagination was not a means of
escaping reality, but a means of venturing beyond it. While especially a
quality of those with religious or artistic interests, the imagination was
not a fool's crutch for those who could not cope with practical living.
Rather it was a power, "mighty as a hero," to overcome the limitations
of hidebound, materialistic reality.[62]

It is not surprising that, given the thrust of these thoughts, there was
a considerable interest shown by Harvard men in "The Place of Mysticism in Modern Life." Addressing himself to this topic, Paul Frothingham
(one of Stone's fellow editors on *The Daily Crimson*) acknowledged to
his Harvard readership in November 1891 that scientific empiricism, not
mysticism, was still the order of the day. Science, however, "by the very
necessity of its methods, is confined to the outward world of the senses.
It does not go below the surface, as it were, and makes no pretence to
investigate what lies behind phenomena, holding that whatever may exist
as the background to the world of things is by its very nature 'Unknowable.' " Rather than accepting the limitations of the scientific method,
Frothingham maintained that the mystic was able "to penetrate the inner,
spiritual realms of human nature" left unsounded by the scientist. The
mystic, by exploring an inner self that was not of the senses, "may still
meet and commune with the Infinite, may listen to the whispers of the
moral sense, and feel with overpowering force the intercommunion of all
things." His findings "may not satisfy the stern demands of the modern
intellect, nor wholly commend themselves to the understanding, but, in
the absence of absolute truth, they have their place." Science held no
"absolute truth" because it left so much of life unaccounted for. It could
not "convey comfort to the heart," or give "wings to the spirit," or "feed
the imagination," but the knowledge of the mystic could. "Not until the
spiritual nature of man can be reduced to a chemical process, and the
conviction of its unity with the world-spirit proved a baseless dream, will
this form of thought [mysticism] utterly perish."[63]

One contemporary mystic who enjoyed popularity within the literary
circle of Cambridge, and whose work Stone & Kimball would later promote, was the Belgian author Maurice Maeterlinck. Combining "the pure,
simple lines of mediaeval thought with a style and a method that are the

refinement of the most extreme *fin de siècle* ideas,'' Maeterlinck appealed to the Harvard student because his "obtrusive virility of a strong character" would not content itself with mere sensual satisfactions and perceptions. A "prophet of the Unseen," he belonged "to that mediaeval mysticism, which looked not upon the earth, but upon what was beyond." Through his "intense imagination" rather than with his senses, "he reaches forward into the invisible world, and lifts for a moment the veil that hangs between the supernatural and the finitude of human apprehension." It is particularly noteworthy that contemporaries were aware of the similarity between medieval artistic expression and that of current avant-garde Symbolism, with which Maeterlinck was identified. "As his lifetime falls within the period of the Decadence, his imagination [which in the fourteenth-century would have made him a disciple of the mystic Ruysboeck] expresses itself in the language of the Symbolistic schools. The symbolic and mystic spirits are so closely allied that it is impossible to exactly define their differences."[64]

Symbolism was not synonymous with mysticism for all Harvard men. To some it was a literary movement that went beyond it. Henry Copley Green explained to the readers of *The Harvard Monthly* in May 1894 that, in the past, literary schools "have treated the separate aspects of human life: the Naturalists, the physical aspect; the Psychologists, the mental; the Romanticists and the Mystics, the emotional and spiritual." Now the time had come for the Symbolists' attempt to integrate these different approaches into one synthesis of the whole man. Their four-fold aim was: "to unite in literature the effects of the other fine arts, to combine all former literary methods, by their aid to treat all the aspects of man, and finally, always to incarnate some ideas." Their notorious interest in sensuous impressions was always counterbalanced by the mystic's realization of "the unreality of time and space." Sensory impressions were not ends in themselves as they were for the realists, but important as "forms of thought and characteristics of man," knowledge of which could lead the Symbolists closer to expression of what was essentially a "pantheistic philosophy" of revealed ideality.[65]

Whether the ideality was the God of the medieval mystic, the power of a Kantian moral imperative, the functioning of a Roycean world-spirit, or the aesthetic expression of a Nortonian imaginative faculty, its essence was beyond the realm of the merely scientifically or realistically knowable. Only through symbolic representation, emanating from the personal imaginative creativity of each man's "spirit," coupled with his actual sensory perceptions (physical, mental and emotional), could one begin to express a synthetic knowledge of the totality of human experience. Art, even more specifically literature, could no longer be content with expressing only one facet of living reality. Realism in art was as insufficient as rationalism in philosophy. Both had merit, but were not capable of providing a whole view of life. In recognizing the importance of imaginatively penetrating life's spiritual dimensions, the integrationist approach of the Symbolists (much like the integrationist approach of Royce) could move beyond former limitations of compartmentalized spheres of knowledge.

This quest for a more comprehensive expression of the realities of human life, realities which included living spiritual factors, was a staggering task for even the most mature individuals. How did Harvard's young men of the nineties go about responding to this challenge which they felt had been put to them? Norton urged them to begin in the simplest of ways, by concentrating on their own conduct as an expression of their spirit made manifest. Principally concerned with introducing his students to the fine arts, all "arts of expression," he took the time in his first lecture to Stone's class to note: "Expression is every mode which a man adopts for utterance of his spirit or character, utterance of thought or emotion." Art was but one form of expression, a man's conduct was another. As moral creatures, "we are responsible to others for the character of the expression we use [towards] them." And as in art, so too in conduct: "The most beautiful is the best. Any habits which are selfish are ugly: for in so doing you are not doing what you can to make the best of yourself. Every act is an expression & every expression has a reflex-action on the soul to confirm the quality from which it proceeds."[66] Sounding curiously like the moral to Oscar Wilde's notoriously decadent *The Picture of Dorian Gray*, Norton challenged his students to integrate aesthetic theory into their active lives, stimulating many of them to enter careers which attempted to give public testimony to the vital presence of spiritual concerns in contemporary life. Though not a Symbolist himself, he in essence was charging them to evidence in their lives and works symbolic expressions of the cultured imagination's contact with the real world. "Unless you are struck by the relation of these things to your own lives you will go through life ignorant men. . . . The world cannot go on unless you Harvard men become more serious."[67]

Two ways that Stone and his friends found to relate seriously their ideas on art to their lives were the production of finely crafted books of high quality, and the publication of magazines reflecting similarly high artistic standards. Neither endeavor was unique to Herbert Stone and his collaborators. Indeed, they were following the leads of older members of their group, consistent with the interests they shared in common. For instance, in the spring of 1893, Charles Townsend Copeland (Class of '82 and later contributor to *The Chap-Book*) taught a voluntary course on books to interested Harvard undergraduates. This was no literature course of the regular curriculum, but focused attention instead on the aesthetics of the books themselves. *The Harvard Monthly* reported that it was "so well attended as to give strong evidence of the need felt by undergraduates for an artistic appreciative treatment of literature apart from its scholarly study."[68] And an "artistic appreciative treatment of literature" could be most tangibly demonstrated in the physical creation of those books. Towards this end Herbert Copeland and Fred Day, recent Harvard graduates and friends of Stone, set up their own book publishing firm in Boston in the early nineties. Dedicated to the art of fine craftsmanship in both printing and binding, this firm was to be one of Stone & Kimball's most closely associated rivals.

Not surprisingly, as concern grew for the production of books which would illustrate their publishers' views that literary book art should be finely presented, a similar concern developed over the unified artistic expression of periodic literature. Ralph Adams Cram, who documented many of the activities of Cambridge's literary coterie, especially their bookmaking interests, noted the motivations behind his own first abortive attempt to establish a magazine, sometime around 1890[69]: "there was the underlying conviction [at this time] that it was a great world—that romance and poetry and beauty were coming back to a drab century, and that in some way I was to find my place amongst the bearers of glad tidings. The time-honoured organ of such an evangel always has been, I suppose always will be, some sort of magazine." His idea was to issue "a monthly publication dealing with all the arts, including letters, postulating the unity of art and its basic importance in the scheme of life."[70]

Cram's journal never came into being, but another one, in which he was involved, did. *The Knight Errant*, carrying a publication date on its first issue of April 1892, was the unofficial organ of Cambridge's book worshippers. Seven of its first ten contributors would later write for *The Chap-Book*.[71] Cram, whose own contribution to the first number was entitled "Concerning the Restoration of Idealism and the Raising To Honour Once More of the Imagination," called it: "one of the earliest and most potent . . . factors in the recreation of the bookmaker's art."[72] Self-proclaimed literary "godmother" of *The Knight*, as she would later be of *The Chap-Book*, Louise Imogen Guiney wrote to a fellow contributor on April 21, 1892: "The *Knight Errant* is said to be out today, being a belated, moonstruck, and unmethodic arrival, who was due months ago. He is as mediaeval as possible, by way of representing the rebound from progress and science and agnosticism and general modernity." And their aesthetic guide, for what she called this "seraphic joke" in a "vulgar old world," was Harvard's own Charles Eliot Norton. "Prof. Norton lends glory to the first number. He is our scholar to swear by."[73] Their aim, as Cram later defined it, "was to be not only an expression of the most advanced thought of the time (the word [advanced] meant then something radically different from what it means today), but, as well, a model of perfect typography and the printer's art." As its cover, both "decorative and symbolic," attested, this periodical was meant as a statement of faith in the efficacy of art as a guide to contemporary life. Supported by no radical fringe, "This venture was made possible by a group of guarantors, the list reading like a 'blue book' of the New England intelligentsia of the time."[74] When in 1894 *The Knight* was preparing to cease publication, *The Chap-Book* lamented the demise of this work of "men of much culture," with its "decadent" but "delightful . . . opposition to commercialism."[75]

While there was much in *The Knight Errant* that appealed to the later publishers and editors of *The Chap-Book*, it was an example of similar interests more than a model for emulation. Stone had been preparing himself for some time for a literary career, and did not need the example of *The Knight* as an impetus to move in that direction. However, the timing of its release coincided with a distinct shift in his own career plans. An active contributor at least since the beginning of his sophomore year to Harvard's student newspaper, *The Daily Crimson*, Stone had fallen into the predictable pattern of preparing himself to follow in his father's footsteps, anticipating a career in newspaper journalism. His work for the *Crimson*, as distinct from Harvard's other more literary publications, he thought would give him "perhaps the most valuable practice of any of the college papers" given his future plans.[76] Midway through his sophomore year, Stone's interest had expanded to the point that not only did he feel he could handle his *Crimson* work (he was now a member of its editorial board) besides his studies, but he was also writing for the *Lampoon*, anticipating election to its board, and planning to try for *The Harvard Advocate*.[77] He had been approached by the managing editor of *The Harvard Monthly* to try for that paper as well.[78] No mere reporter any longer, Stone's fascination with literature had turned decidedly more artistic.

Perhaps it was due to the fact that he was not elected to the *Lampoon* board, or perhaps it was merely the effects of his increased exposure to alternative journalistic options, but by the spring of 1892 Stone had begun to think of publishing his own magazine, a magazine that would, in his own words, "rival the *Lampoon*." His plan was to make it "an illustrated, humorous bi-weekly paper—$2.00 per year. There will be a short story in each number, illustrated in pen and ink or sepia."[79] Unable to convince his father of the timeliness of such a venture, Stone was forced to put his magazine plans in the back of his mind. His energies were in no way diminished, however; and following his spring's vacation in Chicago, he devoted what time he had to the production of his first book, a guide to the Columbian Exposition. It was an important first step towards his career as a book publisher, and eventually to the founding of *The Chap-Book*.

Norton had complained to the students in Stone's Fine Arts class, that: "If this community had a sense of beauty and its influence, it would not allow you and me to be cooped up in this room."[80] Stone felt cooped up, not just by an aesthetically unpleasant classroom environment, but also by the practically inactive regimen of a student's life. Introduced to the world of book publishing by his fair guide, Stone immediately began amassing materials for a second guide—this time for books—and he revelled in this creative and practical work. By January 1893 he was writing his family regarding his college studies: "I think it would be much better if I were to give up this life of tiresome idleness and go to work seriously." It was no longer his wish but his family's that there be a Stone with a Harvard degree. "I wish you were not so anxious to have [me] get a degree at Harvard for I believe I could make much better use of my time in some way other than pretended study." Tantalized by his recent exposure to the active world of publishing and discouraged over his own lackluster performance as a student, Stone reported: "I have come to the conclusion that the best thing I can do is to get expelled from Harvard and then go into the book-publishing business in Chicago."[81]

Curiously, this first note of dissatisfaction over the idleness of academe was written on the stationery of H.I. Kimball, and it was the relationship he formed with Kimball later that month[82] that helped, along with the pressure of his family, to keep Stone at Harvard. But Harvard had now become an opportune place from which to do business, the business of making finely bound and printed books. It was also a place filled with prospective authors. Within a little over one year, the new firm of Stone & Kimball had twenty titles bearing its imprint. Both Stone's and Kimball's academic careers were in serious jeopardy, but their publishing prospects were booming. Even Harvard officials, while frowning on the deficiencies of Stone's scholastic record, gave encouragement to the young man's creative enterprise. Stone explained to his mother that the faculty was "in perfect sympathy with our work and one of them was good enough to say—as perhaps I wrote you—that this was the first piece of real enterprise ever connected with Harvard College. You know the Faculty is trying to do away with the prevalent idea that Harvard is not practical and so they are mighty glad to have us here."[83] Not so glad to be there was Stone, who in early 1894 petitioned the university's Administrative Board for a leave of absence in order to pursue his publishing interests. Stone told his father that the Dean "told me I had the sympathy of the entire board and that they would have given me my degree in a second if they had dared." The faculty was apparently "delighted" with his guide to *First Editions of American Authors*, and the Dean advised Stone to withdraw from Harvard. "He said if I would go away from here until they could forget my record and remember only the firm (I shall regularly send them catalogues and prospectuses) they would grant me my degree out of pure sympathy."[84]

It was at this time, when Stone was trying to negotiate his withdrawal from Harvard, that the idea of publishing a magazine again came under serious consideration. This time Stone did not ask his father's permission but presented him with a fait accompli. On letterhead stationery that read "The Chap-Book," Stone wrote to his family: "I use this paper on purpose to show you what we are doing. I fear father will not be pleased with the announcement but when I have explained just what it is, I think he will agree with me in thinking it a good plan." Much weight has been given, by the historian of Stone & Kimball and Herbert S. Stone & Co., to a further statement of Stone's in this letter that *The Chap-Book* was begun as "no more nor less than a semi-monthly advertisement and regular prospectus for Stone & Kimball."[85] Given the elder Stone's reluctance to sanction his son's earlier plans to issue a magazine, it was not surprising that young Herbert may have tried to make his magazine appear as inconsequential as possible in his family's eyes. But the fact of the matter is, as is plainly evident from the magazine itself, *The Chap-Book* never functioned as merely an advertising medium for its publishers. It was from the beginning an independent literary journal: witty, brash, pleasing to the eye and provocative to the mind.

Advertising itself as "a MISCELLANY of Curious and Interesting Songs, Ballads, Tales, Histories & c.; adorned with a variety of pictures and very delightful to read; *newly composed by* MANY CELEBRATED WRITERS: To which are annex'd a LARGE COLLECTION of Notices of Books,"[86] its poster was nearly as eclectic as the pages of its one hundred issues. The word miscellany aptly describes this semimonthly which ran from May 1894 through July 1898, for its interests ranged over a variety of topics, expressed by a potpourri of seemingly unrelated artists working in diverse genres and mediums. If its advertisement appeared slightly antiquated to some, it reflected an important thrust of its publishers' concerns and the magazine's character. Likewise, if to other critics a magazine that would hire Toulouse-Lautrec to design a poster seemed modern and daring, it was that as well.[87]

Upon close examination, and in the light of the background of Stone's Harvard education, it soon becomes apparent that *The Chap-Book* while appearing miscellaneous was far from that. It was quite methodically drawn together by the unifying editorial vision of its principal guardian, Herbert S. Stone, and his similarly oriented associates in light of the lessons they had learned at Harvard in the early 1890s. Its pages did not schizophrenically alternate between the old and new, but attempted to bring together in a meaningful synthesis what was valuable and instructive in both categories. Essentially romantic Symbolists, who were willing to experiment with a compatible variety of realism, Herbert Stone and his associates produced a magazine that defies easy categorization. Not interested in compartmentalizing art, they used their magazine as a means of showing their readers that romance still had vitality, that realism need not be materialistically squalid, and that art could symbolically reveal insights into realms of knowledge which postmedieval intellectual thought had left largely ignored. Their magazine was neither morbid nor dispirited; on the contrary, it was an experiment in buoyant optimism. It was a statement of faith, a testament of the cultured imaginations that Harvard had nurtured. In articulating their concerns to a national and to some extent international readership, they were fulfilling Harvard's charge to help educate the larger community on intellectual and moral issues of fundamental importance to contemporary life.

The Romantic Vision:
A Familiar Perspective

When *The Chap-Book* first appeared on May 15, 1894 it was a small and spritely literary balloon. Slight in size and slim in contents, it attracted attention because it was both pleasingly new yet pleasantly familiar. Herbert Stone's journalistic enterprise, from its inception, managed to present to its readers a relatively stable mixture of contributions from established literary figures as well as aspiring newcomers to the field. In part, this simply reflected the composition of the environment, Boston's book world, from which the magazine sprang. It also reflected a willingness to entertain a measure of diversity in its pages and the ability to find working areas of intellectual agreement. One such area of agreement was its pronounced fidelity to a recognizable romanticism. Within the freedom offered by an established set of presumptions, *The Chap-Book*'s authors were able to explore tentatively an expanding area of intellectual interest without cutting themselves loose from the secure moorings which grounded, and to that extent limited, their flights.

In launching his new journal, Stone was dependent upon the help of his Cambridge friends. Since he wanted his scheme well under way before turning to his father with any requests for assistance, financial or literary, Stone was temporarily left to his own devices and intellectual inclinations. Not surprisingly, he looked to one of the "older" members of his young literary set for advice and counsel, as well as for contributions to fill his new magazine. Bliss Carman, a most compatible young poet and essayist well known among the Cambridge literati, became Stone's coeditor for the first several numbers and, ultimately, *The Chap-Book*'s most frequent contributor.[1] The influence which he was able to exert on Stone and Stone's magazine through his prose, poetry, editorial scrutiny, and circle of friends confirmed the aspiring publisher's drift toward romanticism.

Coming from an old New England family which had emigrated to Canada when the American colonies declared their independence, Carman's background, both in lineage and locale, helped condition his over-whelming attraction to the romantic vision. Born in the provincial capital of Fredericton, New Brunswick, just fifty miles from the New England border, Carman grew up in a town that boasted its own university while enjoying a secluded setting in one of nature's idyllic fertile valleys. His family was Tory, his heritage New England Puritanism, his home the benign forests of a remote but civilized intellectual center, his education the writings of the nineteenth century's most respected authors. All these factors combined to impress upon the young boy a sense of beauty un-tainted by the artificial, of nature embued with spiritual significance, and of ideals to be reverenced.[2]

When Carman later reflected in *The Chap-Book* on the factors which conditioned the works of his fellow Canadian poets (and by inference his work as well), he attributed considerable significance to their isolation "from the centers of thought and civilization" which had enabled them to keep alive "a very real and pure worship of Nature." Describing the lyric poetry that they produced, he noted: "With their Loyalist traditions, their romantic history, their untold resource, their beautiful land, their vigorous climate, their future all to make, their days of immeasurable leisure, it is little wonder their songs should have all the genuine assurance of youth, the freshness of the fields."[3] Carman was echoing common romantic refrains when he claimed that he and his countrymen were free from the corrupting influences of the decaying, artificial urban environ-ments that were the places of nurture for so many of the literary men of the United States. In their natural environment, these Canadians had become devoted "imaginative interpreters of the beautiful outward world, not unworthy children of Keats and Emerson and Wordsworth." No un-lettered rubes, they knew that what they aspired to was a combination of Keat's sensuality and Emerson's spirituality, to sound "the note of a worship of Nature from which modern knowledge has cast out fear, the note of a religion that was on the earth before Paganism had a name."[4]

While writing for *The Chap-Book,* Carman was also writing a series of essays that would be combined with others to form the volume *The Kinship of Nature.* Here he specifically noted his debts to both the en-vironment of his youth and the intellectual tutelage of one of his early teachers, George Robert Parkin. Before reminiscing about the impact of the *Idyls of the King, The Blessed Damozel,* William Morris, Matthew Arnold, and Charles Algernon Swinburne, all of whom Parkin slipped into the classroom to relieve the study of the classical curriculum, Carman acknowledged the conditioning effect of his surroundings. "Those were the days when we were all young together, whether at Greek or football, tramping for Mayflowers through the early spring woods, paddling on the river in intoxicating Junes, or snowshoeing across bitter drifts in the perishing December wind,—always under the leadership of your [Parkin's] indomitable ardour. In that golden age we first realized the kinship of Nature."[5] Youth, ardor, nature, romantic idylls, aesthetic theorists and lyric poetry all combined to impress Carman with qualities which he would later reflect in his own writing.

By the time Herbert Stone came to Harvard and came to know Carman, the young Canadian's native romanticism had gone through a rather extended period of refinement. He had spent a year in Edinburgh, taught school for several years, and finally ended up pursuing advanced studies at Harvard. Harvard provided, in the words of Carman's biographer, "the awakening impulse" for Carman's artistic creativity. His friends, particularly Richard Hovey (whose knowledge of the European Symbolists would later be of great importance to *The Chap-Book*) and others "of an intellectual or artistic type," were all anxious "to get at and assimilate the best and highest within their reach in the American culture of that day." Their reaching, particularly Carman's, was guided by his contact with Professor Josiah Royce. Royce taught Carman "a form of Spinozistic idealism" which served "as a philosophic substructure for the mystical contemplation and reverie which make up so large a part of his poetic world."[6]

Carman's love of nature, filtered through Royce's idealism, also produced a rationale for art that served as the philosophic substructure for *The Chap-Book*'s editorial choices. He was concerned with nature—the beauty of natural form in its simplicity—primarily because of the spiritual significance he attributed to it. No aesthete, Carman cherished heroic values and ideals, nature's spirit rather than its reality, and the emotional, instinctual and unconscious more than the rational.

Art and life, in Carman's view, should be inseparable. Like Stone's mentor at Harvard, Charles Eliot Norton, Carman believed that art was the expression of self.[7] Inherent in each individual, as in every physical phenomenon, was some spark of the creative spirit, and art, unlike other specialized (or fragmented) approaches to knowledge, was capable of expressing the complex nature of the spirit's life. Carman believed that "good art is the expression, not only of the rational waking objective self, the self which is clever and intentional and inductive, but of the deeper unreasoning self, as well." This belief elevated art to a religion, told of its ability to "pass the threshold of the outer mind and pass in to sway the mysterious subconscious person who inhabits us."[8] Each individual was an important manifestation of the spirit. Each living creature could probe the mystery of creation by exploring his inner self. The artist's task was to document the results of this spiritual quest.

Sounding like a mystic, Carman extolled the values of self-exploration, particularly solitary contemplation. "For it is when we are most alone and withdrawn into our profounder selves that we are most completely in accord with the spirit of the universe, by whatever name it may be called." The great danger to contemporary society came from the fact that it had become preoccupied with partial truths, or worse yet distracting materialism, neglecting life's primary, spiritual meaning. "When we allow ourselves to be engrossed unceasingly in the smaller outward, trivial details of existance, and in superficial human intercourse . . . [we] become so thoroughly habituated to living on the surface that we seem to have no core of being left in us." Carman felt that this was "the real cause of the vapidity of society" and that "we cannot too constantly be giving ourselves away without replenishing our individuality from that deeper intercourse which solitude affords."[9]

Reacting against the dominant tendencies that had been guiding the progress of Western civilization for several centuries, the intellectual advancements of which the Enlightenment was so proud and the industrial advancements of which his own century boasted, Carman championed a revival of individual spirituality. He made of art a religion, because through art he hoped to recapture an awareness of life's endangered spiritual essences. In claiming that art "is the worship of the manifestations of spirit taking shape in forms of beauty, just as our enjoyment of nature is the worship of spirit manifest in the plasticity of sap and cell,—the lovely forms of the outer world,"[10] he was reasserting a primal need of his basically religious nature. For him, as for so many of his contemporaries, traditional Christianity's credibility had been badly damaged, but his will to believe in the efficacy of life's spiritual dimensions remained intact.

In explaining the contemporary significance of Christianity's most important religious celebration, Carman demonstrates a religious persistence that frankly, stubbornly, and even irrationally, refused to die. He rallies all of romanticism's distinctive ideological supports not to bolster a particular doctrinal system of an institutional church. Rather, his concern is for the faith that originally inspired men to create that system. No matter what evidence science and the rational mind can marshal against the claims of revealed religion, deep within the individual soul there remains a need to believe that life is not merely a brief material accident.

At Easter we celebrate the immortal fancy of an imperishable life. It is the season of rapture, of lyric belief in more than human possibility, the day on which the timorous soul is summoned to put trust in the very frailest probability, yet with the stoutest, most stubborn faith. Laying aside doubt and the prosy mind, the soul now and again asserts her right to an hour of pure idealism where the solid and sage of actuality can have no part. She insists that conviction is enough, that proof is not necessary, that her beloved dream must come true because she has dreamed it so often and so hard. She will hear no cold discouragement from her scientific sister mind; she persists in being fondly wilful in her own sweet way. What do the plain deductions of all the doctors, of all the schools count with her? Is not her own intuition more reliable? Shall she forsake the warm, comfortable doctrine of a beautiful immortality for the barren desolation of the fleeting fact?[11]

On other occasions Carman was to rail against "the tyranny of facts,"[12] but in the fact of art's tangibility he found a viable substitute for traditional religion. He saw the danger of those "artists or preachers or teachers or reformers" who in pursuit of some ideal vision or dream "become wholly absorbed in the emotional and mental life, neglecting the material." Men must recognize that "we are creatures so strangely compounded of dust and dream, that we can never wholly give our allegiance to either one." Nature had taught Carman that "the very core and gist of human life," its "miracle," was "the union of mind and matter." It was the moral duty of the artist to make his visions real to others, just as the spirit had made them real in nature. "It will avail you nothing to stand face to face with the vision, if you cannot in some way make actual and apparent to men the beauty you have beheld."[13]

Writers were particularly fortunate in the medium in which they worked, because words were distinctly appropriate to the task of expressing ideality. Words had an advantage over natural manifestations of the spirit because words could never be misperceived as being mere matter. "The word is that which has both meaning and melody, both sense and semblance; it is that which informs us; it is neither matter alone, nor spirit alone, but the dual manifestation of the two in one. It is the symbol of the universe that we perceive, and the universe that we are." As such, words became the very heart of Carman's religion: "The Word is the Lord of Creation, the unresting master of life, the great vagabond, our substantial brother and ghostly friend."[14]

Knowing Carman's background and artistic predispositions, it is not surprising to see how he guided Stone in the choice of literary fare that was to introduce *The Chap-Book* to its readers. Nor is it surprising that the guidelines laid down in the beginning held for *The Chap-Book*'s entire life. While Carman may have been an editor for only the first few numbers, his contributions in poetry and criticism spanned the magazine's complete run. And Stone, who had deliberately chosen Carman to help him get started, managed to maintain final editorial control of his journal until its demise. In the following analysis of a sampling of the contributions published on *The Chap-Book*'s pages, the concerns of Carman can be seen to have been shared not only by Stone but by many other contemporaries. They did not always take it as their task to give critical exposition to the intellectual theories that undergirded their work. But the products of their creativity show that his thoughts were theirs as well.

Leading off the first issue of *The Chap-Book* was a selection of poetry by Carman's fellow Canadian, and cousin, Charles G.D. Roberts. Roberts's verses were a logical choice for two reasons. In the first place, given his relationship to Carman, they were available, no small factor considering *The Chap-Book* was a periodical experiment of a virtually unknown publisher. But more importantly, they reflected the concerns that Stone's editorial vision, supported and enhanced in its early numbers by Carman, was to promulgate in this magazine. Entitled "The Unsleeping," Roberts's six stanzas of verse are a personal avowal of the power and meaning of spiritual reality inherent in all natural reality. More than that they are a testament to the creative imagination which is capable of perceiving the spirit, and through this perception acts as the motivating agent which keeps the spirit alive.[15]

At first the poet is apparently establishing the presence of the spirit, "I," in all natural phenomena. It is this "I" which determines the nature of these phenomena and regulates their natural rhythms, as in the first stanza:

> I soothe to unimagined sleep
> The sunless bases of the deep;
> And then I stir the aching tide
> That gropes in its reluctant side.

Concurrent with the spirit's confirmation as the determining factor in the creation of all the natural phenomena of the universe—from the highest volcanic mountain to the smallest "sightless germ," from the atoms that compose that germ to the comets fixed in deepest space—comes an affirmation of the spirit's continuing presence after creation. Like the heart of a volcano, the spirit's power simmers, ever present, active, ready to burst forth with a new show of energy: "But ever at its heart of fire I lurk, an unassuaged desire." This core of energy is not some impersonal force, but a paternal spirit. Natural phenomena are not merely within the spirit's control, they are within its "care."

While the poet has devoted himself largely to the task of establishing the presence of the spirit within natural phenomena, he closes the poem by cautioning the reader against attaching too much importance to these physical manifestations of the spirit. Also in the final stanza, for the first time in the poem, he draws attention to the personal identity of the "I" who has been speaking.

Space, in the dim predestined hour,
Shall crumble like a ruined tower.
I only, with unfaltering eye,
Shall watch the dreams of God go by!

When material reality has been obliterated, all that will be left will
be spiritual reality. This spiritual reality is not, however, simply the distant
reserve of some deity, "the dreams of God." The "I" who is watching
is finally seen to be the individual spirit who can perceive those dreams,
and it is the perception of the spirit in all natural phenomena which has
been the motivating force throughout the poem. The artist, in this particular instance the poet, graced with the power of creative imagination, is
able to discern the spirit's presence and in so discerning becomes a co-
creator. Making use of Emerson's favorite image of the seeing eye, the
poet has linked the visions of the artist with those of an eternal spiritual
reality.

These verses by Roberts were the kind of serious poetry that most
appealed to Carman and were representative of the art that Stone promoted both through publishing opportunities and through attention in
critical reviews. The artist was more than a lover of beauty. He was both
a perceiver and transmitter of spiritual truths. He was a creator of physical reality that could reveal to others life's most significant spiritual realities. Nature was a teacher, but its lessons could only be learned by those
who could see more than its surfaces. The poet, in creating a poem could
recreate physical reality in such a way as to illumine its spiritual dimensions to others who might otherwise have been ignorant of its presence.
As Carman wrote in a subsequent *Chap-Book*: "poetry is at its best
[when] it is doing for us what nothing else can; . . . interpreting for us
the beauty of the outward world and the inward mysterious craving of
the human mind."[16] In speaking of poetry, Carman did not mean to limit
himself to one specific literary mode: poetry was any act of the imagination which transported man beyond the realm of the material, practical,
rationally knowable universe.

Not content to let the message of Roberts's poetry stand alone without any critical support in that first issue of *The Chap-Book*, Carman
followed "The Unsleeping" with his own review of the poetry of Francis
Thompson.[17] In this essay Carman commented on how the spirit, through
the poet's use of his imaginative faculty, manifests itself in literature. As
a good romantic, he naturally focused first on the individual self as the
seed germ containing all the important secrets of the universe. As an
artist it was his task to reveal to others what he himself discovered in
probing his individual being: "art is the outcome of expression, and
expression is the revelation of self,—sincere or nothing."

Sincerity of expression, for Carman, was virtually synonomous with natural revelation. Nature never lied or deceived or distorted reality; its representations were always faithful expressions of that which had to be. Carman was no natural determinist, but he was an organicist of sorts. For instance, in his criticism of Thompson's style, he complained that it was labored and full of affected mannerisms. These were inexcusable faults in a true artist because they did not result from the "compelling blind necessity the person has felt for just that expression and no other."[18] Part of Thompson's problem was that he did not trust his self enough to realize that its natural expression would have been more profound than any artifically contrived construction that had no roots in his own personal experience.

One problem led to another. Lacking the sureness of self-expression, Thompson's work, in Carman's estimate, became elaborately distorted. Like the scientist who mistakenly thinks that the dissection of one material object will yield a total picture of life's meanings and mysteries, Thompson had concentrated his efforts on the complex exploration of what Carman considered to be poetry's material objects: that is, artificially conceived literary images. Thompson had become a materialist, focusing his attention on isolated man-made constructions that were totally removed from any natural, life-sustaining and spirit-filled context. "He treats a fancy or a conceit as a child might treat a butterfly. He pulls the gauzy wings apart until the poor thing is wracked beyond all hope of loveliness forever."[19] Poetry as revelation of self, and self as revelation of spirit, could not be broken down into its component physical parts, analyzed and explained, in the hope that such an empirical dissection would reveal that which makes its wholeness meaningful. That manner of ratiocination bore no relationship to the functioning of the "compelling blind necessity" of the spirit to find expression. As Carman noted in another context: "Scientific formulae are an admirable means of communication between mind and mind, but art is a means of communication for the whole being,—mind, body and spirit."[20] Thompson's verses were more like scientific formulae than poetry. They communicated only the mind, not the whole being.

Dissatisfaction with attempts to intellectualize, and in so doing to materialize, literary art was further expressed in the next prose contribution to *The Chap-Book*'s first number. Just as it was fatal to become too intellectual in the imaginative process of creating art, it also was destructive to become too intellectual in the receptive process of appreciating art. In an unsigned "Bitter Complaint of the Ungentle Reader," Louise Imogen Guiney[21] vented her outrage over the "diabolic suggestion" that an essay should be written on "How to Read a Book of Poems so as to Get the Most Good out of It."[22] Guiney was a close friend of Carman's,[23] and it was to be expected that her thoughts would be compatible with those of her editors.

Reading poetry, according to Guiney's "Bitter Complaint," was not something one should have to learn how to do, or be forced to do for self-improvement. It should be as natural as eating when one has the appetite to do so. Our "too educated world" was not content to let reading be a natural function of individual and instinctive inclination, something to be done for pleasure and not for profit. When done for profit, reading, especially the reading of poetry, destroyed the very essence of the art being scrutinized. Reading for profit turned poetry into a product. As such it would be highly unlikely for the reader to appreciate it as a mystical happening, a miraculous creation, a manifestation of the spirit.

Using as a foil Cardinal Newman's theory of education, Guiney complained that the schoolmaster's mentality of necessary knowledge was ruining our appreciation of art by overloading our minds with unnecessary information. The schoolmaster "would have us in a chronic agony of inquisitiveness . . . with minds gluttonously receptive, not of the little we need (which it is the ideal end and aim of a university education, according to Newman, to perceive and to assimilate) but of the much not meant for us." Cramming our minds with trivial facts left no room in which the spirit could live and grow. "The Muse is dying nowadays of over-interpretation. Too many shepherd swains are trying to Get the Most Good out of her."[24]

Elaborating on this nonutilitarian, nonintellectual approach to poetry, Guiney took note of the contrast between the nature of poets as creators of art, and that of modern intellectual readers as its consumers. She chose to place her remarks within the nineteenth-century's romantic tradition by equating that which was good and natural with unspoiled youth, and that which was corrupt and artificial with decadent old age. "Even in a sophisticating age, it is the nature of poets to remain young. Their buyers are always one remove nearer to the sick end of the century, and being themselves tainted with the sense of the importance of the scientific, are in so much disqualified to judge of the miracle, the phenomenon, which poetry is."[25] Miraculous phenomena were the substance of the spiritual world, not the world of scientific facts. It was a world of beauty and wonder and enchantment, all qualities dear to the heart of every romantic, as to every child.

Carman was to write in a later *Chap-Book,* "Poetry, the poetic quality in all art, has in it something of the hushed wonder of a child in the face of the unknown; it is the rapt, not quite coherent, exclamation of the spirit, awakening to a consciousness of itself, allured at once by the outward passion for beauty, and teased by the inward curiosity for knowledge."[26] The child was for Carman, as for his fellow romantics, the perfect embodiment of nature's mysterious possibilities. He was a thinking creature not yet tainted by worldly sophistication and practical rationality. He was searching for knowledge yet not afraid to learn from that which he did not totally comprehend. He was both awed and delighted by mysteries. By not foreclosing his mind, the child was capable of free flights of creative imagination, flights in which the real and the imagined, the factual and the spiritual were integrated into a poetic whole. He was not only a favorite of Carman and Guiney, but a recurring figure in *The Chap-Book*'s cast of characters in search of the true meaning of life.[27]

If *The Chap-Book*'s new readers had not already ascertained by the time they finished reading Guiney's article that the artistic predisposition of this fledgling periodical was opposition to what it considered to be a materialistic intellectualism, Carman closed out the first issue with some additional clues. In the unsigned "Notes" section, Carman lavished his praises[28] on lyrics about nature, romantic illusions to exotic peoples, the nonintellectual appreciation of poetic images. Complaining that most magazine poetry was "ghastly twaddle," he called attention to one "priceless treasure" in the current issue of *Scribner's*. After quoting two stanzas of some lyrics called "Afoot," regarding the call of nature to be on the move in springtime, Carman singled out two lines that he claimed had swept him off his feet: "He shall chase the fleeting campfires/ Of the Bedouins of Time." Of particular significance was his following commentary: "What are the 'Bedouins of Time'? I am sure I don't know. What matter is it, what they are? If you will only give yourself up to the influence of the poem you will be exhilarated and refreshed; and when you come to the last line: 'Sink to sleep the nomad years,' you will be full of dreams and peace." What Carman considered almost perfect poetry, found in one of the standard journals, transported the reader beyond the realm of conscious mental activity into a reverie of repose, contentment and well-being. "Why do you wish to torture yourself with thought? Is it not enough that you should be made glad and happy?"[29] Surrendering control of the mind to the incomprehensible spirit produced a sublime state of euphoric unity. This was the function and effect of true art.

The Chap-Book's romantic concerns in its first issue were not limited to the message of its poetry, or even to poetry's critical appraisal. Capitalizing on the immediate identification in readers' minds of the name Robert Louis Stevenson with his romantic tale of adventure, faraway places, mystery and heroics, the one full-page illustration in *The Chap-Book*'s first issue was the title page from Stevenson's new book, *The Ebb*

Tide. Designed by Thomas B. Meteyard, another Cambridge colleague of Stone and Carman, this stark black and white pen and ink drawing of a desert island, inhabited by a lone tortoise amidst beach grass and palm trees, was evocative and appropriate. It captured in its simplicity a sense of the author's romantic concerns and the outlines of unspoiled nature.[30] It also established a style for the new magazine.

Illustrations in *The Chap-Book* would be predominantly woodcuts or pen and ink drawings. The only other illustration to appear in *The Chap-Book*'s first issue was a woodcut, by Herbert Stone, of the startling new fin de siècle artist Aubrey Beardsley. These two examples of the visual arts were clear portents of the melding of traditions that was to characterize so much of *The Chap-Book*'s aesthetic. Fundamental art forms were used to remind the reader of the simpler days of the earliest chap-books,[31] as well as to put him in touch with the newest trends in the decorative arts. They served as visual examples of *The Chap-Book*'s ability to be both old and new.[32]

Pessimism and despair, thought to be so common in the work of the artists of the 1890s, were almost totally absent from the pages of *The Chap-Book*. Certainty regarding the presence of spiritual realities was the basis not only of *The Chap-Book*'s romanticism but of its larger intellectual system. Romanticism had taught poets, such as Clinton Scollard, that in nature the perceptive observer could find the divine manifestations of life's essential spirituality. In Scollard's poem "The Walk," published towards the end of the magazine's first volume, the narrator climbs among the hills, filled with morning's "light and song," announcing his intention to:

> . . . hail as 'comrade mine'
> Each soul soe'er that seeks and sees
> The overture of One divine
> In dawn's antiphonies.

Talking of spirits laughing and leaping in joyful freedom, the poet proclaims that his journey shall not be limited by any mere physical barriers. He and the soulmates he anticipates encountering along the way shall only be limited by the highest reaches of their own imaginations:

> The wide outreachings of our sight
> Yon purple ridges shall not bind,
> But only some Andean height
> Horizoning the mind.

Relying on traditional religious myths and sacred liturgical signs to symbolize the spiritual transformation of physical reality, the poet concludes:

By radiant apotheosis
To Eden earth shall seem re-born:
So shall we find the chrism of bliss
Upon the hills of morn.[33]

Nature could function as a cathedral for these romantics, a place where they might commune with the divine spirit. But actual physical reality, nature in all its glory, remained a poor physical approximation of a more perfect spiritual world. As Archibald Lampman wrote in the second volume of *The Chap-Book*, he sought "a land where no hurricane falls." Using adjectives such as "infinite," "forever," "limitless," "perpetual" and "spiritual," he described a land that was, in the words of his title, "Inter Vias." It was a land that was not readily accessible to those who had become worldly-wise: " 'T is the land that our babies behold,/ Deep gazing when none are aware." Only "the great-hearted seers of old/And the poets have known it," because they possessed, and had been able to maintain from the time of their births, the ability to dream.[34] In their dreams both prophets and poets were able to perceive a spiritual world more real than the natural world they lived in.

Dreaming became a form of divine guidance. The romantic recognized that all of man's unaided efforts to know are limited, and throughout his history he had been forced repeatedly to look for spiritual assistance in living out his mortal existence. In *The Chap-book*'s third volume, Theodore Wratislaw wrote of the proverbial sailor who prayed to "Ave Maris Stella" for illumined direction in his journey on the sea of life. Aware that his destination was other than a physical port, and that without the aid of a divine navigator he would be left hopelessly adrift on an ocean of natural phenomena, the poet cried out for help:

Alone thou shinest forth to show
The hope of dreams man may not know.
O heavenly star, guide even me
To haven and home beyond the sea![35]

For those who were able to see, nature could illumine dreams that were beyond man's ability to fully understand or to actualize. And while some poets and prophets had been able to transcend the world of nature to behold a more perfect spiritual world, most men were not only blind to these visions, but were also blind to the spirit that even nature worshiped. Nature was always one step closer than man to spiritual reality because nature never deviated from its testamentary attitude of worship before the divine. Strange as it may seem, it was Stephen Crane, best known for his naturalistic *Maggie* (1892) and realistic historical novel *The Red Badge of*

Courage (1895), who gave *The Chap-Book* in its fourth volume (March 1, 1896) one of its most dogmatic assertions of nature's constant attitude of spiritual worship.

Crane's "Verses" outline the course of natural history, the eternal presence of the divine, man's insignificant materialistic strivings, and nature's reverential devotion. In four separate sections, Crane describes the earth before man's advent (night), man's early efforts to build his own world (morning), man's later efforts to enlighten his existence (evening), then nature once more alone with God (night). Night—nature and God without man—is at both the beginning and end of the poem. It is a condition where the only appropriate pose before a shrouded spiritual presence is one of worship. Throughout the poem nature continues to sing praises to the divine: "Give voice to us, we pray, O Lord,/That we may chant Thy goodness to the sun." Man, during his brief appearance, first disrupts the worship with the noise of his materialistic labors in creating "little black cities" that mar the natural landscape. After all his work is done, after his brief day of existence, man has only managed to "sprinkle" mere "tiny lights" across his world, in direct contrast with the sun-filled creation of God. Man's preeminent representatives, his "kings," are relegated to a position of value alongside the tiny swallows. But in their self-proclaimed glory, these kings, who bend their knees to no man, are insignificant before the "Humble, idle, futile peaks" of nature. It is the peaks, physically incapable of bending their massive heights, that "bow" in natural majesty before the wisdom of the divine. Night returns and the peaks are left alone with God.[36]

Over and over again nature is portrayed as the devout worshipper of the divine. Most often nature's rituals are seen as a direct parallel to those of conventional religion, as when John Bannister Tabb, Catholic priest and poet, closed out *The Chap-Book*'s fifth volume with "A Rubric" explaining the liturgical meaning of nature's seasonal rites.[37] But at other times, in keeping with Crane's belief that nature ministers more faithfully to the spirit than does man, the human priest is actually replaced by a more competent mediatory spiritual agent. George Woodberry closed out *The Chap-Book*'s sixth volume with the flowers of the field acting as the poet's only possible confessor.

> Only the lily shall shrive me
> Of my passion and my pain;
> Only the rose shall revive me
> From death unto life again.
> O lily, white to see,
> O rose of mystery,
> Hear me confess![38]

Nature was never distracted by its own pretensions. Its constancy was uncluttered by human attempts to usurp the role of God or explain away spiritual phenomenon. While some *Chap-Book* romantics flirted with what amounted to a kind of pantheistic natural religion,[39] most merely utilized images from nature to describe the workings of an otherwise unseen spirit, as had their fellow romantics for a century. In so doing, they were able to capitalize on a known identification that was clearly antithetical to the materialism and idolatry of science which they felt were the prime causes of the decay of Western civilization. Too often in contemporary society worship of the spirit had been replaced by worship of man's own ability to solve the riddles of the universe, to create a world that was perhaps more to his liking than the natural world he had inherited. This sacrilege *The Chap-Book* repudiated. Science, the pinnacle of man's rational knowledge, was but a puny hill from which to get a vantage point to see through the fog of life's mysteries. As Ruth McEnery Stuart and Albert Bigelow Paine wrote in the April 1, 1897 issue:

> The planets are the tireless wheels of Time,
>   That move obedient to a mighty will—
>   A boundless force, unseen, immutable—
> That hurls them on in harmony sublime.
> And through all ages men have sought to climb,
>   By devious ways, dim mountain peaks until
>   They might behold from Science' topmost hill
> The hidden scheme of God's eternal rhyme.
>
> Perhaps when Life's poor story had been told,
>   Beyond these sequences of flower and snow—
>   Earth's limitations and the pain of tears—
> God's universal score may be unrolled,
>   And with a larger vision we may know
>   The technic of the "music of the spheres."[40]

Alternate romantic approaches to the acquisition of knowledge found expression in *The Chap-Book* repeatedly. Concentration on the spirit made manifest in nature was but one way of focusing attention on the ideal reality these artists knew to be present beneath all natural phenomena. The magazine's fascination with tales of love and death, dreams and mysteries, and music likewise testified to its romantic presumption that life was more than what it appeared to be on the surface. Man did not simply mate woman, he loved her with emotions that transformed his very being. Life did not simply terminate with the cessation of mortal functions, it was transposed to another realm. Wisdom was not the rationally knowable; fragments of incomprehensible truth were often revealed obscurely in dreams and mysterious occurrences. And music, the most intangible medium of artistic expression, was capable of translating the mute voice of the spirit into a audible form.

Love, perhaps the favorite topic of all romantics, was a recurrent theme in *The Chap-Book*. It began with the first issue and ended with the last. At times it was banal, at times thoughtfully critical, but always it advocated emotional vitality as distinct from intellectual sterility. Emotions revealed truths, truths that could be perceived in no other way because so often they ran counter to every logical, practical, sometimes even moral requisite of day to day living. As one of life's most powerful emotions, love had traditionally been accepted as both the motivation and excuse for various unpredictable and otherwise unsanctionable deviations from what was considered sane and sensible conduct. It broke the bonds of a closed system of behavior.

When Maria Louise Pool contributed a simple, sentimental story of an old man and his dog to the first issue of *The Chap-Book* in May 1894, most readers would have been unaware that it represented anything more than an explication of the time-tried axiom that a man's best friend is his dog. In Pool's story, Lemmy Little, a crippled pauper, presents himself and his dog, Maje, to the keeper of the town's poorhouse requesting admittance. A peddlar of sweet flagroot, the flagroot carried about in a basket by his dog, Little is destitute and alone, too crippled now even to continue his most primitive occupation. Forced to resort to public charity in order to sustain himself, Lemmy Little will only accept the help he needs to survive if that help is also proffered to his dog, Maje. Maje is the only living creature that Little has to love, both his wife and son being dead. The desperate old man recognizes that he could never be so desperate that he would sacrifice love merely to live. Unless he is allowed to share his portion of alms with Maje, Little will not stay. His emotional appeal to the keeper of the poorhouse eventually is effective, to the point that the resolute guardian of the town's beneficence is willing to risk the livelihood that she and her husband, Abram, depend upon: "I tell you what 'tis. I've made up my mind to take you 'n' the dorg. 'N' if the town don't like it they may jest turn me 'n' Abram out. That's all there is about that."[41] A simple dog story, but that is not all there is to it. It is a story about an emotion that gives meaning to a life totally devoid of any other meaning. And it is a story of society's acceptance of that emotion as meaningful, even worthy of being subsidized.[42]

If, in its first issue, *The Chap-Book* had emphasized a rather vague nonintellectual approach to the appreciation of good poetry, by its last issue of July 1, 1898 the emphasis had become an explicit advocacy of love. Aesthetic enjoyment took precedence over intellectual significance:

before any reviewer could criticize a work of art he first had to become emotionally engaged in the mood responsible for its creation. Sounding very much like Louise Imogen Guiney in one of *The Chap-Book*'s first essays, John Burroughs wrote in one of the magazine's last essays: "It is no doubt a great loss to be compelled to read any work of literary art in a conscious critical mood, because the purely intellectual interest in such a work which criticism demands is far less satisfying then our aesthetic interest."[43]

In order to appreciate a poem the reader had to be moved by the same emotions which had inspired its creation. Professional reviewers relied too heavily on their critical faculties: "They call into play a conscious mental force that is inimical to the emotional mood in which the work had its rise; what was love in the poet becomes a pale intellectual reflection in the critic." Burroughs's opinion was that "Love must come first," creating impressions on the reader's subconscious. Only after this "emotional process" had fixed its images in the mind should the intellect be allowed to try to analyze them. "Probably in all normal, well-balanced minds the appreciation of a work of the imagination is a matter of feeling and intuition long before it is a matter of intellectual cognizance."[44] And if intellectual cognizance never came, as it did not come for Carman in *The Chap-Book*'s first number when he extolled the image of "the Bedouins of Time," that did not diminish the value of the imaginative creativity that was capable of stirring the emotions.

Burroughs likened aesthetic engagement, arising out of the emotions, to faith. It did not matter what it meant, it only mattered that it existed. "Not all minds can give a reason for the faith that is in them, and it is not important that they should; the main matter is the faith."[45] Just as the true believer must not let a religious creed, imposed upon him from outside his own experience, dictate the terms of his faith, so the reader of literary art should not let fixed critical standards bar his appreciation of any creative work which would otherwise emotionally engage him.

Emotional engagement meant taking risks, and *The Chap-Book* romantics were well within the limits of their intellectual tradition by repeatedly linking emotional love with the risk of loss of self or loss of loved one. Most often this loss was equated with physical death.[46] The close association of love with death was not a negative relationship, but an affirmation that the loss of material being did not diminish the substance of ideal reality which had been enlivened in the initial act of loving. If there was no diminution in death, then materialism was void of meaning.

Nature had taught the romantics that death was not terminal. Spring annually brought the renewal of life that the winter months had buried beneath its snows. There was no real loss in nature, merely transformation. In its simplest form this idea was presented in *The Chap-Book*'s seventh volume by Wallace de Groot Rice's verses "The Lesson." A young man mourns over the grave of his loved one, cursing God for his loss. His grief is assuaged, however, when he chances to see one day the white hyacinths, which had been placed on his lover's breast when they buried her, blooming anew, "and at the core/ Of every bloom a honey-bee."[47] The recurring vitality of nature's cyclical rebirth, and the added (if hackneyed) dimension that his love's blossom was still contributing nectar to life's sweetness, had served to remind the young man that he had not lost the beauty of his love. It still lived.

While *The Chap-Book* published a good bit of poetry as banal as Rice's, it was astute enough to reserve its critical praise for the same romantic themes expressed in a slightly more refined form. For instance, in a critical review of the new poems of Stephen Phillips, which appeared in *The Chap-Book*'s eighth volume, the reviewer was so impressed with Phillips's ability to communicate the mystery of love's immortality that he quoted the poet at length.

> I love thee then,
> Not only for thy body packed with sweet
> Of all this world, that cup of brimming June,
> That jar of violet wine set in the air,
> That palest rose sweet in the night of life;
> Nor for that stirring bosom all besieged
> By drowsing lovers, or thy perilous hair;
> Nor for that face which might indeed provoke
> Invasion of old cities; no, nor all
> Thy freshness stealing on me like strange sleep.
> Not for this only do I love thee, but
> Because Infinity upon thee broods;
> And thou art full of whispers and of shadows.[48]

All the physical, natural attributes that make love sensually exciting are noted, but they are the mere outward manifestations of the infinitely more enticing spiritual mysteries which they embody.

Often it is only when the distraction of the actual physical love has been removed that the spirit of love can fully live and be instructive. Love might be the emotion which awakens in an individual the awareness of eternal spiritual bonds, but grief confirms a completely immaterial reverence for life's essential ideality. Death was the logical corollary to love in a work of art because, in a hierarchical scheme, it was progressively more likely to concentrate attention on spiritual concerns rather than physical matter. H.H. Boyesen pointed this out in his review of *Little Eyolf*, "Ibsen's New Play," which appeared in *The Chap-Book* of February 1, 1895.

It took the death of little Eyolf, and the suffering and remorse which it engendered, to make his parents aware of a higher "spiritual life" than the passionate physical love which had given rise to Eyolf's birth.

> RITA (Nodding slowly)—There is a change in me now—I feel the anguish of it.
> ALLMERS—Anguish?
> RITA—Yes, for change, too, is a sort of birth.
> ALLMERS—It is—or a resurrection. Transition to a higher life.
> RITA (Gazing sadly before her)—Yes, with the loss of—all life's happiness.
> ALLMERS—That loss is just the gain.[49]

Reaffirming the same belief that love and passion were often not enough to awaken true spirituality, John Davidson in a later *Chap-Book* explained how the best art was a product of "Beauty [woven] from anguish." In "A Ballad of an Artist's Wife," Davidson outlined the creative struggles of a painter who "shunned the world and worldly ways," capturing on canvas the passion of both his body and mind. But his art was not good enough: "few would look, and none would praise,/ Because of something lacking still." Only after the death of his wife and children, due to his own neglect of them, was the painter capable of producing really great art.

> Then, as he wrought, the stress of woe
> Appeared in many a magic stain;
> And all adored his work, for lo,
> Tears mingled now with blood and brain![50]

If the themes of love and death were frequent topics of concern on *The Chap-Book*'s pages, it was not surprising that at some point attention should be directed toward the works of Richard Wagner. What might seem more surprising was that this attention came from Hamlin Garland in the form of poetry, within months of his manifesto proclaiming the need for literature's fidelity to real life.[51] In the October 1, 1895 issue, after some preliminary descriptions of the "bitter North," Garland wrote of the "Voices, everywhere voices!" of that region "Where the gods sorrowed." These voices were the outcries of life's highest emotions: vengeance, defiance, love and anguish caused by death. Garland recognized that for Wagner these cries represented the voices of the spirit-world of the gods, and the only way they could be communicated was through the medium of music.

> Symphonies infinite, sad, wide as despair,
> Deep as regret, arose from the earth and water
> And blew in strenuous streams of harmony.

Unavailing beauty, strength and youth,
Valkyrie, Dwarfs, Demi-gods, Wotan, Loki,
Imperial Brunhilde and her Siegfried
All waking, moved and sang and fought again
In the golden, rose-shot mist of music-land,
And wondering, in horror strange as sweet,
I cried
    "O dreams of darkness, who hath conjured you?"[52]

Music as an expression of divine spirits—not simply malevolent "dreams of darkness," but reveries of unrevealed spiritual mysteries—was an ideal medium for the romantic artist. Only occasionally would *The Chap-Book* reproduce musical scores on its pages, but often in its prose and poetry it drew attention to music's essential spirituality. Like poetry and love, music transported those who were moved by it to a higher, nonmaterial level of consciousness. Precisely because of its intangibility it appealed to the romantics as the ineffable utterance of supreme ideality.

Consistent with the idea that music was most important as a spiritual communication and not as a man-made composition, *The Chap-Book* tended to concentrate its attention on individuals who were graced with the ability to hear these divine harmonics. John Davidson, in his "A New Ballad of Tannhaeuser" which appeared in the July 1, 1896 *Chap-Book*, traced the course of spiritual guidance which led Tannhaeuser to find the Queen of Love. At first Tannhaeuser was afraid that the music, the "dulcet melody," had merely directed him to a sensual orgy of emotional pleasure. Awakened to these concerns by a different music, the chimes of the Church's matin bells, he appealed to Pope Urban for absolution from his sins. Such absolution the Pope could not give, as he was bound by institutional (man-made) formulae that circumscribed those areas in which the spirit was thought to be able to intervene. Thus it took a miraculous sign to show both priest and penitent that Tannhaeuser had no need of forgiveness. The music which he had originally heard had led him right, and he left the Pope's sacred city to follow once more the music of the spirit which had directed him to the Queen of Love.

Davidson's poetry is a romantic paean, a portion of which suffices to show its essential elements:

    The air, a world-enfolding flood
      Of liquid music poured along;
    And the wild cry within his blood
      Became at last a golden song.

"All day," he sang—"I feel, all day,
  The earth dilate beneath my feet;
I hear in fancy far away
  The tidal heart of ocean beat.

"My heart amasses as I run
  The depth of heaven's sapphire flower;
The resolute, enduring sun
  Fulfills my soul with splendid power.

"I quiver with divine desire;
  I clasp the stars; my thoughts immerse
Themselves in space; like fire in fire
  I melt into the universe.

"For I am running to my love;
  The eager roses burn below,
Orion wheels his sword above,
  To guard the way God bids me go."[53]

Nature was alive with spirit, and enlivened by love and led by music Tannhaeuser was able to follow the dictates of that spirit which enfused all natural reality.

Not all of *The Chap-Book*'s romantics were so sanguine about music's ability to withstand the threat of materialization. Before Garland had published his tribute to the great romantic composer Wagner, and before Davidson had sung his ballad glorifying the new spiritual journey of Tannhaeuser, another romantic had written a short story for *The Chap-Book* about mystical dreams as the source of divine music. In this story Gilbert Parker reiterated many familiar romantic themes (spirit-filled nature, mystical dreams, soul-elevating emotions), but his final message was one of caution against the presumption of man's attempt to transpose a perfect spiritual utterance into a circumscribing musical form that was a human creation.

Parker's story, "The Golden Pipes," was about a physically crippled man, Hepnon, and his efforts to reproduce the music "which was played by some son of God when the world was young" on nature's perfect organ pipes. Hepnon could still hear the music while no one else could. His contemporaries' inability to verify Hepnon's perceptions was not taken as any disproof of the existence of these mystical melodies. Rather "no one laughed at Hepnon, for you could not look into the dark warm eyes, dilating with his fancies, nor see the transparent temper of his face, the look of the dreamer over all, without believing him, and reproving your own judgment." Hepnon was acknowledged to be a privileged seer. "You felt that he had traveled ways you could never travel, that he had

had dreams beyond you, that his fanciful spirit had had adventures you would give years of your full life to know." His assertion that the music of the gods' still emanated from the golden pipes of the Voshti Hills "became a truth, though a truth that none could prove."[54]

Hepnon built an organ, completely fashioned from nature's woods, sundried and patiently worked by hand, so that he might play for others the music of his spiritual reveries. "At last it all was done . . . now the hour was come when he should gather down the soul of the Golden Pipes to his fingers, and give to the ears of the world the song of the morning stars, the music of Jubal and his comrades, the affluent melody to which the sons of men in the first days paced the world in time with the thoughts of God." Hepnon prepared for days for this great revelation of spiritual utterances, "and who may know what he was doing: dreaming, listening or praying?" The day was set, the concert to take place on the Feast of All Souls.

One might have expected that the achievement of artistic perfection, in the true representation of spiritual reality, would have been an occasion for great joy. This was not the case for either Hepnon or his audience. Those who heard his music, rather than being filled with joyful elation, were rendered acutely somber. Like love that was deeper and more meaningful than giddy infatuation, this music struck chords so deep that the listeners vibrated with the pain of impossible emotions: "the air ached with the incomparable song; and men and women wept, and children hid their heads in the laps of their mothers, and young men and maidens dreamed dreams never to be forgotten." Such intensity could not continue for long: "Presently the sounds grew fainter, and exquisitely painful, and now a low sob seemed to pass through the heart of the organ, and then silence fell, and in the sacred pause, Hepnon came out among them all, pale and desolate."

Realization of his dreams had broken Hepnon. All he could say was: "O, my God, O, my God, give me back my dream!" But a dream that was turned into reality, even the reality of music, was no longer a dream. Hepnon had taken the music of God and made it man's, and in the process he destroyed that which was most important about it. The only possible conclusion to the tale was either the death of Hepnon or his effectual extinction. The author chose the latter option. After falling into a sleep from which no one could wake him, "Hepnon and the music of the Golden Pipes departed from the Voshti Hills, and came again no more."[55] The spirit had to remain intangible in order to maintain its ideality. Hepnon violated this sacred canon, he made the spirit real.

Davidson's poem of Tannhaeuser and Parker's story of "The Golden Pipes" share several common elements. Both reveal a firm belief in the presence of spiritual realities inherent within natural phenomenon. Both maintain that music can be an expression of that spiritual presence. And both direct attention to the problem of the tension between the material world and the ideal. Tannhaeuser, while revelling in the emotions that were brought forth by the music he heard, was plagued by fears that his senses were leading him astray from more important spiritual concerns. His problem was quite simply solved, and his tensions resolved, when he learned that it was true spirituality that had guided him to the delights of the Queen of Love. The story of Hepnon, however, is a story of more complex tensions. Hepnon began by knowing that the emotions wrought by the music he heard were truly spiritual. His problem arose when he successfully revealed (with the materialization of his music) that which by its nature should have remained an undefined dream. Davidson's poem portrays the basic romantic problem of identifying the spirit and then following its dictates. Parker's story portrays the problem of the artist who wants to usurp the power of God by creating a perfect expression of ideality.

Earlier in this chapter, Bliss Carman's advocacy of a "union of mind and matter," of artistic expression that would be a product of both the "dust and dream" of human existence, was discussed. This synthesis was the most difficult task faced by *The Chap-Book*'s contributors. Parker was clearly afraid of the achievement of such a synthesis—of artistic perfection that gave form, through the work of human hands, to that which always had been solely the work of an illimitable spirit. Perfect form meant circumscription and termination more devastating than physical death, because it signified that ideality could be perfectly expressed through imperfect material means. The contradiction proved the lie of either the existence of perfect ideality or man's ability to perceive it perfectly.

Coping with the effects of an artistically perfect synthesis of dust and dreams was a dilemma with which most of *The Chap-Book*'s artists would have gratefully struggled if their art could have risen to that level. Approximating the goal of this ideal was the challenge they really faced. Through the variety of forms at their disposal they attempted to meet this challenge in different ways. Some tried to fuse the facts and fancies of human existence into historical and realistic forms. Others attempted to fashion their fancies into materially symbolic and meaningful forms. How successfully they met their respective challenges can be seen in the following chapters.

4

Facts and Fancies:
The Fusion of Realistic Literature

In its advertisements, *The Chap-Book* claimed that it was: "A MISCEL-LANY of Curious and Interesting Songs, Ballads, Tales, Histories,&c."[1] Inclusion of the category "histories" was not inaccurate—and not without qualifications. If art and life were inseparable, then it was logical that literature, documenting the lives of real people, could instruct contemporary readers in this fusion. The facts of human existence served as the basis of meaningful art. They were, however, only raw materials until refined by an act of creative imagination.

As will be seen in the following analysis of *The Chap-Book*'s attitude toward both history and the new literary realism of its day, the journal espoused a belief that reality, past and present, was only meaningful when the lessons it taught transcended the material limitations of "facts." An essential component of life, as of its artistic expression, was the intangible workings of the spirit. There were ideals striving to manifest themselves, and any picture of reality which failed to recognize these spiritual facts was deficient in its perspective. If history and realism were to be true representations of the complex reality that constituted life, they had to effect a fusion of the material and the ideal, the physical and the psychical, the factual and the fanciful.

Given its public proclamations regarding the publication of "histories," it was to be expected that *The Chap-Book* would look backwards to examine traditionally appointed historical periods. Nor was it surprising that the periods upon which it chose to focus were those that most obviously reminded contemporaries of the interplay between the real and the ideal. Biblical stories, visual images reminiscent of the Middle Ages, and hopeless calls for the restoration of the House of Stuart combined, in *The Chap-Book*'s pages, to create an impression that history was indeed a witness to the struggle of the spirit to assert its presence. Christianity, gothic cathedrals and knightly heroism, and the last stand of England's divine right monarchy all stood as examples of ideality doing battle against the forces of materialism. *The Chap-Book's* "histories" were primarily settings for spiritual dramas.

When *The Chap-Book* turned over its entire eleventh issue, October 15, 1894, to a story of Mary Magdalene, it left no doubt as to what were its primary concerns and how history illustrated them. With no warning in previous numbers, nor explanation in this one, "The Passion Flower of Magdala" by Walker Kennedy served as the magazine's complete votive offering to the divine spirit. Tracing the life of the infamous woman of Magdala who came to be a devoted follower of Jesus, Kennedy outlined for *The Chap-Book's* readers the struggle of the perceptive, passionate soul to find fulfillment. Divided into five separate sequences of events, the tale of Mary Magdalene is the narration of five different approaches to life, not just of Mary but of all mankind. Each alternative is punctuated for Mary by death, near death, desertion or madness. Each, that is, except the last.

Upon first introduction to Mary, the woman from Galilee, the reader finds her filled with natural passions, "magnificently animal," "wild" and "beautiful," and "savagely" in love with an earthy and sensuous man. Her passion, "grounded on the earth," was embued with beauty, but it was purely the beauty of natural reality. "It was the highest, the frankest resultant of the senses, candid as the love of the tigress for her mate."[2] Inevitably, such a love fell victim to the senses' inconstancy: Mary's lover deserted her, attracted to the beauty of another woman. Her passion had been beautiful, but like all natural phenomenon it was easily destroyed by competing natural forces.

Love betrayed bred vengeance in the soul of the Magdalene, and Mary was impelled by new emotions she could not control to seek the destruction of those who had robbed her of life's elemental joys. She embarked on a sea journey to find her vanished love, only to be engulfed by a deadly fever which drove her into delirium, then total unconsciousness. When put ashore by the ship's captain, Mary was nursed back to health by a doctor of philosophy who was living in the port city. He purged "the fever demon" from her "troubled flesh" and taught her the peace of "passionless" wisdom, the "pleasures of the spirit."[3]

At this point Mary recognizes that her earlier approaches of giving life over to sensual gratification or emotional revenge are hopelessly inadequate and even destructive means of passionate engagement. The philosopher has taught her that she has a mind as well as emotions, and she is enticed by the possibility that what she has come to share with him is love of a higher sort than that which she had previously experienced. Mary, however, still remembers the emotions which her first lover, "a warm, breathing animal," aroused in her; and, in comparison, the philosopher "seemed a statue on which a cold light shone."[4] The woman realizes that love without emotions is incomplete. As her hope dies that a life of mental stimulation can completely replace the sensual passions she has lost, so too does the philosopher die. Mary again is forced to continue her journey, looking for a passion that can truly make her life complete.

Disillusioned by the insufficiency of the pleasures of either nature or knowledge alone, Mary Magdalene next becomes enticed by the possibility that heroic action, flying in the fact of practicality and rationality, is the supreme passion for which everything else can be willingly sacrificed. She watches Rome's triumphal warriors parading through the city's streets, thinking that death has been defied, glory and fame promising immortality. "Swept away by the magic, the sublimity, the superbness of war," she is enthralled with "the music of heroic achievement" now filling her soul. Mary is suddenly forced, however, to stop to consider the fact that war, like love, also has its victims. Death is not defied by those who are forced to pay the price of another's immortality, those who have to die in order to secure the victor's fame. Finally, "the cruelty of this splendid thing called war smote her with despair and utter helplessness."[5] An egotistic passion that could only survive by eating away the existence of others is a passion that Mary sees is no better than the alternatives she has already found wanting.

Driven back to her native city by the Sea of Galilee in utter despair of finding any lasting meaning in life, any permanent passion that could fill her soul and unite her disparate longings, Mary succumbs to "the seven deadly fires of animal madness." Unkempt and uncaring, both her mind and her senses shut down, until the "sweet, insistent music" of Jesus's voice is able to penetrate her unconsciousness. Jesus's words of "infinite love" satisfy both her need for emotional involvement and spiritual peace. She becomes "transformed" by a divine passion that seeks no material benefits, claims no victims, and even survives death. Taught by the wisdom of the philosopher to acknowledge the existence of the spirit, that divine essence takes on a vital reality for the Magdalene only when it is infused with the emotional power of love, synthesized with the reality of her individual being.[6]

At the beginning of her story, Mary is likened to a natural flower. At the end, concern for the petals gives way to concern for the "perfume." It is the essence of life which can not die, its intangibility that conveys real meaning. In its author's estimate, the story of Mary Magdalene is "a manifestation of the Divine tenderness to the flying generations of man." It is a record of a personal history that has, in the author's mind, taught successive generations the futility of the body, the emotions, the mind or the ego to independently give lasting meaning to life. Faith rather than fame or flesh or philosophy is the only successful means of conquering physical death. Through faith one links one's own life with the Divine Light which penetrates "every crevice of the Universe," unifying mind, heart and spirit in the common pursuit of ideal reality.[7]

Mary's story is history only in the sense that the narrative places the imaginary events of a legendary life into a known, historical context. Virtually no facts are known of the real woman, the "natural" woman.[8] As the story concludes, however, this is not important: it is her essence that makes her real. Nevertheless, by placing the imaginary events of her life in an actual historical context, the author invests her essence with additional credibility.

Traditional Christianity and its well known set of historical circumstances provided abundant material for the artists of *The Chap-Book* in their attempts to portray the existence of a divine spirit manifesting itself in the lives of real men and women. Biblical history was of interest to Stone and his magazine because it was unconditionally didactic, and the lessons it taught were lessons of ideality. They had no use for historical biblical scholarship that minimized the traditional emphasis on the miraculous, the spiritual, the ideal. In fact, when contemporary tales of biblical themes failed to conform with the older tradition, they came under *The Chap-Book*'s censure. In one of only three instances when Herbert Stone identified his authorship of a piece, it was to take exception to a modern interpretation of *The Story of Jesus Christ*.

As the author of this new history, Elizabeth Stuart Phelps-Ward had taken upon herself the task of making "the figure of the Saviour more real and more appealing to persons to whom the formality of the Biblical narrative was merely—or at least primarily—awe-inspiring." To Stone, however, always concerned that the form be appropriate to the subject, and very much in favor of awe, Phelps-Ward's "humanization of the figure of Jesus" was a disaster. It destroyed his divinity, making him "less inspiring, less godlike, and unbearably commonplace." He became merely the man Jesus and not the Christ. Naturally Stone felt that the author's "account of the crucifixion" in consequence left the reader "wholly unsatisfied." Phelps-Ward had torn apart what in Stone's mind was an artistic whole that was "already beyond improvement." In its fusion of both the human and divine elements in the story of Jesus Christ, the Bible for centuries had been able to express an inexplicable mystery that gave meaning to human life. Phelps-Ward's book expressed no mystery, no meaning: it was an "unfortunate" collocation of common facts that never rose to the level of art.[9]

Consistent with *The Chap-Book*'s pronounced tendency to utilize topics that would remind the reader of the integral part the spirit played in the lives of men, the magazine's historical vision was often focused on pre-Enlightenment Europe. Art students of Norton while at Harvard, it would have been surprising if Stone and his friends had not shown such an interest, or if that interest had not in some way taken the form of visual representations. The Middle Ages, as evidenced by the writings of Harvard's historian Henry Adams, had come to represent for Stone's contemporaries a time when the efficacy of the spirit was not in doubt. Indeed, in medieval life the spirit and its Church stood at the center of every individual's world. Faith, while often threatened, remained in the ascendency, together with its divinely appointed earthly minions, until the seventeenth century. At that juncture, the fall of the House of Stuart represented a fatal separation of the spirit from European history. The facts of this extended historical period were not so important to *The Chap-Book* as was its ability to convey the impression that this was the time of heroic valor, of godly monarchs, of martyred saints, and of spirit-filled cathedrals. In its first volume alone, the magazine's illustrations included a gothic cathedral, a stained-glass window design celebrating the rosary, and a knight in mail. Later there were more knights, griffins and unicorns, and a selection of saints.[10]

One of the chief visual characteristics of *The Chap-Book* was also its identification with the fine art of early printing. As a publishing company, Stone & Kimball (and later Herbert S. Stone & Co.) made its reputation in large part on the artistic quality of its books. It was critical, if *The Chap-Book* was to serve in any way as a house organ, that it also give physical evidence that a publication could be a fine work of art. Looking backwards to the fine craftsmanship of artisans in a premechanized society, the magazine chose woodcuts, black and white drawings, elaborate border designs and handmade, uncut paper to create the impression that it belonged more to the printing traditions of the past than those of the present.

That these past traditions came to be the avant-garde in contemporary printing was an irony that was sometimes amusing and sometimes exasperating. In its "Notes" of September 15, 1895, *The Chap-Book* reported one occasion "when the distinguished president of a Women's Club, spying an elaborately printed volume, which lay open on my desk, exclaimed, 'What curious borders and initials! More of your Beardsley *fin-de-siècle* art, I suppose,' "[11] The volume was St. Jerome on Genesis and the Prophets, printed in the sixteenth century. Jerome, whose Vulgate Bible was published in the sixteenth century, was one of *The Chap-Book*'s favored saints, receiving a full-page illustration in the March 15, 1896 issue.[12]

Championing a return to the principles of sixteenth-century printing, and to the faith of the men whose work inspired such fine art, *The Chap-Book* also championed one of the great lost causes of that century. A call for the restoration of the House of Stuart was sounded during the magazine's first summer of publication, August 1894, and was to be picked up later as a minor refrain in both its poetry and its editorial comments. Medievalist Ralph Adams Cram was the first to draw attention to the Jacobite cause in his "The Ride of the Clans." Cram's poetry was accompanied by an article on a recently published "Legitimist Kalendar" detailing Jacobite beliefs and listing the true heirs to the British throne. As *The Chap-Book* explained, this "Kalendar" was "a record of forlorn faiths and bygone loyalties."[13]

Neither the faiths nor the loyalties were completely defunct, however, in that *The Chap-Book* chose to remind contemporary readers of their existence. Louise Imogen Guiney, *The Chap-Book*'s resident Catholic and perhaps best known Jacobite, was certainly partly responsible for the magazine's fascination with the Jacobite cause.[14] But it was a concern that had captured the imaginations of a number of other *Chap-Book* contributors. Perhaps the most unlikely was Thomas Hardy, whose short story on the unsuccessful attempt of the Duke of Monmouth to recapture the throne, appearing in the December 15, 1896 issue, combined a bit of history with tantalizing mystery.[15] It was in the select group of Stone's friends at and around Harvard, however, that the Jacobite cause had become linked with the cause of art.

Stone's magazine had been born in close proximity to Boston, the Boston of his literary friends who had already taken up the Jacobite banner in the whimsical periodical, *The Knight Errant*.[16] When *The Knight* was in imminent danger of demise, *The Chap-Book* endorsed its editorial creed and prayed that it might continue to live. *The Knight* had looked to the past in its fight against the "heresies and treasons" of the present. At war with "the kings of this earth" whose reign glorified the material at the expense of the ideal, this forerunner of *The Chap-Book* proclaimed that it would "fly the banner of yesterday, which is that of the morrow." It believed that the fight against materialism was not lost as long as some were still willing to ask art to be both heroic and moral.[17]

The Jacobite cause became an elaborate metaphor for the cause of art in contemporary society. The Jacobites were fighting the heresy that man could choose his monarch rather than abiding by the choice of God. The House of Hanover represented the "kings of the earth," and their cause was that of a materialistic political liberalism which had overthrown the divinely appointed representative of the Mother Church. Overly simplified and highly romanticized, the cause of the House of Stuart came to stand as an affirmation that spiritual concerns should be unified with politics and other dimensions of real life. *The Chap-Book* stood as a similar affirmation of the unity of the spirit with art.

It would be misleading, however, to construe *The Chap-Book*'s interest in history as evidence that it was primarily oriented toward the past. It chose selectively those historical periods that it liked, mostly to illustrate ideals or faith. If it liked these periods, it was because it was in love with art. And only within certain prescribed limits would it utilize the facts of history toward more important artistic ends. In its essays and critical reviews, *The Chap-Book* spelled out the limitations of both history and historians as interpretive guides to the real meaning of life.

Life's bare facts were inconsequential bits of information until they had been fused into an interpretive whole by some individual's discerning imagination. Essentially this was the act of artistic creation. Jeannette Barbour Perry wrote in a *Chap-Book* essay of November 15, 1897: "There was a dangerous tendency [in the past] to regard even history as a collocation of facts, and the author as only another, and humbler, one. We have made, at least, the advance of caring more for the spirit and less for the substance, more for Carlyle and less for the French Revolution." There was no objective history. Unless the substance of reality could make an impact on a perceptive interpreter, and then be used as the material for a new creation—an artistic creation—that reality, that historical fact, was insignificant. Perry emphasized this point by claiming: "without Carlyle, the French Revolution would have been a poor, inadequate affair."[18]

Mere facts could not make sense out of human history, and those writers who merely gathered together facts, as a scientist gathered together empirical evidence, belonged to what *The Chap-Book* referred to as "the pig-iron school of historians." These historians, the monograph writers,[19] represented an unfortunate trend in American historiography: "The present school of American historians, being scholars and not litterateurs, dig out historical ore and leave their readers to do the smelting."[20] It took the litterateur, the artist, to bring together the facts into a meaningful whole. Smelting was a process of intimate personal engagement, fired by the imagination.

History was not the only literary genre subject to *The Chap-Book*'s criticism. The new literary realism had a dangerous tendency to believe that the facts of human life could, without any qualitative sorting or subjective combining, unify themselves into a work of art. There was a current vogue among a certain group of realists, made popular by the pioneering work of such men as Jacob Riis, of going to live among the poor to observe and record their lives. Unfortunately, many of these literary realists thought that the factual records they published were art. In a review of a book of this type by Walter Wyckoff called *The Workers,* Dorothea Moore reiterated *The Chap-Book*'s point that mere facts do not make a complete picture of real life. She complained that Wyckoff's work was flawed by his detached objectivity. He was always an outsider taking notes, never part of the "oxidizing current" that energized these peoples' lives and made them real. He was a molecular scientist examining individual particles, not complex people. Not until the writer becomes both emotionally and intellectually engaged by his subject, not until "the thing gets hold and grips one hard," will his writing add anything constructive to our understanding of human life.[21]

One of the basic problems with Wyckoff's brand of scientific realism was the premise that any slice of life could serve as the material substance for a work of art. Bliss Carman refuted this contention for *The Chap-Book:* "A scrap of real life, say the realists, is always interesting, however humble or tame. But it is not. The commonplace in life does not interest us as much as the dramatic."[22] If a subject does not interest us, it will make no impression on our perceptions. It will not engage us either emotionally or intellectually. Without personal engagement there is no art, no knowledge, no meaning.

Dramatic realism was an entirely separate issue for *The Chap-Book.* It represented an artistic rendering of some facet of reality that had been capable of stirring the imagination of a perceptive observer. It was not mere reality, it was the product of a fusion of reality with the spirit of the artist. Carman noted: "If the landscape painter would move us as the sunset moved him, he must put more on the canvas than an exact copy of his scene; he must add something of himself." What he added was a "commentary;" and the "commentary comes of imagination alone," allowing realism to "reach beyond the actual" with "the touch of wonder and unreality" to fix a "picture in our mind." Carman did not object to realism as a form of artistic expression. He objected to realism that failed to recognize that life was both real and imaginary, "dust and dream." Conceding that, "Realism touched with imagination may become poetry," he cautioned "prose without imagination cannot even be rightly realistic."[23]

Two separate contributions illustrate *The Chap-Book*'s concurrence with Carman's point. In one, *The Chap-Book* itself took exception to the war correspondence of the famed realist Stephen Crane. Crane had been sending back to American newspapers accounts of the war in Thessaly, and in its commentary on these letters *The Chap-Book* gave its explicit approval of literary or dramatic realism (that is, facts fused into an artistic whole, a new reality, by the creative imagination), and disapproval of mere realistic journalism. *The Chap-Book* believed that Crane, as an observer of war, had been engaged in a private war of his own. This war was one of his "eyes" against his "imagination." Regrettably, his eyes won: "instead of an electric impressionist sketch of battle, worthy of the author of *The Red Badge of Courage*, he forced himself to give us an accurate, colorless description of what was actually passing beneath him." In so doing, he failed to make war as real as it had been in his fiction. "Mr. Crane imagining a battle is a writer, an artist; describing a battle, he is merely a reporter, and not, it must be added, an especially clear or capable one."[24]

A second noted realistic journalist showed that his fictional prose, accepted for publication in *The Chap-Book* of June 15, 1896, could rise above commentary of mere material reality. Lincoln Steffens's short story, "Schloma, The Daughter of Schmuhl," presents a brief impressionistic sketch of the Jews working in New York City's sweatshops in the 1890s. There are, of course, the realistic details, including the Yiddish dialects of the ghetto. But there is also an evocative picture of a young woman, Schloma, whose spirit refused to be deadened by the toil of her labor or the repressively sexist role expectations of her ethnic community. Against all reason and contrary to the conventions of her people, Schloma expressed her irrepressible spirit in song. She refused to follow the dictum of her culture: "Let the women work and be silent that our sons' sons may be glad." Her song was taken as evidence that she had fallen victim to "the Christian love of pleasure," and she was ostracized by her fellow Jews and branded a "Schickse."[25] Steffens heightened the reality of the squalor and drudgery of Schloma's life not so much by calling attention to its particular details, as by contrasting it to an optimistic faith that the spirit could transcend its circumstances. Schloma's ability to sing strikes chords of sympathy in the reader that resonate with forceful, personal meaning. She becomes real because her song has stirred the reader's imagination.

While Carman was arguing in *The Chap-Book* for what he called dramatic realism, Israel Zangwill was complaining about contemporary attempts to make drama "real." Zangwill was often labeled a realist for his stories of London's Jewry; but in his commentary on the contemporary theatre for *The Chap-Book*, he showed himself to be of one mind with the magazine regarding realism. He noted the current trend which advocated that, "People are to 'act' on the stage as they would 'act' in real life." As Zangwill went on to explain, following this principle would present tremendous problems for the actor or actress who wished to play parts from the classic dramas. The problems would be so great, in fact, that they would either drive the works of a genius such as Shakespeare off the stage, or else destroy his artistic creation.

Illustrating his point, Zangwill stressed that in the works of Shakespeare "the natural methods strike a jarring note." Natural methods were jarring because drama was not a natural creation: "After all, as Goethe says, we call Art Art because it is not Nature." Zangwill was not apologizing for Shakespeare when he acknowledged that his work was "as artificial as the masks and buskins of the Greek stage." By its very artificiality it was able to transcend reality while speaking reality's greatest truths. Shakespeare's poetry aimed at the creation of "an artistic heightening of reality, and, indeed, quite as much an aloofness from reality as an approximation to it." He recognized that the finest poetry was "but the quintessence of reality," and in the balcony scene from *Romeo and Juliet,* Shakespeare demonstrated what this meant. In this scene Shakespeare gave the world an articulation of love that the world's most gifted lovers could never have uttered: "it is the genius of Shakespeare interpreting for humanity—as by exquisite music—the full poetry of young passion, itself in reality mute, and incapable of translating itself into felicitous expression."[26]

Translating into artistic form that which had no form in reality was the task of the artist. His work was realistic only insofar as it truthfully corresponded to both the tangible and intangible forces which impelled human actions and gave them meaning. That there were intangible forces at work, more potent than any mere material concerns, *The Chap-Book* had no doubt. The realists that this magazine published were all engaged in attempts to translate these "mute" forces into articulate forms. Their realism was consistently undergirded by their belief that reality was both material and ideal, that knowledge was both conscious and unconscious, and that art was capable of unifying these bifurcated elements into a more meaningful whole.

Realism as a tag of identification lacked precision in the 1890s, as can be seen from Carman's attempts to qualify it. Some practitioners of the art, on whom the title "realist" stuck, objected to its use as a means of describing their literary method. Arthur Morrison, author of the "realistic" *A Child of the Jago,* published in America by Herbert S. Stone & Co., insisted in a letter to *The Chap-Book* in 1897 that the only definition of the term "realist" he could accept was: "that the man who is called a 'realist,' is one who, seeing things with his own eyes, discards the conventions of the schools, and presents his matter in individual terms of art." Through his own vision, utilizing his own personal perception, the realist could see things differently, giving them "a new reality and an immediate presence."[27] Notwithstanding Morrison's objections or Carman's qualifications, "realism" had been defined in considerable detail (prior to *The Chap-Book*'s initial publication) by America's foremost realist, Hamlin Garland. And Garland was an author Herbert Stone deliberately sought to capture for his publishing company and his magazine.

When *The Chap-Book* first went to press in the spring of 1894, the young publishing firm of Stone & Kimball was already marketing the work of Hamlin Garland. Garland was Stone & Kimball's first "real" author, and the adjective in this context has nothing to do with Garland's literary philosophy. Only Stone's own guides to the Columbian Exposition and his *First Editions of American Authors* predate the firm's publication of a new edition of *Main-Travelled Roads*. Garland had already established his literary reputation with the first edition of this book, so that when Stone acquired the rights to it, he secured the work of a known writer.

What Garland was known for was his realism, and his reputation had not made him welcome in the literary circles that Stone frequented in Boston. Young Stone may have been an acceptable guest at Boston's literary afternoon "at homes," but Garland was not.[28] This, however, did not stop Stone from jumping at the chance to secure a revised edition of *Main-Travelled Roads,* together with an introduction by William Dean Howells, as the first piece of fiction to be released by Stone & Kimball. Stone, it must be remembered, was only twenty-one years old, a student, and a publishing nobody. If he had shunned his father's help in starting his journal, he had not done so in launching his publishing company. Relying on the friendly contacts of his father and Chicago journalism, rather than the fraternity of Boston literature, young Stone gained an introduction to Garland.

Herbert Stone's father arranged the first meeting in March 1893 between his publisher son and the midwestern author. The senior Stone apprised his son that Garland was working on some new pieces, and told him that Garland, who was then in Boston, would be expecting Herbert to call.[29] Stone's father, an experienced businessman, must have known what a commercial advantage it would be if his son could secure the rights to publish a well-known literary figure. The younger Stone was not insensitive to this fact, nor to his novice standing in the business and the distance this represented between himself and Garland. Herbert mused to his father: "I wish I had enough of a 'pull' to get a chance at publishing them [the works of Garland] myself. . . . But I suppose Mr. Garland would hardly wish to have a new firm take hold of the thing—much less a boy."[30] As it turned out, Garland did wish the new firm to take hold of his work.[31]

Publishing the works of Hamlin Garland was not an ambition strictly motivated by Herbert Stone's desire to capitalize on an established author's reputation. The young publisher was shrewd enough to accept his father's help in soliciting authors, but Garland was an author whose work was artistically compatible with the aims of Stone & Kimball, and—within a year—those of *The Chap-Book*. In one of the early original manuscripts Garland brought to Stone & Kimball for publication, the midwestern realist issued his artistic manifesto. *Crumbling Idols* was released just two weeks before *The Chap-Book*'s debut; and in it Garland called for a new literature true to the reality of the American peoples' lives. Garland's distinctive brand of realism, or "veritism" as defined in this book, championed the cause of the West, the woman, the ethnic immigrant and modern art. Yet it was romantic idealism at its core, and the first clue lay in its epigraph:

> To love the truth in an age of lies;
> To hold fast art when hunger cries;
>   To sing love's song in spite of hate,
>   Keeping his heart inviolate,—
> These are the artist's victories.[32]

Garland was an advocate of art as the creative expression of individuality: of the individual self encountering the facts of his existence, then recording those impressions in an effort to acquire self-enlightenment and to share his enlightenment with others. Such self-exploration had to be free from conventions if the pursuit of knowledge was to be fruitful and true to experience. Garland was modern in his conviction that there was not one "Truth" to be found but many different truths filtered through the perceptions of many different individuals. He affirms: "The sun of truth strikes each part of the earth at a little different angle; it is this angle which gives life and infinite variety to literature."[33] Yet if this phenomenal relativity made him modern, his equally firm conviction that the emotions contained the key to life's significance linked him to a romantic past. "The secret of every lasting success in art or literature lies, I believe, in a powerful, sincere, emotional concept of life first, and, second, in the acquired power to convey that concept to others."[34]

Veritism, like romanticism, found love to be life's essential emotion because love transported the individual out of his selfish concerns and allowed him to see a new ideal, a new conception of life. "A man must be moved by something higher than money, by something higher than hope of praise; he must have a sleepless love in his heart urging him to re-create in the image the life he has loved." It was fidelity to this image, this dream, that made him an optimist. The artist experienced a "keen creative delight" in reflecting in his work "his own concept of life;" and the realist used the facts of everyday life to point up, by contrast, how much they differed from his ideal.[35]

Admitting that the facts of life failed to coincide with its ideals, the artist nonetheless had to love the world he lived in, love the beauty of nature rather than grovel in its deficiencies. He should not write of "crime and abnormalities," but should turn his attention to nature. The "new literature" would come from those persons, "rightly educated," who (like traditional romantics) turn their eyes "naturally to the wheat-fields, the forests, the lanes of orange-trees, the ranges of unsurpassed mountains." Instructed by their natural surroundings, and impelled by a positive love of life, they would engage in the task of "working out the drama of life in a new way, thinking new thoughts, building a happier, sunnier order of things."[36] They would, in effect, be working towards a new ideal.

Tension existed between the real world and the ideal, and Garland was not insensitive to its presence. He felt it in his own life, and reflected it in the work he submitted to *The Chap-Book*. Garland, the publicly avowed and branded realist of his day, contributed a poem to *The Chap-Book* of November 15, 1895 setting forth the struggle of the artist torn between the real and the ideal, between what the artist wanted—his ideals embodied in art and song—and what he feared—his base passions and materialistic concerns.

Entitled "The Cry of the Artist," Garland's poem is a plea of salvation. The narrator likens himself to a swimmer afloat on the ocean's surface, the horizon line separating the heavenly sky above from the monstrous sea of passion below. He feels himself to be within the grip of some spiritual force ("O strange and treacherous power,/ Where will you carry me?") and turns his eyes upward: "I see my ideals soar like eagles above me—." Where once such a swimmer would have petitioned God for deliverance from the sea of life's "green caverns of silence," from the "cold hand" waiting to pull him down, there is now an appeal to art for redemption.

> O art and song, wheeling high up there
> To you I lift my eyes!
> For you my arms still throb and swell—
> O, shadow me with your promises,
> Let your wings drop down on me
> Their dapples of purple light!
> Shadow me, lure me,
> Strengthen me![37]

If Garland had been converted to the religion of art, it was Stone who had done the work of proselytizing. Garland had been a Henry George single tax advocate and propagandist of diverse social and economic reforms for B.O. Flower's publishing company and journal *Arena*.

By Garland's own account, when Stone first met him, Stone told him that his attentions were misdirected: "Herbert said, paternally, 'You started right, Mr. Garland, but you've gone wrong.' I listened meekly. He went on: 'You're a bit of the preacher where you should be only the artist. The *Arena* was all very well once, but you need a different kind of publishing now. You must write for the *Chap-Book* and forget your 'cause'." Stone's temerity was only slightly less astonishing than Garland's acquiescence. "He was right. My reforming zeal had led me astray. I put aside economics and gave myself up unreservedly to my work as literary historian." Garland also gave Stone & Kimball the rights to *Crumbling Idols* as well as the rights to a new work of fiction.[38]

In his attempt to acquire an author, Stone had shown Garland that his ideals could most effectively be expressed through art, and should be addressed to an audience whose primary interest was art. Economic theories had their role to play, as did journals of social reform, but neither was capable of shouldering the emotional burden necessary to convey the vital reality a new ideals. Art, as presented on the pages of *The Chap-Book,* could. Garland became again an artistic historian, revealing the facts of life, as he saw them, struggling to come into accord with life's ideals.

More familiar than Garland the poet, or Garland the art critic, was this Garland the chronicler of life. Most particularly, Garland was known for his realistic renderings of life on the Midwest plains. *The Chap-Book* serialized one of these plains stories, "The Land of the Straddle-Bug," which began on November 15, 1894 and ran for seven consecutive issues.[39] It revealed the ideals of the author in the form prescribed by their natural setting. It also validated a radical denial of the legitimacy of one of society's oldest conventions, marriage, in the face of more primal human emotions. It represented for *The Chap-Book* an artistic expression of the critical insights Stone & Kimball had just published in *Crumbling Idols.*

True to his theories, Garland depicted the struggle of unseen forces in their natural setting. The unspoiled wilderness of the plains not only embodied these "mystical" forces, it was to call them forth in the individuals who came to populate the plains. Blanche Burke and her husband, Howard, had come to the prairie land just outside "Boomtown" in the spring of 1883 to homestead. They were awed by the "new world" into which they entered, "everything wild and mystical and glorious." Through sensitivity to her primitive environment, Blanche becomes the protagonist of the story, vibrating sympathetically with forces so elemental that they were beyond the means of human articulation. Blanche, from her first night on the prairie, was aware of their attraction. They "appealed to something primeval in her."[40]

Far from intimating that these elemental forces were of base origin, Garland was quick to establish their divine significance. After introducing them in the first chapter of the story, and before relating how they would come to influence the lives of the plains people, the author clearly delineates the presence of God as the motive force behind all natural phenomena. Blanche, looking skyward from within the frame skeleton of her new home, felt a "great awe" come upon her. "It seemed as if she had drawn a little nearer to the Almighty Creator of the silence. When they spoke it was in low voices. It was as if God could hear what they said. That He was just there behind the western glory."[41]

Uncluttered by man-made intrusions in the East which blocked natural perceptions, the virgin territory of the plains provided an arena wherein these settlers could freely commune with the spiritual forces lying deep within their individual selves. "Tyranny was behind them, the majesty of God's wilderness before them, a mystic joy within them." Freed from the restraints imposed upon them by the artificial environment of the East, the homesteaders were to find that they were also free from the constraints of society's conventions. "Out here it doesn't matter much what you do. . . . Of course I don't mean wrong things. Some things are wrong anywhere, but there are other things that people *think* are wrong that are only unusual."[42] Blanche and the people closest to her were to find, when they concerned themselves less with rational thinking and more with instinctual feeling, that one of the worst "wrongs" of society was the "right" course of human action. They came to find a new ideal.

Blanche was the victim of a barren marriage, her maternal instincts smothered from lack of use. Encountering another woman holding a newborn baby, a scene that "had a sort of sublimity—it was so old, so typical, and so beautiful," awakened in Blanche "a strange, hungry, envious passion."[43] She was to satisfy this passion by conceiving a child with a man other than her husband. Against the backdrop of the storms of winter, Blanche explored the nature of the new emotions raging through her body as both she and nature endured a period of turbulent gestation, trying to ascertain the meaning of an "unusual" season.

As her fellow homesteaders left the prairie for the winter, Blanche remained. She had become one with her environment, its passions were hers, its elements composed her being. The wind was like the newly arisen maternal spirit, blowing through her body and carrying her into the unknown recesses of her womanhood. "Now the wind had dominion over the lonely woman, wearing out her soul with its melancholy—vast and wordless sigh. It seemed to enter her soul, filling it with hunger, unrest, never conceived before. Day after day it sighed in her ears and wailed about the little cabin, rousing within her nameless, inarticulate desires and despairs. Obscure emotions, unused powers of reason and recollection came to her. She grew in sombre womanhood." Somber, indeed, because Blanche knew that she had deviated from the direction society laid out for her when instead she chose to follow her instincts. Nature was not to be denied, however. "Her terror and shame gave way at last and she allowed herself to dream on the mystical joy of motherhood."[44]

Once Blanche had come to terms with her emotions and her actions it only remained for Garland to resolve society's response, effecting an accommodation to a new ideal. This was accomplished in the story's "Conclusion," which appeared in *The Chap-Book* on February 15, 1895. Blanche left her husband, driving off into a terrible storm with the father of her yet unborn child. At the height of the storm they were forced to encounter Bob Bailey, whose mercantile store figures as the drawing room of Boomtown's society. Bailey "typified the world" to Blanche, as he does to the reader, and he was the the one who would sit in judgment over her deeds. Not unexpectedly: "To his clear sense the whole thing seemed monstrous. He had been brought up to respect the marriage bond and to respect women. The illicit was impossible to his strong soul and the passions incidental to buoyant manhood he had kept under perfect control . . . it seemed natural."[45]

Natural it was not, however, but of this neither Bailey nor society were yet aware. Accustomed to assuming that adherence to any legitimate ideal should be capable of justification through rational articulation, Blanche was challenged by Bailey to present her case. Unable "to formulate . . . in her mind" any defense, unable "to voice her deepest emotions," Blanche was an unconvincing witness in her own behalf. "She felt herself in the grasp of forces as vast, as impersonal, and as illimitable as the wind and the sky, and plain; but reduced to words her pleas for mercy from Bailey would have been, 'I could not help it.' "Intellectual and verbal forms, just like society's strictures, were inadequate to encompass the reality of this woman's situation, of the formless forces she was following. Even Bailey, at his most disapproving moment, was compelled to admit that this case did not seem to fit the facts of similar situations about which he had read in the newspapers. Blanche showed "no signs of degradation." On the contrary, she "seemed more refined and dignified."[46]

Weighed down by the shame that was thrust upon her by Bailey's judgmental presence, deprived by society's unnatural conventions of the exaltation she had experienced when she first gave herself up to the dreams of motherhood, Blanche is driven to the point where rationality ceases and the emotions alone hold sway. As the winter storm continued to assault the prairie, "she lay listening to the storm, thinking strange disconnected thoughts. The strain upon her was twisting her toward insanity . . . . She saw no end to this elemental strife. . . . It filled her with emotions far below words." Only when Blanche reached this nadir was transformation possible, a transformation that was to free her from the constraints which stood as a barrier to her own fulfillment. "As she lay thus, a sudden mysterious exaltation came upon her and she grew warm and happy. She cared for no man. No man's opinion was of consequence to her. She was a mother, and God said to her, 'Be peaceful and hopeful.' . . . She lay lovely and careless and sinless as a prattling babe, her eyes fixed upon the gleam of lights in the dark."[47] Emotional fulfillment of her maternal nature had shriven her of any societal sins. Inarticulate as an infant, she had no need of words to express her conformity with divine purposes.

Just as Blanche had passed a night of elemental struggle, so had Bailey. Just as the forces of nature had worked their way into her soul, so had they come to influence the man and bring him to a new insight. "Lying there in the dark, with the elemental war and wind and snow filling the illimitable arch of sky, he came to feel in a dim, wordless way that this tragedy was born of conventions largely." Man was like an insect in the infinitesimal process of life; and Bailey "came also to feel that the force which moved these human insects, was akin to the ungovernable sweep of the wind and snow,—all inexplicable, elemental, *un*moral." In true conformity with Garland's theory of veritism, Bailey came to see "that each case must be judged by itself." His final judgment of Blanche was that she had "the right to be a mother."[48]

Garland's story was not a throwback to the romanticism of an earlier era, although his portrayal of a spirit-filled nature was strikingly traditional. Rather, "The Land of the Straddle-Bug" was a careful application of the artistic theories set forth in *Crumbling Idols,* which had appeared just six months before the "Straddle-Bug" began its serial run. The presence of divinely motivated, inarticulate forces was never in doubt. But these forces were manifesting themselves in ways that cast doubt on traditional truths. When seen in their natural context, when felt at their deepest, most inexplicable level, they invalidated conventional wisdom and set forth a revised ideal for human behavior. Bailey may have been forced to conclude that since his old morality was no longer operative, he was now in a situation that, casting the best light on it, was unmoral. But Garland was explicit in repeatedly noting that while the men in the story may not have understood the workings of these elemental forces, they were the forces of divinity. Idealism was not divorced from God, replaced by an amoral naturalism or mechanistic determinism. It was simply seen to be, in contemporary situations, more complex and less capable of rational explication than had been hitherto thought. It operated on levels "far below words," and consequently far beyond the realm of rational thought.

Even though words had their limitations, even though facts could not create a complete picture of reality in and of themselves, they were the means whereby the literary artist communicated. If realism was to be true to its purpose of, in the words of Garland, interpreting the verities of human existence, it had to be as true to actual life as possible. Factual precision was imperative; but these facts were only important as they formed an "impression," produced an "effect" on the perceiving consciousness of individual persons.[49] Facts which did not possess the power to capture the imagination had no significant reality. Conversely, if some other phenomena, such as dreams or visions, emotions or spirits, could make an impression on any single, perceptive observer, they became real. The role of the artist was to reveal the reality which he perceived, material and/or immaterial, for the benefit of those who lacked the artist's heightened sensitivity. The means he had at his disposal were the words of traditional human discourse.

Few artists have equalled the precision or perception of Henry James, and James was the one writer for whom Herbert Stone was willing to risk financial embarrassment in order to insure the privilege of publishing his works.[50] James, as it turned out, was only to be exceeded by Carman in the number of issues of *The Chap-Book* in which his work appeared; and, along with Garland, was one of only two writers to have lengthy fictional works serialized.[51] His contributions dealt with the problem of knowledge, of facts and fancies which made an impact on the consciousness of his characters, delineating the nature of the realities in which they lived.

Garland may have called himself an historian, but James, in describing his major work which appeared in *The Chap-Book*, referred to himself as a "painter of life." Like Garland, he recognized that the fixed standards and inherited wisdom of the past only represented a partial picture of reality. He aspired to paint a larger picture, a picture that would include that which was not understood or which was only incompletely comprehended. "The effort really to see and really to represent is no idle business in face of the *constant* force that makes for muddlement. The great thing is indeed that the muddled state too is one of the very sharpest of the realities, that it also had colour and form and character, had often in fact a broad and rich comicality, many of the signs and values of the appreciable."[52] James was embarked on an exploration of what constituted reality and how that reality was perceived. On his journey in the mid-1890s he took with him the readers of *The Chap-Book*.

On May 1, 1896 James made his first appearance in *The Chap-Book* with a short story, later compiled into a book of *Embarrassments,* called "The Way It Came."[53] He proposes the existence of phantoms which have the power to alter drastically the course of human lives. His characters are nameless, his narration that of diary reflection recounting events after they have transpired. The anonymity of the characters suggests that they could be anyone. The narrative form lends credibility to an otherwise incredible sequence of events. "The Way It Came" combines spiritual visions and everyday life in a complex and ambiguous picture of the composition of reality.

After a short introduction in which the existence of the diary was established, James let the diary entries themselves tell the story of three people: the diarykeeper; another woman, who was the diarist's friend; and a man, who was the diarist's fiancé. Their interrelationship revolves around the occurrence of previous spiritual visitations experienced by the friend and fiancé, and the attempts, principally of the diarist, to effect a meeting of these two people who have so much in common but are unacquainted with each other. The keeper of the diary forms the connecting link between the two spirit-sensitive individuals, serving as a kind of medium who acts as the arbiter of the reality of their eventual encounter.

Intrigued by the "strange adventure" of communion with the spirit world that both her friends had experienced, the diarist recalls how she had endeavored for five years to bring her two friends together. A series of "extraordinary" accidents continually thwarted all efforts to introduce the pair. "A cold, a headache, a bereavement, a storm, a fog, an earthquake, a cataclysm, infallibly intervened," until it began to seem that only "some lurking volition" could "account for anything so absurd."[54] Once the diarist accepts the man's offer of marriage and feels that she can definitely insure his presence at a designated rendezvous, a date is arranged with the other friend for a long-awaited meeting. Suddenly aware of the danger to her own happiness of bringing together her future husband and a woman with whom he has so much in common, the jealous diarist prevaricates to prevent their tryst until after she and her fiancé are safely wed.

Moved by remorse at her own mean deception, the diarist goes, the morning after the aborted meeting, to the home of her female friend to confess her subterfuge. She is greeted with the news that her friend died the night before. When she returns to tell her fiancé that now he will never get to meet the elusive lady, she is astonished by his assertion that they have met, the very night of her friend's death. Two issues preoccupy the rest of the story. The first is whether the fiancé met the living woman or whether he was merely visited by another spiritual apparition. The second, and ultimately more important, is the determination of which relationship is more meaningful, more real to the man: the one with his living fiancée or the one with the dead friend.

Initially the diarist attempts to establish the fact that her fiancé could not possibly have met her friend while the friend was still alive. She empirically researches her friend's movements on the night of her death, and is convinced that an actual meeting could not have taken place. The fiancé, when presented with this data, is unconvinced. He insists: "I saw her living—I saw her to speak to her—I saw her as I see you now!"[55] When pressed that it was a representation of death he saw, a vision of a woman, whereas the woman (his fiancée) who stands before him at that instant is a living woman, he remains adamant: "It was life! it was life!"[56] In truth, to him it was life, no matter whether the woman's substance was corporeal or not. His comparison between the friend and his fiancée confirms the point for the reader: the spirit of the dead woman is as real to him as the actual, living woman who stands before him.

Whether or not the spirit-sensitive couple ever met in reality becomes a moot point, as the reader learns how their spiritual relationship grew in importance and assumed a reality of its own. The diarist discovers that her fiancé continues to meet the spirit of the woman whom he had never known while she was alive. His love for the dead woman becomes filled with "passion," while he begins to act towards his fiancée "mechanically, compunctiously." The engagement is terminated by the diarist, who leaves him "to his inconceivable communion." Six years later, apparently by his own hand, the man dies. "It was the result of a long necessity, of an unquenchable desire. To say exactly what I mean, it was a response to an irresistible call."[57]

Reality is a product of the perceiving self, and in the case of the man in "The Way It Came," he possessed an "accessibility to forms of life," a "command of impressions, appearances, contacts closed—for our gain or our loss—to the rest of us."[58] His unique ability to perceive what others could not meant that his reality was different than theirs, but no less real. The sequence of events transcribed by the diarist documents the facts surrounding the relationship of her two friends. If at the time of their first meeting a question was raised as to whether the occurrence was physical or spiritual, there was no question as to whether or not it had transpired. Only the form of the encounter was ever in doubt, not its occurrence. After their initial introduction the relationship was unequivocally spiritual, but no less real. It was so real, in fact, that it replaced the man's relationship with his living fiancée and ultimately forced him to terminate his physical life, presumably to share finally in a relationship that was totally spiritual.

In James's other contribution to *The Chap-Book* he was also concerned with perception, but this time it was a detailed and systematic exposition of the actual act of perception and growth of knowledge. On January 15, 1897 the first chapters of *What Maisie Knew* began a serialized run that was to last for eight months and span fourteen issues.[59] Appearing in this American magazine slightly ahead of its British periodical publication and before its release in book form, *What Maisie Knew* was an extremely important literary staple in the offerings of the newly enlarged and somewhat altered *Chap-Book*. If James's reputation seemed as established and respectable as the magazine's new format, the outward appearances of both were deceiving. *The Chap-Book* had not changed its intellectual orientation. It was continuing to evidence the same concerns as had been promulgated in its first years as a "little magazine." James, however, was changing in that he was moving into a new phase of literary creativity that would produce his greatest works. *What Maisie Knew* was part of this movement, and was most appropriately first printed on the pages of *The Chap-Book*.

Concerned with psychic phenomenon of a phantasmagorical nature in his earlier contribution to Stone's magazine, in the tale of Maisie James probed the psyche of one small girl, beginning when she was six years old and concluding with the end of her childhood. Maisie met people, not ghosts, and the knowledge she grew into came in response to the reality she encountered in her relations with the individuals who inhabited her child's world. Yet in the first chapter, James described her "little world" as "phantasmagoric," and the people who formed images on her developing consciousness were like "strange shadows dancing on a sheet."[60] To the young girl, the real world was as fantastical and inexplicable as was the world of spirits to the adults in James's earlier story. She did not have the cognitive sophistication to comprehend rationally either the nature or the meaning of everything she encountered. However, she was extremely perceptive and, notwithstanding her limited intellectual development, grew in knowledge.

Maisie's first great lesson was that words failed as a medium of communication: they were not to be believed as factual representations of reality, and they precipitated dangerous and explosive situations. Used as a mouthpiece to voice the hatred of her estranged parents for each other, Maisie discovered that their words could be defused of their lethal, and misleading, meanings if they were buried in silence. She assumed the pose of "a little idiot," puzzling out her own knowledge but not verbally evidencing it to others, or trusting the evidence of other's words.[61] Once, under the charm of unaccustomed maternal attention, Maisie was deluded by a false sense of security into abandoning her pose of silence and believing the words that were spoken to her. She was forced to relearn the lesson that words were unreliable and, worse, that they could rob her of the small tokens of security that her elders were capable of giving to her. The young girl forgot momentarily "that she had never been safe unless she had also been stupid."[62] Paradoxically, as Maisie pretended to be stupid she became more astute, and came to learn how she herself could manipulate words, bending them to her own purposes as the diplomat did in delicate negotiations.[63]

For a writer so obviously competent in the use of language to express precise meanings and to describe exact situations, James's attitude toward language in *What Maisie Knew* was particularly revealing. If Maisie learned at the beginning of her education that the meanings of words could not always be relied upon to be true or total representations of reality, she also learned towards the end of her childhood that verbal communication could arise spontaneously, without prior instruction, and be completely comprehensible. When Maisie, a young English girl, stood at the point of crisis in her life poised on the platform of a French train station, she was able both to understand the meanings of the French words she had never been taught and to respond appropriately in that same language. "It was the most extraordinary thing in the world: in the intensity of her excitement she not only by illumination understood all their French, but fell into it with an active perfection."[64] Illumination came to Maisie through her perfectly attuned perceptivity of all the subtle, and often mute, nuances of a situation, heightened by her emotional involvement. In such contexts, she was able to respond to an entire picture of reality. When words masked or confused reality rather than revealing it, she dismissed their evidence. When words helped her to express her sense of a situation, she utilized them, even when they may not have been factually true or when they were the words of a language of which she had no intellectual knowledge.

To define a situation or a person by naming it, by giving it a word or words which meant that its essence was understood by the person who had captured its meaning in verbal symbols, is one of the most important functions of language. Yet in the history of Maisie's childhood which James gave to *The Chap-Book,* the girl was rarely recognized as a distinct personality with her own name. Often she was referred to as an animal— a monkey, pig, donkey, chick or duck[65]—or as a monster, horror or fright,[66] or even more inappropriately as a boy.[67] Her real parents never take account of her as a person by calling her by name. Her stepmother only addressed her as such when Maisie posed a real threat to the stepmother's own selfish interests.[68] James heightened the reader's sense of Maisie's essential namelessness by calling attention to an incident when a total stranger made a point with the girl by using her name: "He called her by her name, and her name drove it [his point] home."[69] Only two other persons ever recognized Maisie as a person in this way; and it was between these two, her stepfather and her governess, Mrs. Wix, that Maisie was ultimately forced to choose.[70]

The fact that the adults who were responsible for the child's well-being regarded her as such an anomalous and indistinct entity played a large part in creating a feeling of confusion and insignificance within Maisie's consciousness. She had no fixed place where she belonged, just as she had no fixed identity recognized by a name. One moment she was a "precious pet,"[71] the next she was a "dreadful dismal deplorable little thing."[72] Her world was one of "restless change,"[73] and increasing knowledge of the precariousness of her situation filled her with terror.[74] Maisie's search for knowledge was also a search for meaning and stability. She was looking for a reality that she could count on, something that in the face of all life's variations and confusions would remain true.

In her verbally suspect environment, Maisie learned that she could rely on her own acute sensibilities to further the cause of her education more than she could rely on any thing else. She trusted "the unmistakable language" of that which she could see and feel; and only when words were corroborated by her own sense perceptions did she believe them.[75] Often Maisie was guided by a look, sometimes by the mere tone of a voice. For instance: "It was something in Mrs. Wix's tone, which in spite of caricature remained indescribable and inimitable, that Maisie. . . . drew this sense of support."[76] It was in the "sense" of a situation thus perceived that Maisie acquired a truer picture of reality than in the facts which that sense often confounded. Maisie knew from the beginning that Mrs. Wix was the one real parent among all her adult relations: "What Maisie felt was that she [Mrs. Wix] had been, with passion and anguish, a mother, and that this was something Miss Overmore [her stepmother] wasn't, something strangely, confusingly, that mamma was even less."[77] Ultimately, when Maisie was forced to choose who her real parent would be, she not surprisingly chose Mrs. Wix, although that woman was the only one to whom Maisie was not tied by either legal or blood relations. Maisie had been told that both her natural mother and her legal step-mother were her parents, but she knew through her own perceptions that only Mrs. Wix was capable of fulfilling that function.

If knowledge came to Maisie as a result of her own perceptive abilities heightened by intense emotional engagement, it was only natural that she should have expected that the answer to her dilemma of insignificance lay in the senses' most powerful capacity, the ability to love. It was Maisie's dream that her love for her stepfather, and his love for her, would prove the salvation of them both. It was a dream incapable of actualization because only Maisie's love transcended the realm of self-serving gratification. Maisie's love for her stepfather assumed "heroic" proportions when she willingly sacrificed her own self-interests for his sake.[78] His love for Maisie never rose to such heights, as he was willing to sacrifice what was in Maisie's best interests so as not to have to sacrifice his own sensual indulgences. Later, Maisie was forced to choose between her ideal conception of love and a compromise with reality. She had matured enough, developed a critical "moral sense," to know that only in adherence to an ideal was there security. Maisie gave up everything, in her words gave up everyone,[79] to remain true to her ideal.

Both of James's contributions to *The Chap-Book*, "The Way It Came" and *What Maisie Knew,* form parts of the corpus of works treated by Leon Edel in his fourth biographical volume, *Henry James: The Treacherous Years, 1895–1901.* James's writings during this period demonstrate, in Edel's estimate, "the ways in which the imagination endows reality with realities of its own."[80] In *The Chap-Book* stories, James's central characters sacrificed the security of material reality because the realities which their imaginative perceptions had created were more vital to their lives. Meaning lay not so much in material reality as in fantastical or ideal creations that took note of facts unperceived by less sensitive observers. James's art, as *The Chap-Book* promoted it, paralleled the perceptions of his characters. He dealt with the "shadows" of reality, and in the shadows found life's "substance." And as his characters learned new truths about life that were incapable of rational articulation, so too did his readers:

> The splendid voice still rings in one's ears, the splendid emotions still vibrate in one's heart, but one is not yet ready to explain or to translate them. Indeed, the ultimate emotion set vibrating in our hearts by a supreme work of art is never explicable or translatable—any more than love and faith are explicable or translatable."[81]

Following closely on the heels of the author's unsuccessful attempt as a playwright in 1895, James's *Chap-Book* works, especially *Maisie,* demonstrate a change in their author's literary perspective. He was influenced by contemporary playwrights, particularly Ibsen,[82] to adopt a "scenic method" of exposition. By creating a total picture of reality he was able to infuse the facts of a situation with additional significance. His imagination, like the imaginations of his characters, was no longer bounded by literal verisimilitude. He could, like Bliss Carman's landscape painter, add something of himself to his creation, a "touch of wonder and unreality'' that was the essence of great art. For James had learned, as Leon Edel so rightly perceived, ''that he need be neither a 'realist' nor a 'naturalist'; the new symbolism, especially as Ibsen and Maeterlinck used it on the stage, gave him a freedom from material things and a liberty to imagine: if what he created was real to him it could be real to others.''[83]

5

Symbolic Imaginings:
A Search for Meaning

Philosophic brooding over the ultimate meaning of life has been a perennial pastime of successive generations of American college students. When Herbert Stone started publishing his small literary magazine, his collegiate environment was a perfect incubator for questioning minds challenging materialistic conceptions of reality. Stone's instructors and fraternal associates thought it an essential part of their intellectual duty to propose and then explore alternate methods of perceiving reality. They were not imbued with any devotion to science or to its disciples in the fields of literature and art. They believed science was limited to perception of "empirical" facts. It did not allow for the play of the imagination, and the imagination alone was unlimited in its ability to move beyond the tangible barriers of knowledge. In pursuit of a greater awareness of life's unknown dimensions, of life's essences rather than its elements, Stone and his *Chap-Book* turned attention to the revelations of the creative imagination. Most often these revelations came in the form of symbols, some sacred and some profane.

Stone was a student of languages, literature and the arts. He had begun his studies as an observer of his father's literary work and world, and continued this education in classes in a European preparatory school and in his courses at Harvard. Thus by the time he was ready to launch his publishing enterprises, he had a fairly well-established knowledge of foreign writing and a familiarity with foreign art. French literature was his area of special interest. In his academic studies, active involvement in La Conférence Française at Harvard, and association with others who had personal knowledge of contemporary French authors, Stone developed an abiding fascination and appreciation for French artistic expression. His was not an adolescent flirtation with the merely sensual and pessimistic indulgence of an infamous fin de siècle decadence, but an engagement with an idealistic search for forms with which to continue an inherited romantic quest for symbolic significance.

Within the first two months of its publication, attention was directed in Stone's *Chap-Book* to the works of the French Symbolists. On July 1, 1894 Gertrude Hall translated three stanzas of Paul Verlaine's "Moonlight," and these verses were followed by a critical essay of Anatole France on "Paul Verlaine: A Propos of his Book, 'My Hospitals.' " Hall's translation of Verlaine presented the sobbing melancholy of contemporary French poetry, with its pessimism muted in a suitable imaginative solution. This was to be the pattern of the magazine's appreciation of that symbolic literature which its critics called decadent and despairing. The works of the Symbolists which *The Chap-Book* chose to publish and promote were the works which could stand as supports for the magazine's intellectual position. These works fit within the larger context of *The Chap-Book*'s artistic offerings, and, for the purposes of this study, must be seen within this context. The July 1, 1894 issue of the magazine serves as a good model.

When *The Chap-Book* in this issue first introduced the work of Verlaine, just six weeks after it began publication, it did so by carefully juxtaposing the poet's verses with explanatory critical commentary. The message was unequivocal that this form of symbolic poetry, created by this poet, was but another example of the magazine's concern for the imaginative world tentatively explored by so many nineteenth-century romantics, as well as a host of religious seers. France's essay called attention to Verlaine's art by highlighting the spiritual qualities of its creator, qualities with which *The Chap-Book* could identify, not those by which it was repelled.

"Moonlight" led off the magazine's fourth number:

> Your soul is as a moonlit landscape fair
> Peopled with maskers delicate and dim,
> That play on lutes and dance and have an air
> Of being sad in their fantastic trim.
>
> The while they celebrate in minor strain
> Triumphant love, effective enterprise,
> They have an air of knowing all is vain—
> And through the quiet moonlight their songs rise.
>
> The melancholy moonlight, sweet and lone,
> That makes to dream the birds upon the tree
> And in their polished basins of white stone
> The fountains tall to sob with ecstasy.[1]

In the first stanza, the comparison between a "soul" and a "moonlit landscape fair" could have been a simile found in any number of earlier romantic lyrics. Verlaine was creating an interior landscape of the soul, "peopled with maskers delicate and dim." His fantastical players, disguised behind masks that hide their true appearance, celebrate "triumphant love, effective enterprise." Yet the landscape is filled with "an air of knowing all is vain—." Verlaine has learned that two common solutions of the nineteenth century are not sufficient to give the soul's life meaning. Neither the emotions nor purposive action are capable of transposing the songs of the players out of their "minor strain." Punctuating this thought, the poet employs a frequent Symbolist technique of combining antithetical states and inappropriate adjectives for heightened effect: the light is quiet, the songs that the players raise fail to break the silence.

Pessimism over these futile endeavors is not the final message of the poem. One sound is capable of piercing the stillness, of articulating the voice of the soul. It is the "sob," a wordless cry of "ecstasy" which accompanies the reverie of the birds that "dream" while the players revel. Perched above the concerns of those other inhabitants of this interior landscape, the birds are essentially creatures of the air, capable of flights of fancy. Not grounded by material concerns, as are the dancers of the senses, they alone are privy to the secret exclamation of divine utterance.

These were the first verses of a known Symbolist to appear on *The Chap-Book's* pages. It is important to note that they appeared, not with a fanfare championing their decadence as might have trumpeted their appearance on the pages of England's *Savoy,* but rather appropriately intermingled with other works of similar intellectual focus that were neither startling nor unsettling in their known romanticism or acceptably compromised realism. Verlaine, who was to so many others a symbol of the most degenerate aspects of contemporary society and literature, was to *The Chap-Book* an appealing example of the familiar romantic hero. Anatole France's essay described him for the magazine's readers as: a "singularly robust old vagabond"; "a spectator at once *naif* and full of insight"; "a superb and magnificent savage"; a "primitive, natural man."[2] Possessed of a "poetic" if admittedly "bizarre imagination," Verlaine was capable of the great romantic feat, transforming a cold, bare room into "a place of enchantment" filled with "the magic of a Thessalian moonlight."[3] What was most significant to France, and to *The Chap-Book,* was the poet's ability to look beyond the real world to see the realm of the spirit.

Casting off the material world to be a "mystic,"—"whose kingdom is not of this world"—Anatole France likened Verlaine to the medieval mendicant friar and saint, Francis of Assisi, who "would have recognized him, you may be sure, as one of his spiritual sons, and perhaps would have made him his favorite disciple."[4] For all his infamous vices, Verlaine was to *The Chap-Book* a man of faith, in France's words a man of "pious simplicity," a proselytizer like St. Francis. France's essay contributed a picture of the aging poet that the magazine adored. It recounted Verlaine's own words describing his efforts to convert an unbeliever: "What a terrible man! all mustaches and believing neither in God nor the devil. I reasoned with him from time to time that there must be someone above cleverer than we, and that he was wrong not to believe in Him and to trust in Him."[5] As if to reinforce both France's image of Verlaine—the imaginary Franciscan—and the poet's own words of traditional piety, on the page facing this text in *The Chap-Book* appeared an illustration entitled "The Rosary." In this design for a stained-glass window, Eugene Grasset pictured an aged friar, in appropriate Franciscan garb, kneeling at the feet of the Virgin and Child, about to receive a strand of precious prayer beads.[6]

Recent criticism, by its emphasis on other personality traits of Verlaine, only serves to highlight both the work and the criticism of the poet which *The Chap-Book* chose to publish. For instance, in the late 1960s William Gaunt, a respected authority on late nineteenth-century aestheticism, described Verlaine in a manner that hardly conjured up an image of sainthood. His representation, while florid, is also faithful to the facts of Verlaine's life.

> Verlaine! squinting and villainously ugly, his suppurating limbs wrapped in vile rags, the consumer of a prodigious amount of alcohol, supported by the earnings of street-walkers and the charitable replies to begging letters; the would-be assassin and self-confessed homosexual; the connoisseur of prisons and the habitué of hospitals. Debauched and snivelling he resembles the old Karamazov of Dostoevsky's novel, in his capacity for an endless degradation lit by flashes of insight and even humour; his fits of mawkish repentance alternating with fits of maudlin ferocity.[7]

A far cry from St. Francis. *The Chap-Book* was willing to concede that the French poet was always pictured, even then, as "a wretchedly dressed and apparently unclean pauper" but this was, for *The Chap-Book,* an acceptable way for a poet to look. When it was rumored that Verlaine had been presented to high society in frock coat and opera hat, *The Chap-Book* indulged in a bit of humorous outrage: "This news is horrible. There was a bohemian sort of charm about the poverty of the poet—but the innocent, childlike Verlaine attired in tall hat and frock is very unpleasant: it suggests decline—or intoxication."[8]

Rather than condemning the old reprobate as a moral degenerate,

The Chap-Book continued to sing Verlaine's praises even after the poet's death. Accepting a request to act as the American representative of an international committee, headed by Mallarmé and Rodin, which was soliciting funds to erect a statue in Verlaine's honor, *The Chap-Book* enthusiastically issued a call for contributions: "I am in hopes the readers of the CHAP-BOOK will respond at once to this note. The number of persons in this country who knew and appreciated Verlaine's work is not great; yet the opportunity to assist in raising a monument to the greatest poet of modern France, and one of the most perfect poets of all time, is remarkable."[9]

Perfect poetry was what *The Chap-Book* thought Verlaine wrote, and in one of his untranslated "Epigrammes," which led off the ninth number of the magazine, its readers were presented with themes recurrent in the journal's intellectual offerings. Mature age, ripe and realizing reluctantly that such a state is quickly spoiled, looks on the foolish and sublime antics that make up the "camaieu" called life. The poet is not part of the action, but indeed a spectator watching the show. He refers to "le joli pêle-mêle" as a ballet, a play. Always unfolding before him as a voiceless presentation accompanied by music, reality becomes "la pantomime" which merely encases the lives of the players. It is not the real essence of life, it is a mere show, a form, a play on a stage that has the semblance of life. Juxtaposed to the "jeux de silence et de mystère," art alone holds the secret of life's real meaning and will reveal it only to such a player as Columbine. Columbine was the invisible wife of Harlequin, a favorite of the French comic opera. Mortal eyes could not see her; mere mortals, likewise, could not perceive the great mystery of life or recognize the reality of art. The "vieillissant poète" enjoys the pleasures of his sight and mind, but he knows that they are only "l'illusion dans le décor."[10]

Behind the illusion, or delusion, of outward material reality lay another world of more momentous illusions, that of the mysterious spirit world. It was Verlaine's perception of this world that made him so attractive to *The Chap-Book*. He was a spiritual man, even if at times in the past the spirit he had followed was that of the devil. By the 1890s, Verlaine was perceived to be penitent and capable of penetrating life's thick cloak of illusions to find ultimate meaning. In the eyes of Chicago society matron and *Chap-Book* contributor Mrs. Reginald de Koven, Verlaine was not only well on his way to effecting his own spiritual salvation, but was also an effective instrument in saving others who had travelled a similar path of depravity.

While never referring specifically to the poet's erstwhile conversion to Catholicism, de Koven was convinced that he had experienced a genuine spiritual rebirth. In his earlier days, because of the extreme receptivity of his poetic nature, Verlaine had been, by de Koven's account, "doubly charged" by the "world spirit" which had poured into him all "the essences and intuitions of the body and the soul." These conflicting influences were evidenced by the fact that he was a protégé of both the nineteenth century's sensual Baudelaire and the Middle Age's spiritual Villon. Verlaine achieved sufficient maturity to assert his own individuality only after undergoing a painful process of spiritual regeneration. He left his old masters behind when he emerged from his experience as a faithful romantic. He was an artist of natural lyricism, isolated in an individual quest to probe the limits of the mysterious, and moral, spirit world.

> Then the whole was set to the vibration of a new rhythm as strange and as remote from the consciousness of men as the songs of interlunar space, so that his utterances with the naturalness of a bird's song or an infant's lisp should have the accents of melody undreamed of. And this is not all—strangest and most tragically terrible in its possibilities of pain—the chrism of conscience burns his sinister brow. The phantom of the of the immortal soul drives him into the outer darkness.[11]

Out in this spiritual darkness, Verlaine found a companion. He found woman. If his song had come to sound like a romantic lyric, he recognized that her's did not. They met in that favorite romantic setting, "the dwelling place of death . . . where love and life live together," that "ultimate spot, occult, remote." But she was not the romantic poet's fair maiden: she was beauty in decay. An expert on vice who was also initiated in the ecstasies of the spirit, Verlaine found a soul-mate in woman. She, like he, lived primarily in a world of spirits. She, like he, knew the depths of depravity. He would become her "prophet and interpreter," because he knew the landscape of her interior life.

Like Verlaine, woman was removed from the real world. She was a spectator, in de Koven's estimate, rather than a participant. Deprived of any active involvement with life, woman had been forced to rely on her imagination to savor vicariously all of life's emotional sensations. Her outward appearance was merely a "mantle of deceit," the cloak of centuries of enslavement, a costume contrived by man to conceal the true reality of her being. De Koven "appreciated" Verlaine because Verlaine was able to perceive both the reality and the unreality of woman's existence. He could look beyond the actual to see that she, having been driven into the realm of the imagination, had developed into not merely the pure spiritual creature that man admired, but also a thoroughly experienced sensational creature. In her mind she had experimented with "all crimes, all horrors, as well as martyrdoms and joys." Out of necessity an imaginative creature she, like Verlaine, knew that there was a devil as well as a god, and that outward appearances often failed to conform with interior reality. She had glimpsed the divine, she had also grovelled in depravity.

Woman—traditionally a symbol of purity, removed from the corrupting influences of the material world—became in Verlaine's hands a more perfect symbol of the irony of appearances. Outwardly the picture of "divine patience," always cheerful, always smiling and compassionate while ministering to the suffering, woman was inwardly possessed of a knowledge of evil which was blacker than any brigande's because her experiences were without tangible limits. Verlaine, "the convict poet, from this heart rotten with all the sins of fancy and of deed," knew woman as his contemporaries did not.

But de Koven's "Feminine Appreciation" of Verlaine came not because she thought he glorified woman's capacity for depravity, but because Verlaine the believer, Verlaine the regenerate, also knew woman's capacity for spiritual exaltation. He could plead for the salvation of her soul. He knew that the "love of the spirit" often "choked in the throats of dumb and suffering women," and his poetry was an articulation of their mute cries. By pointing out the irony of her existence he challenged her to create a symbol for herself that would not be deceitful. It may have been ironic that a man so "vicious and disreputable beyond words" could utter such words of comprehension and faith. But it was entirely appropriate, an appropriately "strange anomaly," that it should have been Verlaine "who had understood."[12]

Strange anomalies were not unusual to *The Chap-Book,* a magazine that repeatedly demonstrated its fascination with the ironical, the anomalous, the paradoxical. If the reality of women's lives was more complex than their surface appearances indicated, *The Chap-Book* did not find that either strange or surprising. If that complex reality was further complicated by its lack of conformance with the accepted symbol which was supposed to represent it, that also was neither strange nor surprising. By devoting considerable attention to ironies and anomalies such as these, *The Chap-Book* evidenced an intellectual awareness that the truth, or truths, of reality were not always what they appeared to be on the surface. A new vision was needed, a greater sensitivity that would broaden one's perceptions of a world hidden from the view of those who only were concerned with surface phenomena. Perhaps there was also a need for new symbols to convey the truths that this visionary perspective would bring into focus.

Traditional rational expectations were shattered when *The Chap-Book* at different times mourned over or mocked those who looked to art in the hopes of finding a simple, literal depiction of an equally simple, comprehensible reality. One of *The Chap-Book's* simplest and most traditional illustrations makes this point so subtly that it almost passes unnoticed. On February 15, 1896 two woodcuts were printed from an old chap-book, entitled "The World Turned Upside Down." Heavy lines and light-hearted humor reverse the natural order of physical life: lovers are trapped in a net set by a bird, and a horse plays the groom to a tethered man.[13] The jest, however, is not mere whimsy. It is but part of a series of illustrations from old chap-books that propose riddles, depict dreams, visualize fables, ask questions and present conundrums.[14] Each solution or situation contains an element of mystery, of truth disguised or unperceived; fragments from "The True Trial of Understanding."[15]

In an earlier volume, *The Chap-Book* had responded with editorial commentary on the "proper interpretation" of one of its other illustrations. Georges Pissaro's contemporary drawing "In the Garden" had appeared in the September 15, 1895 issue. Several numbers later, an anonymous letter was reproduced asking the editors to provide a definitive statement on what the picture was supposed to represent. Confusion had apparently been commonplace among the letterwriter's acquaintances, as he recounted the assertions of those who "insist that since the body and head of the fowl resemble the head of the elephant, the object *is* an elephant; or that as the tail is the tail of a fish, therefore the fowl is a fish." Some others, "unbelievers" relying on the title for a clue, proposed that the object was an orchid. The correspondent, with his own unspecified conclusion, appealed to *The Chap-Book* to settle the dispute.

With characteristic disdain for such a narrow focus that was concerned only with a realistic subject rather than with an appreciation of the artist's vision, *The Chap-Book* indulged in a bit of sarcastic ridicule. Like the illustration in the old chap-book, this *Chap-Book* suggested to its readers that if they did not understand the reality that was presented to them, perhaps it was because the picture they saw was upside down. "It had not been my intention to refer to the matter—but since the subject has been brought up, I am forced to acknowledge that through a stupid mistake in the office the drawing was printed upside down. If my readers will take the trouble to examine the picture anew, its interpretation will doubtless be plain."[16] The illustration, of course, had not been printed upside down. Nonsensically proposing that the picture be turned so that those looking for literal meaning might find what they sought, *The Chap-Book*, with humorous condescension and carefully chosen words, ridiculed those who could not see the absurdity of the letterwriter's request. So intent on the "matter" of art, they were blind to its meaning. *The Chap-Book*, tongue in cheek, suggested a different angle of vision that might help their perception. In all seriousness, they truly would have to turn their world upside down before they would be cured of their materialistic myopia.

Pedants pondering only the affairs of this world also drew the attention of William Butler Yeats in his one contribution to *The Chap-Book*. Yeats combined, with some fine ironical twists, threads of medieval Christianity, Druidical paganism, fantastical enchantment, and mythic metamorphosis. His story, "S. Patrick and the Pedants," was an attempt to illustrate "the doctrine of the gods set out in new symbols," just as St. Patrick had done by other means in early medieval Ireland. It was a serious artistic portrayal of *The Chap-Book's* intellectual vision that made use of many of the magazine's most frequent themes.

Two characters comprise the story's cast: Michael Bruin, an aged smuggler living outside an Irish coastal village; and a medieval Ollamh, cursed by St. Patrick to assume the form of a heron. Bruin "had little communion with mankind" and "had no thought for anything but the making of his soul." Possessed of two artifacts to help him in this process, the smuggler cherished his Spanish crucifix and French rosary, symbols not only of his spiritual aspiration but of his trade in material thievery. While awaiting the arrival of a schooner, prey for further plunder, Bruin caught sight of a flock of heron. He determined to shoot one so as to acquire his sustenance for the next several days. Raising the sight of his gun to his eye and taking aim at the heron, "to his wonder and terror, a man of infinitely great age and infirmity stood in its place." When Bruin dropped the gun the "enchantment" vanished and the heron reappeared. After repeating his previous movement, only to have the apparition return, the thief performed a set pattern of spiritual ablutions (crossing himself, reciting a *Paternoster* and *Ave Maria,* and promising the recitation of a succession of rosaries). Believing he had exorcised the evil spirit, Bruin took aim and fired. The old man lay fatally wounded.

Moving to the place where the old man had fallen, Bruin attempted to investigate the nature of his prey. As he looked on the figure clothed in robes of an ancient pattern, an arm reached out trying to grasp the rosary hanging around the smuggler's neck. Bruin drew back protesting: "Wizard, I will let no wicked thing touch my blessed beads!" The dying man asserting that he was no wizard, attempts to explain why he wants to "kiss the cross before I die." He and the other herons, many generations before, had been Ollamhs of King Leaghaire. They were pedants, "busy with a dispute about the merits of the great and little metres," unimaginative workers intent only on the oaken staves upon which they carved their precious knowledge: "we neither hunted, nor went to battle, nor listened to the Druids preaching by their grey stones, and even love, if it came to us at all, was but a transitory fire." When the "Druids and the poets" told them of the new symbolic utterances of "a new Druid Patrick," they "yawned in the midst of their tale." And when Patrick came to preach to King Leaghaire, these Ollamhs's "hearts were deaf, and we carved and disputed and read," and paid no attention to the saint.

Patrick, however, sought them out and spoke to them in a voice that they recognized as being filled with "rapture." He complained: "I preached the commandments of the Maker of the world," and "within the foss of the king and from the centre of the earth to the windows of Heaven there was a great silence." All the creatures of nature were silent in their attention to the wisdom of God's new prophet, all creatures except the Ollamhs who continued in their own noisy pursuits: "all else being silent, the sound shook the angels with anger." In anger, Patrick vilified the Ollamhs: "Oh, men who have no part in love, who have no part in song, who have no part in wisdom, but dwell with the shadows of memory where the feet of angels connot touch you as they pass over your heads, where the hair of demons cannot sweep about you as they pass under your feet, lay upon you a curse, and change you to an example for ever and ever." Patrick doomed them to a heron's life of futile pondering, condemned to stand for hours in grey pools unillumined by either the stars or the sun.

Having listened to the old Ollamh's history, "the voteen [Bruin] bent over his gun with his eyes upon the ground, trying in vain to understand something of this tale." He was aroused from his reverie, "his dream," when the Ollamh again grasped the rosary. With a cry of: "You must not touch my blessed beads!" the thief struck the old man a final blow with the barrel of his gun. Bending down over the figure, which was vanishing before his eyes, Bruin became intent on expropriating the clothes of the dead Ollamh: "Surely, he thought, if that ample cloak, and that little tight-fitting cloak under it, were warm and goodly, St. Patrick would take the enchantment out of them and leave them fit for human use." The clothes, however, vanish as completely as had the old Ollamh.[17]

Brief, but pregnantly compact, Yeats managed to relate the major intellectual concerns of *The Chap-Book* in this short symbolic narrative. Bruin, a thief of material goods, is ironically concerned with the salvation of his soul. The irony does not cease here. Bruin's obsession with "the making of his soul" focuses his attention on the mere material evidence or artifacts of a spiritual life. When he is presented with a true vision of spirituality, a vision that confounds the evidence of material reality, he does not understand it. He destroys it, and then attempts to rob it of the material substance it momentarily leaves behind. As a thief his purpose was always the acquisition of material things. As a seeker of spiritual rewards, he is never able to transcend his addiction to physical goods.

The history of the heron serves several purposes. On one level it functions in the same way as the histories of *The Chap-Book*'s realistic literature, linking a spiritual vision with a more tangible and comprehensible reality. By making use of a familiar historical figure, St. Patrick, the author can also take advantage of all the associations traditionally brought to mind by the mere introduction of the saint into the narrative. St. Patrick is a symbol of vibrant spirituality. Linked with an earlier form of Irish spirituality, the natural paganism of the Druids, the "new Druid Patrick" serves the additional function of establishing the continuing historical succession of spiritual seers. He preaches the same "doctrine of the gods" as had the Druids, only now it is "set out in new symbols." The symbols might change, as do the historical characters, but the spiritual force which inspires them remains the same.

History, as *The Chap-Book* employs it, also serves a didactic function, and the story of the heron is a forthright explication of the facts of one man's life. These facts are very specifically meant to serve as "an example for ever and ever" to other men so that they might be more cognizant of spiritual concerns. If others, like Bruin, are to avoid the curse which befell the Ollamh, they must have hearts that can burn with emotions; they must experience life rather than merely reading about it or remembering it; they must love and sing and listen, along with nature, to the spiritual commandments of the universe. Poets and priests, conversant with angels and demons, attuned to divine utterances, are the teachers. The lessons they teach are thoroughly and traditionally romantic.

Lastly, the history of the heron is also an interpretation of a vision. It is a verbal account of a mythical metamorphosis, a rational explanation of a fantastical enchantment, a guide to the perception of an imaginary creation. Bruin sees a vision. Twice some kind of magical transformation of reality occurs before his eyes, and his only thought is to have reality reinstated in its natural guise. Resorting to rote formulae to rid himself of a spirit foreign to his perceptions, he closes his eyes to this new manifestation of spiritual reality. With eyes closed to the vision, he makes use of the material means at his disposal to destroy its representation. Rather like a museum painting that has failed to stir the imagination of a dull observer, this imaginative creation comes complete with critical commentary, a catalogue to the exhibit, explaining the nature and inspiration of its composition. But if Bruin is not perceptive enough to recognize and appreciate the reality of the vision, he also turns out to be incapable of comprehending its verbal message. Even a straightforward narrative detailing a spiritual history fails to convince the materialist that the vision has substantive reality. Bruin is a worse pedant than the Ollamh ever was.

Enchantment was an unwelcome element in Bruin's world. He prayed to St. Patrick to remove this apparition from his sight, characteristically bartering the recitation of four rosaries in exchange for the saint's intercession. When the enchantment was finally destroyed, the unillumined Bruin still hoped to reap some tangible good from his encounter. What he believed to be the "real" goods, of course, the Ollamh's clothes, disappeared when Bruin denied the reality of the spiritual enchantment. Bruin is left with his "blessed beads," but they are untouched by any spiritual encounter.

Enchantment was the substance of *The Chap-Book*'s artistic world. It was the infusion of divine inspiration into an otherwise unmeaningful set of material phenomena. It was both a recognition and representation of a state suspended half-way between the uncompromisingly real and the incomprehensibly spiritual.[18] It was not unlike the process of artistic inspiration. *The Chap-Book,* just a few months before it ceased publication, voiced its conviction that Yeats not only wrote of enchantment, but also inhabited "the shadowy borderland between the known and the mysterious."[19] His art was inseparable from his own individual search for meaning; and the search led him and his readers into a world where mystery and matter mingled. It was the world Bliss Carman had said was composed of dust and dream. Enchantment was the breach in the dike of life's material defenses. Once this point of vulnerability had been exposed, once the mysterious and fantastical were accepted as credible phenomena, a flood of all sorts of physically and rationally "impossible" possibilities naturally followed.

Midway through its career, *The Chap-Book* had complained that "moderns" could not believe the impossible. In its "Notes" section of November 15, 1895 the magazine published a take-off on Lewis Carroll's famous fantasy:

> "I can't believe that," said Alice.
> "Can't you?" the Queen said in a pitiful tone. "Try again; draw a long breath, and shut your eyes."
> Alice laughed.
> "There's no use trying," she said, "one *can't* believe impossible things."
> "I daresay you haven't had much practice," said the Queen. "When I was your age, I always did it for half an hour a day. Why sometimes I've believed as many as six impossible things before breakfast."
> Poor Alice, and poor moderns we, of whom she is the type! A whole philosophy of life is told us jestingly, and we cannot see it. Although nothing is so conducive to flexibility of mind and comfort of spirit as this same faculty of believing the impossible, no one is willing even to "draw a long breath and shut his eyes."[20]

Like those other moderns who could only see realistic representations in works of art, so these moderns had to alter radically their natural perceptions, indeed to go blind to the real world in front of them, before they would be able to see and appreciate a new philosophy of life. This new philosophy called for flexibility of mind to understand and accept a reality that fit into no fixed and logical systems, and Carroll's tale of Alice was a favorite illustration and model. In its last full issue, *The Chap-Book* published a short story by Gouveneur Morris, "A Chapter from Alice in Wonderland Lately Recovered." Alice is subjected to the nonsensical conversation of a bizarre group of impossible creatures. She repeatedly is saying, "I don't see," or "I don't know," as the creatures' rhetoric twists, contorts and confuses all logic, syntax and meaning. There is no meaning in this world—that is, no meaning that makes any sense to Alice or to the reader. But the reader learns to expect the unexpected, to accept confusion and contradiction, and finally becomes a witness to the drowning of Alice who is the only normal creature in the entire story.[21] Carroll was, in *The Chap-Book*'s estimate, the father of symbolism largely through his example of using the "marvel of words" to confound all logical knowledge in the presentation of utter "inanity."[22]

It was necessary for these authors to destroy all preconceived patterns and all rational knowledge, to turn the natural world over on its head in order to alert contemporaries to the fact that in the material world there was no real, fixed, or eternal meaning. This world was only an illusion, in many instances a delusion that masked true spiritual reality rather than revealing it. From the notoriously decadent Symbolists to sententiously traditional romantics, the thought was the same: each individual had to recognize that the central reality of life lay in his own personal relationship with some spiritual force or forces. Ella Wheeler Wilcox's art may have been unctuous to the aesthetes, but her ideas were at the base of their artistic credo. Her "Illusion" was also theirs:

> God and I in space alone,
>   And nobody else in view.
>   And "Where are the people, O Lord," I said,
>   "The earth below and the sky o'erhead
> And the dead whom once I knew?"
> "That was a dream," God smiled and said
>   "A dream that seemed to be true.
> There were no people living or dead,
> There was no earth and no sky o'erhead—
>   There was only Myself and you."[23]

These *Chap-Book* authors were inheritors of the well-established romantic belief that through symbolic interpretation nature could yield knowledge of a basically mysterious spiritual reality,[24] but they had become wary of a method that could degenerate into simple nature worship, that is, worship of the symbol rather than its meaning. Wilcox's bald denial of the existence of nature was one alternative. Another was a reorientation of symbolism away from the natural in favor of the artificial. This altered perspective still viewed symbolism as the most appropriate means of expressing that which by definition defied absolute delineation, but it became more efficacious as it became more artificial. The further symbols were removed from direct physical correspondence, the less likely they were of misinterpretation. The less familiar they were, the more compelling they became because of their greater power to startle the unimaginative out of their mental complacency.

Never assuming the pose of decadence, or espousing its position of despair, *The Chap-Book* was willing to make reference to a dictum of the decade's most notorious Decadent in order to emphasize its own perspective on reality. In its "Notes" of August 1, 1894, written by Louise Imogen Guiney[25] and issued that first summer of its existence before it left the environs of Harvard College, *The Chap-Book* reminded its readers of one of Oscar Wilde's epigrams: "Do you recall his admirable creed that nature as well as Life imitates Art?" Of particular note is the magazine's commentary outlining what was axiomatic in this statement, and what contemporaries still had to learn: "That Life is always an imitation of the Art that preceded it is easy to see; but it is not quite so easy to see how nature too is no more than the reproduction of Art." *The Chap-Book* had, nonetheless, come to see the natural world from this perspective: "I have recently had a curious experience which confirms me in my adherence to this apparently wayward artistic theory." The experience referred to was that of seeing new French art work, paintings in which all of nature was shaded blue. After living with these paintings for several weeks, *The Chap-Book*'s "Notes" writer conceded that she too began to see nature as blue. "All this happened some months ago, and Nature still remains obstinately of her strange new complexion. Nothing looks as it did. For better or worse, my old earth is gone."[26] Artistic expression of reality became more real for *The Chap-Book* than the deceptions of artistically uninspired sight. The perspective was new, the old material reality gone.

Art was a teacher of life. This assertion could stand without further elaboration for those artists who had elevated devotion to their craft into a religion. In chorusing this familiar refrain, they were led by their masters in romanticism. On April 1, 1898 Bliss Carman, in noting the high esteem with which he still regarded the poet Longfellow, also indicated the direction in which this venerable master had led his followers: "He was never the priest of nature; he was always the gentle sacristan of art."[27] Art was revelation, inspired by creative spirit, that directed attention towards life's ultimate meaning. The artist was charged with the care of the spirit's vestments. He was the one who made ready for the congregation the symbolic clothes which served as visual testaments to the spirit's presence.

While Carman clearly established Longfellow's elevation above the ranks of the mere worshippers of nature, he failed to accord his contemporary, Louise Guiney, the same status. He praised her for what he termed the "eternal paganism"[28] evident in her nature lyrics, and to this she took exception. "No! I can't answer for Bliss Carman's restoring me to the ranks of 'paganism,' which I think is a word he used erroneously for natural religion. . . . It hurt me, and complimented me not, as it was meant to do." She took it as a failure of her art to have led him "into so queer a conclusion!" Guiney, a "persistent Papist," blamed herself for being "so inarticulate" as to have led Carman into his false assessment of her spiritual motivation. She recognized the problem that artists of the word had to cope with: "Speech was given to man to conceal his thoughts," and only the rare individual, "someone who has strong faith," will be able to see through their surface meaning to perceive the nature of the spirit which lies hidden beneath their traditional forms.[29] Carman's misperception of Guiney's art denigrated it, in her mind, to a primitive romanticism rather than recognizing its foundation in a complex, if highly traditional, set of religious symbols.

Seen within the context of *The Chap-Book*'s own predominant romanticism, it is not surprising that its symbolism should often be the work of its most romantic artists. Their success in moving beyond their inherited tradition was varied. When Richard Hovey, Carman's coauthor for a book of verse, wrote an introduction for Stone & Kimball's edition of *The Plays of Maurice Maeterlinck* in 1894, he helped to articulate his publishers' conception of the nature of contemporary symbolism, and identified which of *The Chap-Book*'s romantic authors could claim the designation of symbolists. His choices, rather than clearly differentiating between an old and new symbolism, show the continuity of symbolic perceptions that has led to what is now the "new school."

As an introduction to modern symbolism, Hovey began by stating: "In a broad sense, all language is symbolism and all art is language. To the artist the material universe is a medium through which to express the immaterial realities of thought and feeling." These two elements, as Hovey called them, must be present in all art: "the immaterial passion, action or reflection, and the material embodiment by which it is made manifest through the senses." Creative fusion in a work of art yields a product, however, that is greater than the sum of its parts. Hovey noted that the artistic manifestation was a product of not only "instinct" and "intelligence," but also of "imagination." That these "immaterial realities" were closely linked in Hovey's mind with the spiritual realities enshrined by traditional religious symbols was evident in his rhetoric: "The one is the symbol—it would not exceed the modesty of prose to say, the sacrament of the other."[30]

Art which was concerned primarily with ideas, with the articulation of life's ethical problems, for instance, had to be symbolic, in Hovey's estimate. "If the abstract idea dominates, art turns to symbolism of necessity. The body is its own majestic speech, and the emotions of the soul have their instinctive and spontaneous language, but for the idea expression must be forcibly created." Noting that the senses and the emotions "find utterance through natural correspondences," ideality could only be expressed by "artificial correspondences," what he termed "consciously invented symbols." These symbols would "imply" rather than "definitely state an esoteric meaning." They would give "an impression of the thing symbolized rather than a formulation." And they could be present in literature that was either characterized as "romantic" or "realistic."[31]

Along with Herbert Stone's undergraduate friend and *The Chap-Book*'s long-time associate editor, Harrison Garfield Rhodes, Richard Hovey was one of the magazine's most knowledgeable promoters of European symbolism. Thus when he identified current members of the new school of symbolism it was not surprising that he should have included such obvious representatives as Mallarmé and Maeterlinck. In doing so he noted, however, that Maeterlinck was conceptually romantic and rhetorically realistic. He was, nevertheless, a master of symbolism as was Ibsen, who had been successively characterized during his career as a romantic, a realist, and most recently a symbolist.[32]

Of particular interest to this study is the fact that the only other contemporary writers Hovey singled out for mention as belonging to the new school of symbolism were three *Chap-Book* romantics: Gilbert Parker, Bliss Carman and Charles G. D. Roberts. Conceding that their forms were "diverse," Hovey believed that their work collectively revealed "a general character that differentiates it from the symbolism of other periods." This character was its suggestiveness rather than its certainty.[33] While they were modern in their realization that the "immaterial realities" could be only symbolically suggested rather than definitively known, Hovey was also careful to point out that their method was merely a contemporary manifestation of a tradition that dated back to biblical times. He closed his introduction to modern symbolism with the assertion that the method which these authors "have adopted, is not likely to become obsolete as long as the world still harkens to the parables of the Man of Nazareth."[34]

Whether one chooses to call symbolism a quest for ideals and ethics or knowledge of a universal spirit, it was, to *The Chap-Book*'s romantics, essentially religious at its core. Symbols were sacred because they were material revelations of an essentially spiritual reality. Bliss Carman recognized what Charles G. D. Roberts was doing when he began a volume of his poetry with an "invocation."

> Thy touch, O grave mysteriarch,
> Makes dull familiar things divine.
> O grant of thy revealing gift
> Be some small portion mine![35]

Calling for divine inspiration, for the revelation of spiritual mysteries, Roberts's poetry published in *The Chap-Book* is a better example, however, of intellectual affinity with the aspirations of symbolism than adherence to its methods. In "Origins," which appeared in the January 1, 1895 issue, Roberts details the symbolic, née romantic, quest for the meaning to individual life. He begins in the land of "dreams," the region of "the dark sublime," where time is endless, a region "beyond the bournes of space." Here there is only "the averted Face" of the deity, the divine creator. In a "dark and mystic heat/Where soul and matter meet," man, the recipient of an "enigmatic Will," is created and set forth on his short physical journey through life.

Man is a slave, during his brief physical existence, to the laws of nature—particularly those of heredity—and subject to the punishment of original sin.

> Inexorably decreed
> By the ancestral deed,
> The puppets of our sires,
> We work out blind desires,
> And for our sons ordain
> The blessing or the bane.

In this natural state man stands in "ignorance" surrounded by the forces of "fate." But he is curious, and "questions stars and earth/Of life, and death, and birth." One might think that he is a scientific empiricist, but more likely he is a romantic looking on nature to reveal the answers he seeks. He surveys "kindred skies," the "common grass" where all mens' "atoms mix and pass," the trees in spring with their sap running, the brooding birds stirred by the same spirit which thrills men's blood, a "vital fire" that animates all of life. Yet man's ignorance is unrelieved until the coming of "a word."

> But in the urge intense
> And fellowship of sense,
> Suddenly comes a word
> In other ages heard
> On a great wind our souls
> Are borne to unknown goals,
> And past the bournes of space
> To the unaverted Face[36]

Only when the "word," presumably some symbolic utterance (perhaps here a conscious reference to traditional Christianity and the "word" that inspired the gospel writers) is heard can man gain release from his physical environment and be transported into the infinite. There he will meet and know the spirit that was not revealed to him even in the dream of his original creation. There he will find answers to the questions he posed to his instincts, emotions and intellect.

Roberts's poetry is not symbolism, however. It reveals through exposition rather than symbolic impression. Its message is similar in intellectual content to that of L. Hereward in a "Rondel" published in the same volume of *The Chap-Book*:

> This place is as a nether world
> Where Time and Life are conquered kings.
> Each ghostly tree in mist shroud curled,
> Its great gaunt arms in wild mirth flings,
> And in my brain a fancy springs—
> "I, too, am dead—the earth scroll furled—
> This place is as a nether world
> Where Time and Life are conquered kings!"
> There is naught real. The moon is swirled
> In clouds which meet the mist wreath's rings,
> The mist itself, by ghost winds shirled,
> More real than aught to which it clings.
> This place is as a nether world
> Where Time and Life are conquered kings.[37]

Both poets know that true reality lies beyond the realm of the physical. Hereward employs a favorite *Chap-Book* device of making his point by direct contradiction of physical reality. The earth, time and life are not real. What is real is a world of mist, of ghosts; the real nether world. These were traditional romantic thoughts, of the same variety as those which inspired Gilbert Parker in his story of "The Golden Pipes." They were also the thoughts that were to lead some of *The Chap-Book*'s romantics beyond their inherited tradition into an exploration of new symbolic representations.

Earlier it was shown how Parker's story "The Golden Pipes" fit within the canon of romantic literature.[38] It was also noted, in contrast to the work of John Davidson, how Parker's tale deviated from the standard romantic expectations. By decrying the realization of a dream, even when that realization was a faithful articulation of romanticism's most cherished beliefs, Parker had distinguished himself as belonging to the new generation of romantics rather than to the old. He was a symbolist, preferring the dream in its unequivocally spiritual state to any physically contrived manifestation.

Symbolism, as Hovey described it, adherred to a philosophy that spiritual reality could only be suggested, not defined. Hepnon, the organ builder and musician in Parker's story, had violated this symbolic principle: he had found a way to circumscribe spiritual reality by enclosing it within some man-made and communicable form. It assumed a quality of definiteness and lost its essential infiniteness. By being so transformed the dream was destroyed, there was no longer any vital spiritual reality in Hepnon's life. Parker was not advocating an abandonment of all artistic aspirations to symbolize in artistic forms the revelations of spiritual mysteries. He was cautioning the artist against thinking that his symbols were more than symbols. If symbols were complete and true representations of spiritual reality, then they were not symbols at all but evidential facts. If they were factual they could not be spiritual.

Symbolism, according to its most important interpreter and apologist in the 1890s, Arthur Symons, contained three essential components: it was mysterious, antimaterial and religious.[39] Only after man recognized that the material world stood as a barrier to more significant knowledge, knowledge of spiritual mysteries incomprehensible to man's rational mind, would he be able to appreciate the value of symbolic forms. Symbolic forms were the antithesis of material evidence. They taught by suggesting more than their surface reality, more than their literal meaning. As they came closer to being perfect symbols of perfect spirituality, they would by necessity become less and less literal (more mysterious), less and less natural (antimaterial), and more and more sacred (religious revelations of the spirit).

There was in symbolism an inherent quality not unlike the snake swallowing its tail. Symons verified the fact that the symbolists went to great lengths to perfect their symbolic forms, but it was with a very specific purpose in mind: "There is such a thing as perfecting form that form may be annihilated. . . . It is all an attempt to spiritualize literature, to evade the old bondage of rhetoric, the old bondage of exteriority. Description is banished that beautiful things may be evoked, magically."[40] Material forms by their very nature were a physical shell that separated man the perceiver (on the outside) from the essential ideal reality (on the inside). Symbolic forms, which were less physical, suffered less from this liability than other linguistic forms, but they nonetheless remained forms trying to approximate, trying to invoke a formless spirit. If the form were ever to be perfected, the result would have to be a formless form.

Support for the belief that man was kept captive behind walls of material or literal forms came not only from the known symbolists, but also from some of *The Chap-Book*'s most traditional authors. Six months after *The Chap-Book* changed its format and enlarged its size, William Watson was writing of the spirit's captivity to the five natural senses. Watson, one of Britain's conservative opponents to the influence of French literature,[41] acknowledged that if there was indeed some mysterious spiritual reality in the universe, man was only able to perceive its existence by means of his senses. His senses, however, served more to isolate man from that spirit than to bring him into closer contact with it. Watson's poem, "The Captive's Dream," begins:

> From birth we have his captives been:
>   For freedom, vain to strive!
>   This is our chamber: windows five
> Look forth on his demesne;
> And each to its own several hue
>   Translates the outward scene.
> We cannot once the landscape view
> Save with the painted panes between.[42]

Watson recognized that a perfect and comprehensive view of life was impossible: man could get only partial views through the windows of each of his separate senses and each of these was colored by the physical limitations of those individual senses, as well as by man's subjective apperception of their messages. But man also had some inkling of a larger view of reality, a perspective that might illuminate areas of knowledge that his senses could not perceive.

> Ah, if there be indeed
>   Beyond one darksome door a secret stair,
> That, winding to the battlements shall lead
>   Hence to pure light, free air!
> This is the master hope, or the supreme
>   despair.[43]

If only man could get beyond the physical barriers which obscured his vision, he might reach a vantage point from which he could explore the true meaning of life. Pure light and free air were symbols of the formless spirit. Yet in Watson's mind, because man's actual knowledge was limited by his physical means of perception, he would always be shut out of the spirit's realm. Neither his hope nor his despair would ever be completely fulfilled or totally banished. Watson was not a symbolist. Were it not for symbols as imaginative windows to the spirit, *The Chap-Book* would have had to agree with Watson.

Agreement was not forthcoming, however, because most of these artists believed that the creative imagination would unlock the door leading to that secret stair to which Watson had referred in his poem. While they did agree that the physical senses alone were not sufficient to reveal spiritual reality, they had what amounted to a religious faith in man's ability to dream and thereby to commune with the spirit. Such faith was not uncommon to romanticism. Neither was the realization that spiritual revelations would never be totally comprehensible. Willian Carman Roberts wrote in *The Chap-Book* of September 15, 1897:

> Behind such various vestures of strange dreams
> Abides my soul, I know not its true form;
> Nor have I faith it is the thing it seems—
> Now hushed in calm, now crying of the storm.
>
> For evermore the dreams are as a veil
> Of strangely-wrought enchantment to my ken,
> Where through my soul's eyes make my being quail,
> Or bid me wanton with my joys again.
>
> I have no knowledge of the thing it is,
> . . . . [44]

What the romantic knew was that love inspired such dreaming. What the mystic knew was that the spirit inspired such dreaming.

Whether it be love of women or love of a traditional conception of God, it was in dreaming—that state of creative reverie—that man found the most satisfaction and significant knowledge. Later Edmund Wilson took as the title for his study of the "Imaginative Literature of 1870–1930" the phrase *Axel's Castle*. Villiers de l'Isle-Adam's poem "Axel," in Wilson's opinion, summed up the position of the Symbolists of the 1890s: they would rather dream of life than live it.[45] Wilson took a negative view of this position. Earlier *The Chap-Book* had contended that this pose helped explain "half the vagaries of the century's end,"[46] but its opinion was not verbalized with the same negative assessment of symbolism that Wilson would later proffer in his book. Wilson, in 1930, juxtaposed the story of the life of Arthur Rimbaud with the story of Villiers's "Axel." Rimbaud, by abandoning his creation of symbolic literature and turning to "a life of pure action," had, in Wilson's estimate, chosen the better way.[47] *The Chap-Book* had not agreed.

On May 15, 1896 *The Chap-Book* published a tribute to the poetic genius of Rimbaud. The tribute came from the pen of Stéphane Mallarmé, and was, as Mallarmé indicated in his text, a response to a direct solicitation from *The Chap-Book*. "Vous ne me demandez pas autre chose que suivre, comme je les perçois et pour y infuser le plus de belle probabilité les *grandes lignes* d'un destin signicatif."[48] And Mallarmé decried Rimbaud's renunciation of art: "et se, l'instinct des vers par quelqu'un renonce, tout devient inferieur en s'en passant, meme vivre."[49] Rimbaud was an innovator, a producer of magical effects, "avec le desordre somptueux d'une passion on ne saurait dire rien que spirituallement exotique." His reverie was an illustration of the Symbolists' complete annihilation of the natural world. It was, in Mallarmé's mind, also a demonstration of the poet's inspired awakening, "un eveil genial," to the mysteries of the unknown visionary world.[50] To prove these points, *The Chap-Book* (by one recent account the only American magazine in the 1890s to publish anything by or about Rimbaud)[51] included fragments of Rimbaud's verses. One was:

> J'ai rêvé la nuit verte aux neiges éblouies
> Baisers montants aux yeux des mers avec lenteur,
> La circulation des sèves inouies
> Et l'éveil jaune et bleu des phosphores chanteurs.[52]

Long before *The Chap-Book* focused on the works of Rimbaud, even before the magazine's "Notes," in its brief analysis of Villier's "Axel," drew attention to the modern proclivity which preferred dreams to their reality, *The Chap-Book* had published a series of "dream" stories by Percival Pollard. Pollard was one of America's few "decadents," and his "Dreams of Today" appeared in five consecutive issues of the magazine. In "The Dream of an Agreement," which appeared in the August 15, 1894 number, Pollard anticipated *The Chap-Book*'s fascination with Villiers's meaningful theme. In Pollard's story the lovers have married, rather than killing themselves before their love was consummated as had the lovers in "Axel." One morning, over breakfast, they decide to part. Their love affair is over. He says it is because she was too perfect: "My ideals— you have realised them all!" She says it is because their life together was too delightful: "you have been so placidly perfect." Ideals that are unrealized give man, as this man noted, something to "yearn for." Once realized they become, as this woman noted, "stale."[53] Their original dream, of a perfect love, had vitality only so long as it remained a dream and not actuality.

In one of its closing issues, *The Chap-Book* began a review by stating: "A dream is a curious thing. While it lasts it is very real; more real, say some psychologists, than waking life. But with most men the reality of dreams vanishes before the reality of everyday life. We can hardly remember our dreams till after breakfast."[54] The review goes on to state that for most men ideas, or ideals, have a similar reality: their reality lasts only until they come "into contact with everyday facts." *The Chap-Book* belonged to that small minority for whom "everyday facts bear no comparison, so far as reality is concerned, with ideas. For them the idea is real, cost what may." This was the basis of the intellectual tradition of idealists, the faith of religious believers, the philosophy of Spinoza, the aesthetics of Pater.[55] This was the creed of *The Chap-Book*.

Calling attention to Israel Zangwill's *Dreamers of the Ghetto* in this review entitled "A Justification of Faith," *The Chap-Book* was concerned with impressing upon the reader the fact that Zangwill was an artist. He was, perhaps, a realist, but the reality he saw was the Jewish ghetto of London peopled with dreamers. "He has seen dreamers and he presents them to us so that we see them. And this is no mean thing, to give the world fresh assurance of the power of faith." Because Zangwill, the artist, was able to see the evidence of man's essential nature, of man's persistent "power to dream," his work stood as "the ever necessary protest of art against fact." It mattered little that these dreams were largely futile when seen in terms of their history of unfulfillment. What did matter was that they existed. They had reality to those who dreamed them. They represented the truths of the moment for those who, from their individual perspectives, perceived them. "For ideas come and go; any particular idea is very real one year and wholly unreal the next. The truth that is lasting is that they can be real at all."[56]

The Chap-Book had no corner on the market of truth. It never proposed that it had any definitive answers to the questions that had puzzled the minds of men for centuries. What it did propose to have was a method. Its method challenged the individual to look beyond surface realities in the hope and expectation that once his vision was cleared of its material myopias, he would be able to perceive the existence of mysterious spiritual phenomena. Precisely because he would be engaged in an exploration of a formless body of knowledge, traditional forms of communicating— and thereby comprehending—the import of this knowledge had to be made more flexible. Flexibility came for some with minor adjustments, such as recollecting the visions and insights of earlier ages when spirits and enchantment were as much a part of everyday life as its material reality. For others the forms of rationalism, scientific empiricism, and deterministic naturalism had become so ossified that the only way of breaking free of them was to destroy them entirely. *The Chap-Book* experimented with different forms, some traditional, some not. All, however, were aimed at the artistic expression of a reality that was essentially ideal.

6

A Chap-Book of American
Intellectual Life, 1894–1898

What seems to be at first glance, is not always an accurate representation
of what actually exists behind the facade of superficial appearances. In
the case of *The Chap-Book,* almost all existing critical commentaries have
been based on superficial appearances, on what seemed to be; and almost
all have failed to understand the reality of this magazine's existence.
When *The Chap-Book* began publication on May 15, 1894 it appeared to
most readers that they were being greeted by a startlingly new and innovative little magazine. When publication ceased on July 15, 1894, most
observers thought they were witnessing the death of a moribund literary
journal. Neither of these observations reveals the truth of either *The
Chap-Book*'s beginning or its termination; nor do they adequately represent
the nature of *The Chap-Book*'s life during the four years and one hundred
issues of its existence.

As an intellectual creation, *The Chap-Book* was more than small
pages, Janson type and heavy black lines; more than the trials and errors
of young and inexperienced businessmen. *The Chap-Book* was a record
of ideas conceived in America's most respected institution of higher learning and promulgated from the nation's most aggressive center of com-
merce. From first issue to last, this magazine presented to its reading
public a mind trying to probe the meaning of contemporary existence.
There was no revolution in its ideas when it began publication, nor was
there any reactionary reversal in its life when it got a little older. There
was a consistent effort, however, to accommodate new ideas within an
older intellectual tradition, to make sense out of the ideas of the 1890s in
light of what was known, and accepted, from the past.

With the approach of the century's end, many speculated on the
future course of this inherited intellectual tradition. There were those
who thought it had no future and there were others who thought there
could be no future without it. Some wanted to cast off everything be-

longing to the old century so as to be able to create something different in the new one, and some wanted to cast off nothing, content with what was and fearful of change.[1] A great division loomed ahead, challenging people to reflect on their own intellectual orientation: were they of the past or the future?

On the surface it appeared that the past consisted of romanticism, transcendental idealism, and fixed moral values, while the future promised realism, empirical pragmatism and ethical relativism. Observers had not yet decided on which side of the great divide lay the intellectual thrust of symbolism. Symbolism in itself was a symbol of the 1890s. Did it mark the decay of the nineteenth century's dominant intellectual tradition of romanticism? Or was it a step beyond even the "future" of that which was real and pragmatic? With no fixed answers to any of these questions came *The Chap-Book,* a little magazine that was frank in its adherence to romantic idealism, pragmatic in finding an accommodation with realism which was acceptably ideal, and avant-garde in introducing the works of the European Symbolists to the American magazine-reading public.

Magazines are a distinctive medium for transmitting ideas. Unlike discreet, single-volume publications, intellectually unified around a coherent theme, plot or interpretive analysis, a magazine is often a collage of autonomous contributions. When unity exists in a lengthy serial run, it is generally the result of either a rigidly defined subject area of concern, or of strict editorial control. *The Chap-Book* claimed that its concern was that amorphous subject "art" as a revelation of "life," its editors' policy to publish only "the best writing they could procure."[2] Within such expansive boundaries *The Chap-Book* did, nonetheless, maintain a surprisingly large measure of intellectual unity, a unity that has gone largely unnoticed.

Perhaps the reason for this critical oversight is that most observers have not been looking for intellectual integration in the 1890s. They have wanted to see revolt by some and stubborn refusals to change by others.[3] They have wanted to see fresh new beginnings and definitive terminations. When they saw the names of known Symbolists, they wanted to see decadence, immorality and sensual preoccupation. When they saw the names of Realists, they wanted their works to read like compendiums of facts dispelling all illusions. And when they were faced with authors of romantic tales, they wanted to encounter only anachronisms from an earlier age. *The Chap-Book* frustrates these expectations. While *The Chap-Book* romantics are strikingly traditional, they seem to be in league with the era's most notorious, avant-garde decadents. The realists are romantic, and the symbolists religious. Neither *The Chap-Book*'s individual contributors nor its editors seem to be aware of the proper intellectual pigeonholes for practitioners of the era's varying artistic disciplines.

Failure to conform to restraints imposed by intellectual stereotypes does not mean that *The Chap-Book,* its contributors, and its editors are so atypical as to lack significance. On the contrary, *The Chap-Book* is highly representative of the mainstream of intellectual life in the 1890s. Consider, for example, the fact that *The Chap-Book*'s earliest issues were almost entirely composed of contributions from Stone's Cambridge associates. His coeditors, likewise, were drawn from this same coterie. These men and women were not intellectual renegades, engaged in a generational revolt against inherited norms. Frequenters of Boston's most respectable parlors rather than bohemian cafés, they represented the pillars of the nineteenth century's cultural establishment. Their failure to fit, individually or collectively, into the standard interpretive categories of this period calls those generalized interpretations into question, rather than the particular misfits that make up this magazine.[4]

When young Herbert Stone was sent to Harvard in the summer of 1890, both he and his parents knew why it was important for him to be there. The nation's preeminent institution of higher learning was not expected to effect an intellectual conversion in young Stone, alienating him from a cultural tradition that was no longer viable. Rather, he was expected to get the education and credentials which would enable him to assume a position of leadership and responsibility in the society which fostered that tradition. This education was not, however, at least for Herbert Stone, a course of study directed to a profession. Stone was schooled as neither a scholar, nor a scientist, nor even a businessman. His calling was that of a gentleman, the proud vocation of generations of Harvard men. His task while at Harvard, as defined by both University president and professor,[5] was to acquire a broad cultural background so as to better understand the nature and duties of his existence. His goal: the achievement of intellectual freedom and spiritual unity. Education at Harvard began a process that was to last a lifetime. The search for meaning was a process too serious to be merely a cliché.

Meaning is a function of language, and language was the focus of Stone's undergraduate education. Courses in Greek, Latin, Hebrew, English, French, German, Spanish and Italian were the foundation of Stone's curriculum.[6] While his intended career was assumed to lie in some form of journalism, these courses—concentrating on literature as well as language—were never meant to nurture linguistic skills for practical purposes. His future responsibilities were not translation but interpretation. Stone was being taught man's means of communicating ideas in times past and present, ideas which served as commentaries on how life was lived and why.

As a student of Western civilization's means of expression, from its Greek and Semitic fundamentals to its contemporary aesthetic effusions, Stone learned important lessons from the Cambridge intellectual community. He learned that man had spirit as well as substance, and that his spirit was in danger of being lost in the pursuit of material goods and rational/scientific knowledge. He learned that before the time of the Renaissance, man had been able to integrate his spiritual and actual life. He learned that there were ideals expressed in this earlier time which were still viable, that there were some mysteries no rational mind would ever be able to fathom, and that ineffable spiritual truths could be expressed and comprehended only approximately and only through symbolic representation. He learned that throughout the nineteenth century there were those who had been trying to pick up the spiritual threads let loose by the rational and materialistic makers of Renaissance and Enlightenment culture. And he learned that it was now his task to continue that essentially "romantic" and "idealistic" endeavor.

At a time when the traditional interpretations of American intellectual life have claimed that our educated class was embracing science and pragmatism,[7] despairing of the reliability of once secure supernatural supports to life's meaning,[8] Stone found himself in an intellectual environment in which these analyses held scant relation to fact. The Cambridge intellectuals, from whom Stone acquired much of his education, found science wanting not because of a fundamentalist fear that it would destroy the underpinnings of an uncritical faith, but because it was intrinsically insufficient as a method in providing answers to questions that probed a reality far beyond the limits of mere physical matter. Even if science could teach man exactly how the natural world operated, it could never answer the ultimate question of why. It could never, by the empirical method, solve a single spiritual mystery or authenticate one genuine mystical experience. It could never explicate the "reasons" that gave life meaning, reasons that had nothing to do with rationality.

Contrary to the interpretation that American intellectual life was divorcing itself from its formerly intimate association with religious thought, the ideas of the 1890s expressed in Cambridge and later in the pages of *The Chap-Book* are rich testimonies of faith. Not a Philistine faith of conformity, the kind that Santayana railed against, but a faith in the efficacy of the spirit. These artists knew that the spirit could manifest itself in a variety of ways, as William James (another Cambridge intellectual) would later document,[9] and art was the way that spoke most cogently to them. Art, as Norton taught Stone, was a vision of the ideal, a manifestation of the imaginative, unconscious spirit.

There was no conscious or disrespectful blaspheming of traditional religious revelation in this aesthetic belief in art as spiritual revelation and in the imagination as an agency of inspiration. The arts had a long history of manifesting spiritual concerns, and the artists of the nineties were well aware of this tradition. They were especially impressed by Europe's many fine Gothic cathedrals, standing as contemporary evidence of medieval man's longing after the spirit, tributary offerings to transcendent omnificence. In the 1890s they recognized, however, that their own testaments would have to be of a different nature. The spirit was no longer central in the life of society, so they turned their concentration not to grand monuments but to moments of personal encounter. Heirs to a century of romanticism, art was for them a means of manifesting the actual workings of the spirit within the individual artist, an immanent expression of communion with that which some called divine, some ideal reality.

Such communion was not limited to doctrinaire romantics like *The Chap-Book*'s Bliss Carman, or aberrant devotional aesthetes like the Symbolist Verlaine. Nor were *The Chap-Book* artists strangely out of step with their contemporaries by adhering to such a belief.[10] *The Chap-Book* has unfortunately suffered from the mistaken judgment that it was too tied to nineteenth-century beliefs to be truly modern, thus talk of spiritual communion is dismissed as a predictable anachronism. Yet many other contemporaries, artists who have escaped this negative verdict and have been judged to be modern, show the same spiritual concerns. A brief comparison of some similar thoughts will be illustrative.

In 1894 Chicago architect Louis Sullivan, recognized later as one of America's first great "modern" architects, wrote an essay entitled: "Emotional Architecture as Compared with Intellectual: A Study in Subjective and Objective." Read before a meeting of the American Institute of Architects in New York in October of that year, just five months after *The Chap-Book* began publication in Cambridge and just weeks after Stone's magazine moved to Sullivan's own city of Chicago, this philosophic essay urged the poet-architect to a recognition of the fact that "an art work to be alive . . . must indeed be animate with a soul, must have been breathed upon by the spirit and must breathe in turn that spirit."[11]

Soul and spirit were catch-words that one would expect to hear in a speech from Sullivan's contemporary architectural colleague and *The Chap-Book*'s contributor, Ralph Adams Cram, leader of the Gothic Revival in architecture. Cram's buildings were blatant reminders of a spirit-filled past, and his contributions to *The Chap-Book* served the same function. Sullivan's architectural achievements were in an entirely different mode than the one pursued by Cram, his critical orientation thought to be the reverse of that verbalized in *The Chap-Book*. Sullivan would come to be hailed as a modern by twentieth-century critics, Cram's distinction would be to be respected and admired as a marvelously talented anachronism, and praise of *The Chap-Book* would be reserved for what it might have been. Yet contrary reputations mask the anomaly, if it is one, that these contemporaries voiced similar concerns for spiritual expression. Sullivan was undoubtedly the more articulate spokesman with his buildings. His words shared with a New York audience in 1894, however, showed a marked similarity with those that *The Chap-Book* would share with its contributors for the next four years.

Just as *The Chap-Book*'s ideas were rooted in romanticism, so were Sullivan's. Addressing the nations' architects, Sullivan called attention to the instinctual knowledge of children, and of nature as a material revelation of spiritual reality. He noted that if architects were to be real artists, it was essential for them to have retained an innocent responsiveness to nature's call first experienced during childhood. "Unless, as a child, with that marvelous instinct given only to children, he has heard the voice of nature murmuring in the woodland or afield or seaward, no after hearing can avail to catch this revelation."[12] Spiritual enlightenment was so essential to the artistic endeavor, in fact, that Sullivan claimed all good artists had to be "born with . . . a hunger for the spiritual." In an age that educated people to disbelieve, hunger (a natural drive to satisfy an essential requirement of life) was the word used by Sullivan to emphasize the importance of spiritual concerns. Without that spiritual hunger, he said, "all other craving avails as naught." With that hunger, the artist would be impelled to "draw on the spiritual nutrition and stored-up vitality of the world" whereby he could enter into "that extraordinary communion that the sacred writers called to 'walk with God.' "[13]

Sullivan's conception of nature, with its spiritual dimensions, and of the artist's function in this sacred environment were rooted unquestionably in romanticism and transcendentalism. From these roots, however, he would propagate new growth, a realistic new growth that would carry art beyond the developments it had achieved during much of the nineteenth century. Sullivan took romanticism's love of personal experience, of the particular, of nature and of spirit and melded them together into a definition of what a work of art must be. "It must stand for the actual, vital first-hand experiences of the one who made it." But it also must be more than this. It "must represent his deep-down impression not only of physical nature but more especially and necessarily his understanding of the out-working of that *Great Spirit* which makes nature so intelligible to us that it ceases to be a phantasm and becomes a sweet, a superb, a convincing *Reality*." Sullivan unequivocally declared that the work of a true artist "absolutely must be . . . as real and convincing as is his own life."[14] Yet notice his paradox that an artistic rendering of nature, without knowledge of its spiritual core, is a representation of a phantasm; only with a recognition of spirituality is there realism.

Reality was for Sullivan, as it was for *The Chap-Book*, ideal at its core; and realism was an outgrowth of romanticism, not a reversal of its intellectual thrust. Careful delineation of the precise details of individual experience was essential, for it was only through truthfulness to the details of life that an accurate picture of reality would emerge. But neither Sullivan nor *The Chap-Book* considered mere material facts as the sole components of either life or life's artistic expression. Art had to be "as unreal, as fugitive, as inscrutable, as subjective, as the why and wherefore of the simplest flower that blows," asserted Sullivan. Nature, and thus realism, was not merely objective and tangible; it was subjective and spiritual as well. Without a recognition of these dimensions of life, the picture would always remain incomplete, inadequate. "Unreality," all man's inner, personal experiences, all life's spiritual mysteries, were essential components of any work of art that would truly represent life in all its reality. "It is the presence of this unreality," said Sullivan, "that makes the art work real: it is by virtue of this silent subjectivity that the objective voice of an art song becomes sonorous and thrilling."[15]

Integration of the ideal with the real was Sullivan's goal just as it was the goal of *The Chap-Book*. What Sullivan termed objectivity and subjectivity (objectivity, linked to the head, was verifiable; subjectivity, linked to the heart, was nonverifiable) were "the two controlling elements of human endeavor" which, unfortunately, for most of recorded history had been pitted against each other in "internecine warfare." Sullivan's recognition of the struggle of each of these elements to supplant the other illustrates the central tension in the aesthetic and intellectual theory of the poet-architect. His commentary also shows that—like Royce and his philosophic system, and *The Chap-Book* and its periodical pages—there were thinkers and artists in the 1890s advocating intellectual synthesis. Their goal was not realism to replace an effete idealism but rather union of the two to produce a complete view of a living reality that was neither mundane in its materialism nor intangible in its ideality.

Sullivan explained:

> They [objectivity and subjectivity] are ordinarily known and spoken of as the intellectual and the emotional, but they lie deeper, much deeper, than these: they lie in the very heart of Nature. Coming into man's being, they have been antagonistic because of the fanaticism and one-sidedness of human nature, because of its immobility. Because from the beginning man has been beset by beautiful, by despicable, illusions. Because

one set of men have believed in what they could see and another set have believed in what they could not see. Because it has too often happened that the man who could see with the outer eye could not see with the inner eye; because the other man, rhapsodizing with the clear insight of faith, had no thought for the things of this world. Neither believed in the virtue of the other. Neither has inferred, from the presence of the other, the necessary existence of a balancing but hidden power.[16]

If Sullivan's work, in both buildings and books, stands today as better art than the corpus of *The Chap-Book*, if it enjoys a better reputation among critics, it is because Sullivan was better able to keep his idealism grounded in reality. He was better able through synthesis to build something new, to expand our conception of reality. Too often *The Chap-Book*'s focus became that of the man of faith, forgetting life's material matrix. Too often what began as a positive assertion of the spirit became primarily a negative rejection of all material worth. Even romanticism's spirit-filled natural environment became subject to abuse, degenerating into sentimental similes or didactic abstractions.[17] The crucial balance was set a-kilter, the ability to see with both eyes, as advocated by Sullivan, impaired.

Recall that *The Chap-Book*'s first editor and most frequent contributor, Bliss Carman, advocated a literature defined by the same precepts as Sullivan's. Carman called for an integration of the "rational waking objective self" with "the deeper unreasoning self" in order to produce art that would express a more complete view of reality than was possible from one of the perspectives alone. He cautioned that "we are creatures so strangely compounded of dust and dream, that we can never wholly give our allegiance to either one."[18] Unfortunately, in his own writing Carman failed to live up to these critical dictums: his pantheistic love of nature turned towards primitive paganism rather than anything more intellectually complex; his romantic idealism too often became an excuse to wallow in emotionalism, drifting off into meaningless fancies totally divorced from reality. Carman was able to theorize about an aesthetic synthesis, in much the same fashion as Sullivan, but as an artist his creations fell far short of his theoretic designs.

Carman's personal failure points up the dangers faced by most of *The Chap-Book*'s romantics, as well as the interpretive problems of the magazine's readers. It was difficult for these antimaterialist artists to create a reality that would be sufficiently ideal to be acceptable; it was difficult for any but the most astute readers to perceive some of the dangerously fine distinctions that composed their attempts at synthesis.[19] If artistic perception was to act as the synthesizing agent, effecting the fusion of dust and dreams, the process for romantics was one of subtle refinement. Too often they were too refined to give life's material concerns their proper measure; and too often when they did try tentatively to ground their idealism in reality, their synthesis was so subtle as to be barely perceptible. Traditional romantics, tied to what had been in the nineteenth century, had the most difficulty of any of *The Chap-Book*'s artists in anticipating or making changes in the twentieth century. Their work, consequently, was the most inconsequential of the magazine's offerings, lacking the vitality of fresh encounters or original creations.

Realism and symbolism served as the more important crucibles in which the metal of *The Chap-Book*'s synthesis would be tested. Artists working in these modes were more successful in their synthesizing than were their romantic counterparts, and their artistic products have proven more permanent. Garland, James, Yeats and Verlaine all contributed in substantial ways toward the establishment of *The Chap-Book*'s critical reputation. They were recognized as artists of considerable skill even before their appearances in this magazine, and that recognition brought recognition to the magazine as well. More than that, their work in *The Chap-Book* represented the best that this magazine had to offer. If their art was the best, their ideas were also compatible with *The Chap-Book*'s overall philosophy. They clearly demonstrate that the concern for intellectual fusion of the ideal and the real into a composite picture of life was one shared by practitioners of different artistic methods. At the same time their careful use of language, documenting art's ability to mean more than the artist consciously intended, more than any given observer might comprehend, likewise stood as testaments of a common belief that there were yet unexplored and unknown dimensions to reality. Reality, even for *The Chap-Book*'s realists, was a fluid, perhaps undefinable term.

Realism in *The Chap-Book* did contain many of those elements that were then associated with the term's common definitions. Secure in the public's acceptance of the local color movement, written dialog tried to capture the sounds of the spoken word, sometimes in regional dialect, sometimes in the broken English of the immigrants. Attention was focused on the everyday lives of everyday people. Fascination with high culture in Boston and New York, or in European drawing rooms, gave way in most instances to the vogue of vicariously savoring poverty, ghettos and the lives of the plain folk of rural America. Paupers, pioneers, tailors, and thieves, once the foci of a romantic vision, now became the subjects of tales that tried to represent authentic slices of the lives of real people. Factual accuracy and compendiums of scenic details were all supposed to lend veracity to the artist's conception of reality.

More than the elements of composition, realism for some was also a way of looking at life. Garland claimed that there were no fixed "Truths," only different truths pertaining to different lives.[20] In his major serial contribution to *The Chap-Book* he attempted to validate this perspectival attitude. Questioning the universal applicability of fixed moral standards did not signify, either for Garland or *The Chap-Book,* however, any disavowal of an underlying idealism. Never did there appear in this magazine any contribution that pictured man as a mere physical phenomenon, caught in the web of a mechanistic and predetermined universe, lacking truth, value or morality. Never was there put forth a belief that life was only material reality, only that which could be seen, touched and tested. Always there was something more, something that might be better understood by faithfulness to the facts of physical reality, but never completely understood by those facts alone. Ideals or spiritual forces, shifting or static, were still there.

Experimenting with different ways of expressing that which was fundamentally inexpressible, of understanding that which lay outside the realm of factual knowledge, outside the real and verifiable, were the symbolists. While not a new tendency in American literature, symbolism had never been fully accepted. Charles Feidelson has traced the difficulties encountered by American writers in embracing symbolism, given the enduring strength of the Puritan emphasis on strict rationality. And he has noted the importance of the rejection, by Protestant thinkers and writers, of the Catholic scholastic tradition which allowed for a multiplicity of meanings, some of which were not necessarily understood at any given time.[21] Without the intellectual possibilities offered by an open-ended intellectual framework, like scholasticism, symbolism could hope to be nothing more than mere correspondence. Even though the Puritan intellectual legacy inhibited the development of symbolic thought in America, however, it could not completely stifle it. Hawthorne, Emerson, Melville, Whitman and Poe were all symbolists, and as Feidelson has pointed out, precursors of America's modern writers. Similarly, F. O. Matthiessen has noted that in symbolism one sees the link connecting Hawthorne to Henry James and T. S. Eliot and twentieth-century literature.[22] Twentieth-century literature has not been exclusively symbolic, but the pervasiveness of symbolism, seen in both the intellectual orientation and works of some of the era's most important writers, cannot be discounted.

In Thomas Stearns Eliot one sees not only the continuation of this important movement in American literature, one also sees an artist with a background remarkably similar to that of Herbert Stone. Since they held such similar influences in common, it would have been more surprising if their ideas did not in some way correspond. Both families traced their ancestry back to seventeenth-century Puritan New England. Both men had grandfathers who were midwestern ministers, and fathers who were prominent businessmen. Like Stone, one of Eliot's parents took an active interest in literature, cultivating a similar interest in the son. And both sets of parents wanted their sons to receive a Harvard education. Once enrolled at Harvard, although a dozen years apart, the two young men came under the influence of Charles Eliot Norton—Stone in his classroom, Eliot by his scholarship. Stone worked his literary apprenticeship on the student newspaper, Eliot on the literary journal. Stone found his cohorts calling for the restoration of the house of Stuart, Eliot enjoyed the contemporary revival of interest in the metaphysical poets. Stone, through travel, course work and club participation, came to know and appreciate the newest trends in French literature. Eliot, following his graduation from Harvard, would also head for France where he became acquainted with many contemporary French Symbolists. Later, as a graduate student back at Harvard, Eliot wrote a doctoral dissertation on the idealist philosopher Francis Herbert Bradley, an effort which called forth the critical praises of Josiah Royce, Harvard's foremost philosopher during Stone's undergraduate years.[23]

Although Eliot's youthful experiences were not far removed from Stone's, and although the ideas with which both men were bombarded were similar, the distance in time separating their two lives was great enough to mean that there could be similarity without sameness. Eliot's academic interest in idealism did not precipitate any serious charges that his ideas were a throwback to the romantic idealism of the last century. Romanticism he publicly disavowed, and nobody disbelieved him. Nineteenth-century idealism was a precondition to his twentieth-century intellectual growth, just as Stone's could have been, but it would have to grow amid historical circumstances different from those of *The Chap-Book* in the 1890s. Eliot's war, for instance, was not the squalid affair Stone was faced with in the Spanish-American conflict. It was a world war that killed many men and optimistic ideas about progress, not just the attention of one magazine's audience. Eliot's war was, in fact, the war that killed Herbert Stone.[24]

Neither Stone nor his magazine lived on into the twentieth century, but their ideas did. While Eliot is only one example of similar intellectual proclivities and continuity, his example is illustrative. Eliot's writing is complex, as complex as his perception of reality. His use of symbols is crucial to his explication of reality, symbols whose meanings change with the poet's or dramatist's changing perspectives. As he matured, he developed a highly religious, and ostensibly conservative faith. It was a faith that would not have surprised *The Chap-Book*. It was not disembodied idealism or romantic sentimentality, it was symbolism rooted in human experience and historical tradition. Eliot's symbolism, similar in intellectual origin to *The Chap-Book*'s, was an outgrowth of his idealism; his poetry and prose, like *The Chap-Book*'s pages, a means of giving expressive life to a fundamentally idealistic, and perhaps inexpressible, conception of reality.[25]

Another example of a thinker, fascinated with developing an idealistic synthesis that would serve as a philosophy of life, was Eliot's teacher at Harvard, Irving Babbitt. Eschewing materialism and naturalistic science, as well as the metaphysics of religious orthodoxy, Babbitt proposed in 1908 a definition of humanism strikingly similar in intellectual orientation to *The Chap-Book*'s earlier attempt at synthesis of the real and the ideal. This "New Humanism" was concerned that man "should have the sense of communion with absolute being and of the obligation to higher standards that this insight brings," while at the same time remembering that he was "as a passing phase of the everlasting flux and relativity of nature."

Worried about the difficulties of maintaining a properly balanced perspective, Babbitt attributed excesses of the past and the present to a lack of appreciation for both facets of human life: ideal and natural reality. Whereas once religion had inhibited man's natural faculties, Babbitt believed that now science was distracting man from spiritual concerns. "Important faculties that the supernaturalist allowed to decay the naturalist has cultivated, but other faculties, especially those relating to the contemplative life, are becoming atrophied through disuse." He complained, "Man has gained immensely in his grasp on facts, but in the meanwhile has become so immersed in their multiplicity as to lose that vision of the One by which his lower self was once overawed and restrained."[26] But if balance was Babbitt's theoretic goal, the fulcrum of his intellectual scale was off-center, weighted by an essential idealism.

Babbitt, like Eliot, and like Sullivan and *The Chap-Book* before them, verbalized a belief in intellectual synthesis. His synthesis, like theirs, was an attempt to express a fundamental belief in life's meaning. Eliot was not a disciple of Babbitt's New Humanism, nor was Sullivan, nor would *The Chap-Book* have been, probably, if it had lived on into the twentieth century. Neither was Eliot's synthesis that of Sullivan, nor Sullivan's that of Babbitt or of *The Chap-Book*. All had their own emphases, each his own synthesis. What they shared though, was a belief that life was more than a material accident, more than a scientific formula, and more than a rational argument. In Sullivan there was passion and realism, in Eliot symbolism and history, in Babbitt ethics. *The Chap-Book* was not as vibrant as Sullivan, as sophisticated as Eliot, or as doctrinaire as Babbitt. But it shared with each one of them an intellectual awareness, verbalized if only imperfectly actualized, of life's composite structure.

Twentieth-century intellectual life with all its complexities cannot be completely understood by examining the history of any one person or magazine, any more than it can be adequately generalized in stereotypic categories. Many ideas make up that life, appearing and reappearing in slightly different forms, at different times and different places among different people. Few, however, have been altered so radically or so quickly as to leave no traces of where they came from or when. The thoughts of *The Chap-Book* were not to be lost with the old century. They would reoccur in a variety of intellectual combinations, linked with some seemingly similar and some dissimilar intellectual, aesthetic, and social concerns. A new agrarianism would find favor with a number of Americans dissatisfied with the effects of increased technological and material "progress"; a sense of spiritual immediacy would revive the faith of some religious thinkers; and increasingly philosophers and thinkers in other disciplines would direct attention toward the myths and symbols men have used for centuries to express in artistic forms their central conceptions of the meaning of life.

Thus when *The Chap-Book* ceased publication in the summer of 1898, its actual life may have ceased but not the life of its ideas. These ideas had never been unique to its pages, so the decision to end its publication had little effect on the future course of American intellectual life. Stone's decision to terminate *The Chap-Book* was based on financial realities, not intellectual preferences: *The Chap-Book* was supposed to make money, and the bottom line of its publishers' balance sheet showed that the magazine required constant subsidization from the bookmaking operation of the firm. Subsidization was required even in the face of general critical acclaim, because, in short, the publishers of *The Chap-Book* were not good businessmen. They were sloppy in keeping accounts and inept in marketing their product, a product that by almost all contemporary accounts was a good one.[27]

Admitting that *The Chap-Book*'s four-year existence stands as evidence of the failure of its publishers to capitalize on the production of a magazine cannot contravene the fact that the product itself was not a failure. *The Chap-Book* had made an impact on the American public: its early design, its willingness to display personality, and its endorsement of new trends in foreign literature all would give courage to others who would follow—others whose design skills might be better, whose sense of personality might be more vital, and whose hospitality to artistic innovation might be more daring. But what was most important about *The Chap-Book,* was, in this author's estimation, its ability to mirror the intellectual make-up of some of America's most literate individuals in the last decade of the nineteenth century. And the image presented had a unity which has gone largely unnoticed. It showed enduring intellectual features from the past blended with certain new intellectual features of the present. *The Chap-Book* was a record of complexity and consistency, of American intellectual life in the process of change.

Appendix

Contributors to *The Chap-Book*

Aldrich, Thomas Bailey: vol. I, nos. 5 & 10
Ashton, John: vol. III, no. 1

Bacheller, Irving: vol. IX, no. 3
Baldwin, Mary: vol. VII, no. 10; vol. VIII, no. 8
Balton, Ethel: vol. V, no. 6
Bangs, John Kendrick: vol. VII, nos. 8 & 12; vol. VIII, no. 4; vol. IX, no. 1
Barnard, William Francis: vol. VIII, no. 10
Bartlett, Gertrude: vol. VIII, no. 10
Bates, Herbert: vol. IV, nos. 6 & 10; vol. VI, no. 7; vol. VII, nos. 2 & 10; vol. VIII, no. 8
Bates, Katherine: vol. II, nos. 3 & 8; vol. VI, no. 5
Beardsley, Aubrey: vol. I, nos. 5 & 7
Beerbohm, Max: vol. IV, no. 7; vol. V, nos. 8, 9, 10, 11, 12; vol. VI, nos. 2 & 3
Bell, Lilian: vol. III, no. 2
Bellini, Giovanni: vol. I, no. 11
Bennett, H. H.: vol. V, no. 2; vol. VI, no. 12; vol. VIII, no. 2
Bennett, John: vol. III, no. 10; vol. IV, no. 5; vol. VII, no. 5; vol. VIII, nos. 4 & 5
Benson, E. F.: vol. VII, no. 1
Benton, Joel: vol. I, no. 9; vol. VII, no. 3
Berthon, Paul: vol. IV, nos. 5 & 7
Bisland, Elizabeth: vol. V, no. 7
Boner, H. Geraldine: vol. V, no. 12; vol. VII, no. 10
Boner, John H.: vol. II, no. 1; vol. IV, no. 7; vol. VII, no. 8
Borie, A. E.: vol. IV, no. 5; vol. V, nos. 7, 9, 12; vol. VI, no. 4
Boyce, Neith: vol. V, no. 1; vol. VIII, no. 4
Boyesen, H. H.: vol. II, no. 6
Boyle, Virginia Frazer: vol. V, no. 5
Bradley, Will H.: vol. II, no. 8; vol. III, no. 8
Bragdon, Claude Fayette: vol. I, no. 12; vol. II, nos. 4 & 11; vol. III, no. 1; vol. IV, nos. 1, 2, 6; vol. V, nos. 1,2,9, 10, 11
Branch, Anna Hempstead: vol. VIII, no. 4
Brewer, Layton: vol. V, no. 4
Brooks, Jennie: vol. II, no. 5
Brown, Alice: vol. I, nos. 4 & 9; vol. II, no. 4; vol. VI, no. 6; vol. VII, no. 3; vol. IX, no. 3
Brown, Anna Robeson: vol. VIII, no. 1; vol. IX, no. 4
Browne, Helen Madder: vol. V, no. 2; vol. VI, no. 9

Bullock, Shan F.: vol. IV, no. 11
Burgess, Gelett: vol. VIII, no. 6
Burroughs, John: vol. III, no. 9; vol. VII, no. 2; vol.IX, no. 4
Burton, Augustus: vol. VIII, no. 11
Burton, Richard: vol. I, no. 8; vol. II, no. 6; vol.IV, nos. 3, & 11; vol. V, no. 12

Cable, George W.: vol. V, no. 9
Caldwell, Eleanor B.: vol. II, nos. 2 & 7; vol. IV, no. 4; vol. V, no. 1
Canton, William: vol. IV, nos. 6 & 10; vol. VI, nos. 8 & 10; vol. VII, nos. 7 & 10
Cardozo, Elizabeth C.: vol. VI, no. 8
Carleton, Emma: vol. III, no. 2; vol. IV, no. 3; vol. VIII, no. 7
Carman, Bliss: vol. I, nos. 1, 2, 5, 8, 9, 10, 12; vol. II, nos. 1, 2, 4, 7, 8, 9, 10, 11, 12;
    vol. III, no. 1; vol. IV, nos. 2, 6, 8, 12; vol. V, nos. 9 & 10; vol. VI, no. 1; vol. VII,
    no. 11; vol. VIII, no. 10
Carpenter, Horace T.: vol. VI, no. 4
Carruth, Edith: vol. VII, no. 5
Cawein, Madison: vol. II, no. 6; vol. IV, no. 9; vol. VI, nos. 2; vol. VII, no. 11; vol. VIII,
    nos. 6 & 10
Cazals, F. A.: vol. II, no. 9
Chaffee, Frank: vol. II, no. 4
Chamberlin, Joseph Edgar: vol. V, no. 10; vol. VIII, nos. 11 & 12
Chambers, Robert W.: vol. VII, nos. 2 & 8
Channing, Grace Ellery: vol. V, no. 7
Chapman, Coates: vol. VI, no. 11
Chapman, J. J.: vol. VII, no. 6
Chauvenet, William Marc: vol. IV, no. 11; vol. V, no. 5
Cheney, John Vance: vol. III, no. 7; vol. VIII, no. 8
Childe, Rheta Louise: vol. II, no. 10
Clark, Cecil: vol. IV, no. 9; vol. V, no. 2; vol. VI, no. 2; vol. IX, nos. 1 & 4
Colyar, W. Douglas: vol. V, no. 8
Connor, Florence G.: vol. VII, no. 8
Copeland, Charles Townsend: vol. I, no. 6
Cram, Ralph Adams: vol. I, no. 6; vol. III, no. 6
Crane, Stephen: vol. IV, no. 8; vol. VIII, no. 9
Crosby, Raymond M.: vol. III, no. 12; vol. IV, nos. 1,2, 3, 7, 10; vol. V, nos. 1, 3, 6, 8, 10
Crowe, John Maxwell: vol. V, no. 11
Cummings, Edward: vol. IV, no. 4
Curtis, William Eleroy: vol. VIII, no. 12

Davidson, John: vol. III, no. 11; vol. IV, nos. 2, 4, 7, 12; vol. V, nos. 2 & 4; vol. VI, no. 5;
    vol. VIII, no. 7
Day, B.C.: vol. V, nos. 3 & 6
De Koven, Mrs. Reginald: vol. IV, no. 6
De Koven, Reginald: vol. VI, no. 10
De Santis, G.: vol. I, no. 3
D'Espagnat, Georges: vol. VI, no. 4
Devoore, Ann: vol. V, no. 11; vol. VI, nos. 5 & 12; vol. VIII, no. 12
Dole, Nathan Haskell: vol. II, no. 1; vol. VII, no. 6
Dorsey, Anna Vernon: vol. V, no. 3
Duffield, Pitts: vol. VII, no. 12

DuFreen, Kathleen Hoy: vol. VIII, no. 1
Dunbar, Paul Lawrence: vol. VI, no. 6; vol. VII, no. 2; vol. IX, no. 3

Earle, Alice Morse: vol. V, nos. 7, 8, 9, 10, 11, 12; vol. VI, no. 1; vol. VIII, nos. 8 & 12;
    vol. IX, nos. 1 & 3
Eastman, Barret: vol. VIII, no. 12
Eckels, James H.: vol. IX, no. 1
Edwards, J. B.: vol. V, no. 11
Edwards, Louise Betts: vol. VIII, no. 9; vol. IX, no. 1
Embree, Charles Fleming: vol. VII, no. 9

Fallows, Alice Katherine: vol. V, no. 8
Fenollosa, Mary McNeil: vol. VIII, no. 4
Field, Etta Dexter: vol. III, no. 7
Field, Eugene: vol. II, nos. 3 & 6
Fitch, Clyde: vol. II, no. 6; vol. III, no. 5; vol. IV, no. 5; vol. VII, no. 11
Fox, John Jr.: vol. IV, no. 11
France, Anatole: vol. I, no. 4
Fuller, Henry Blake: vol. IV, no. 2

Gachons, Andhre des: vol. IV, no. 7
Galbraith, Lettice: vol. IV, no. 6
Gale, Norman: vol. IV, no. 4; vol. V, no. 11
Garland, Hamlin: vol. II, nos. 1, 2, 3, 4, 5, 6, 7; vol. III, no. 10; vol. IV, no. 1
Gates, Lewis E.: vol. II, no. 1; vol. VI, no. 3; vol. VII, no. 12; vol. IX, nos. 2 & 4
Gibson, Charles D.: vol. II, no. 10
Glasgow, Ellen: vol. VII, no. 7
Goetz, Philip Becker: vol. I, no. 12; vol. III, no. 7; vol. IV, nos. 8 & 11; vol. VI, no. 5
Goodhue, Bertram Grosvenor: vol. IV, no. 10
Goodhue, Harry Eldredge: vol. I, no. 8
Gosse, Edmund: vol. II, no. 11
Graham, Kenneth: vol. II, no. 5; vol. III, no. 8
Grasset, Eugene: vol. I, no. 4
Graves, William Lucius: vol. IX, no. 1
Greban, Arnoul: vol. VI, no. 3
Greene, C. E.: vol. IV, no. 11
Grisson, Arthur: vol. V, no. 8
Guiney, Louise Imogen: vol. I, no. 7; vol. II, no. 1; vol. III, no. 3; vol. V, no. 8; vol. VI,
    nos. 2, 6, 10, 11, 12; vol. VII, nos. 1 & 5; vol. VIII, nos. 1, 3, 11

Hale, Edward Everett Jr.: vol. V, no. 8; vol. VII, no. 7
Hall, Gertrude: vol. I, nos. 4 & 8
Hall, Ruth: vol. VIII, no. 11
Hallowell, G. H.: vol. I, no. 6
Hapgood, Norman: vol. IV, nos. 3, 8, 12; vol. VII, no. 10
Hardy, Thomas: vol. VI, no. 3
Harris, Joel Chandler: vol. VIII, no. 9
Harris, Tom: vol. V, no. 4
Hawthorne, Julian: vol. II, no. 12

Hazenplug, Frank: vol. II, no. 5; vol. III, nos. 2, 5, 8, 9, 11; vol. IV, nos. 5, 9, 12; vol. V, nos. 2, 4, 5, 9, 11; vol. VI, nos. 3, 5, 7
Hemenway, Myles: vol. V, no. 9
Henderson, W. J.: vol. I, no. 12
Henley, W. E.: vol. III, nos. 2 & 3
Hereward, L.: vol. II, no. 2
Higginson, T. W.: vol. I, nos. 12, vol. IV, no. 11
Hilliard, J. N.: vol. VII, no. 9; vol. IX, no. 2
Hinkson, Katharine Tynan: vol. V, no. 1; vol. VII, no. 3; vol. IX, no. 1
Hird, Frank: vol. III, no. 11
Holloway, E. S.: vol. III, no. 6
Holloway, William Jr.: vol. V, no. 5
Hollyer, Frederick: vol. I, no. 9
Hopper, Nora: vol. V, nos. 5 & 10; vol. VI, no. 3
Hovey, Richard: vol. I, nos. 7 & 10; vol. II, no. 4
Howe, B. H.: vol. IX, no. 3
Hughes, Rupert: vol. VII, no. 6
Hyde, George M.: vol. VII, no. 8

Jacobus, R. P.: vol. VII, no. 11
James, Henry: vol. IV, no. 12; vol. VI, nos. 5, 6, 7, 8, 9, 10, 11, 12; vol. VII, nos. 1, 2, 3, 4, 5, 6
Jarboe, Kathryn: vol. VI, no. 4
Jenks, Tudor: vol. VI, no. 5
Jerrold, Laurence: vol. V, no. 5; vol. VII, nos. 1 & 8; vol. VIII, no. 6
Johnson, Hilda: vol. III, no. 5
Johnson, Ralph: vol. V, no. 8; vol. VI, no. 1; vol. VII, no. 11
Joliquet: vol. IV, no. 10
Jossot: vol. III, no. 3

Kennedy, Walker: vol. I, no. 11
Kimball, Hannah Parker: vol. I, no. 9; vol. II, no. 5; vol. IV, no. 9
Kobbe, Gustav: vol. VIII, nos. 11 & 12

Lampman, Archibald: vol. II, no. 5; vol. III, no. 12
Lang, Andrew: vol. VIII, nos. 7, 9, 11; vol. IX, no. 3
La Rose, Pierre: vol. I, nos. 7 & 8; vol. V, no. 5; vol. VII, no. 8; vol. VIII, no. 1
Larremore, Wilbur: vol. IX, no. 4
Laughlin, Clara E.: vol. VI, no. 11; vol. VII, no. 10
Lee, Agnes: vol. V, no. 9
Lee, Gerald Stanley: vol. VI, no. 8; vol. VII, nos. 3, 9 12; vol. VIII, no. 4
Lefevre, Edwin: vol. III, no. 1; vol. VI, no. 10; vol. VII, no. 7; vol. VIII, nos. 6 & 9
Leland, Anthony: vol. II, no. 9; vol. IV, no. 7; vol. IX, no. 2
Lewis, Elizabeth Dike: vol. VIII, no. 9
Lighton, W. R.: vol. VII, no. 12
Lloyd, Beatrix Demarest: vol. VIII, no. 1
Locke, William J.: vol. IV, no. 8
Lummis, Charles F.: vol. II, no. 11; vol. IV, no. 7; vol. V, no. 10; vol. VI, no. 9
Lummis, Dorothea (Moore): vol. II, no. 9; vol. III, no. 11; vol. IV, no. 12; vol.V, no. 3; vol. VII, nos. 7 & 9; vol. VIII, nos. 4 & 5

Lummis, Harry B.: vol. IX, no. 2
Lyde, Phoebe: vol.VIII, no. 12
Lynch, Gertrude: vol. IX, no. 4

Mabie, Hamilton Wright: vol. II, no. 9; vol. IV, no. 4; vol. V, nos. 5 & 11; vol. VI, no. 5;
    vol. VIII, no. 2
McCarthy, Justin Jr.: vol. IX, no. 3
McCulloch, Hugh Jr.: vol. II, no. 12
McIntyre, John T.: vol.(IX, no. 1
Macy, Arthur: vol. II, no. 8
Macy, John Albert: vol. V, no. 9; vol. VIII, no. 1
Mallarmé, Stéphane: vol. II, nos. 3 & 4; vol. V, no. 1
Matthews, Brander: vol. V, no. 10; vol. VII, no. 7
Meteyard, T. B.: vol. I, no. 1
Millard, Gertrude B.: vol. VII, no. 11
Mills, Rose Edith: vol. VIII, no. 2
Moody, William Vaughn: vol. I, no. 3
Moore, F. Frankfort: vol. IV, no. 9; vol. V, nos. 4 & 10; vol. VI, no. 2
Morris, Gouveneur: vol. IX, no. 4
Morris, Harrison S.: vol. I, no. 7; vol. III, no. 6
Morrison, Arthur: vol. IV, no. 1; vol. V, no. 6
Moulton, Louise Chandler: vol. I, nos. 2 & 8; vol. II, nos. 4 & 7; vol. III, nos. 1 & 3;
    vol. V, no. 6; vol. VI, nos. 6 & 9; vol. VII, no. 5
Mower, Martin: vol. I, no. 8
Mullin, E. H.: vol. VIII, no. 6
Munn, George Frederick: vol. I, no. 6

New, E. H.: vol. IV, no. 5
Newbolt, Henry: vol. VIII, no. 9; vol. IX, no. 1
Nicholson, Meredith: vol. IX, no. 3
Nordhoff, Evelyn Hunter: vol. IV, no. 8
Noxon, Frank W.: vol. VI, no. 4

Osborne, Duffield: vol. II, no. 10; vol. V, no. 9

Packard, Winthrop: vol. VI, no. 12; vol. IX, no. 4
Paine, Albert Bigelow: vol. VI, no. 10
Palmer, John Williamson: vol. VIII, no. 5
Parker, Gilbert: vol. I, no. 12; vol. II, nos. 10 & 12; vol. III, nos. 2, 4, 6, 8, 10
Peabody, Josephine Preston: vol. I, no. 6; vol. VII, no. 7
Peattie, Elia W.: vol. II, no. 11
Pell, William D.: vol. VI, no. 4
Penfield, Edward: vol. I, no. 10
Pennell, Joseph: vol. VI, no. 1
Pereira, Lyndwode: vol. VIII, no. 5
Perry, Jeannette Barbour: vol. VIII, no. 1
Peters, William Theodore: vol. VII, no. 12
Philips, Roland Edward: vol. V, no. 6
Piatt, John James: vol. VI, no. 9
Picaroon: vol. V, nos. 6, 7, 8, 9

Pickering, Theodosia: vol. VIII, no. 4
Pissaro, Georges: vol. III, no. 9
Pollard, Percival: vol. I, nos. 2, 4, 5, 6, 7, 10
Pool, Maria Louise: vol. I, nos. 1 & 2; vol. III, no. 12; vol. V, nos. 1; vol. VII, no. 6;
    vol. VIII, no. 7
Potts, William: vol. V, no. 6; vol. VI, no. 1
Pratt, Charles Stuart: vol. III, no. 6
Prince, Helen Choate: vol. VIII, no. 2
Prindiville, Mary L.: vol. V, no. 9
Pugh, Edwin: vol. VI, no. 11

Quiller-Couch, Arthur: vol. III, nos. 1 & 9; vol. VI, no. 2

Raffaelli, J. F.: vol. II, no. 11
Ragsdale, Lulah: vol. VI, no. 4
Reed, Helen Leah: vol. II, no. 3
Regnault, John: vol. VIII, nos. 5 & 10
Rhodes, Harrison Garfield: vol. I, no. 10; vol. IV, no. 9; vol. VIII, no. 8
Rhys, Ernest: vol. III, no. 6
Rice, Wallace de Groot: vol. VII, nos 2 & 9; vol. VIII, nos. 4 & 11
Richardson, Fred: vol. II, no. 12; vol. III, no. 9; vol. IV, nos. 8, 9, 10, 11, 12; vol. V, nos.
    1, 6, 7
Ricketts, Charles S.: vol. I, no. 3
Risley, R. V.: vol. VII, no. 10
Roberts, Charles G. D.: vol. I, nos. 1 & 3; vol. II, no. 4; vol. III, no. 4; vol. IV, no. 10;
    vol. V, no. 3; vol. VIII, no. 5
Roberts, Theodore: vol. VIII, no. 1
Roberts, William Carman: vol. V, no. 2; vol. VII, no. 9
Rook, Clarence: vol. IV, no. 12; vol. V, no. 12; vol. VI, nos. 2, 9, 12; vol. VII, no. 7
Roseboro, Viola: vol. IX, no. 1
Rosenthal, Beatrice: vol. V, no. 3; vol. VIII, no. 9
Ross, Clinton: vol. IV, no. 11; vol. VI, no. 7; vol. VII, no. 7; vol. VIII, no. 2

Sabin, Edwin L.: vol. VIII, no. 6; vol. IX, no. 4
Sanborn, Alvan F.: vol. VIII, no. 3
Savage, P.H.: vol. VII, no. 5
Sawyer, Harriet F.: vol. IV, no. 11; vol. V, no. 5
Scollard, Clinton: vol. I, no. 8; vol. III, no. 9; vol.IV, no. 7; vol. VI, no. 2; vol. VIII, no. 2
Scott, Mary McNeill: vol. II, no. 9
Seon, Alexandre: vol. II, no. 9
Sharp, Evelyn: vol. IV, no. 10; vol. VII, no. 8
Sharp, William: vol. I, nos. 3 & 9; vol. II, no. 5; vol. IV, no. 3
Sheffield, Alfred Dwight: vol. VII, no. 10
Sherman, Francis: vol. VI, no. 3; vol. VIII, no. 8
Sherman, Frank Dempster: vol. IV, no. 2
Sherwood, M. E. W.: vol. IX, no. 1
Sigerson, Dora: vol. III, no. 11; vol. IV, nos. 5 & 12; vol. V, no. 6
Simpson, Eve Blantyre: vol. II, no. 8
Sloan, John: vol. II, no. 1
Small, Herbert: vol. I, no. 6

Southall, J. E.: vol. III, no. 11
Stedman, Edmund Clarence: vol. V, no. 4; vol. VII, no. 8; vol. VIII, no. 5
Steffens, J. Lincoln: vol. V, no. 3; vol. VIII, no. 1
Sterner, Albert E.: vol. IV, no. 4
Stetson, Charlotte Perkins: vol. VIII, nos. 6 & 10
Stevenson, Nathaniel: vol. VII, no. 9
Stevenson, Robert Louis: vol. III, nos. 2 & 3; vol. V, no. 3; vol. VI, no. 1
Stoddard, Richard Henry: vol. I, no. 2
Stone, Herbert Stuart: vol. I, no. 10; vol. II, no. 2; vol. VIII, no. 6
Stuart, Ruth McEnery: vol. VI, no. 10

Tabb, John B.: vol. V, nos. 1, 5, 12; vol. VI, no. 10
Taylor, J. Russell: vol. I, no. 6; vol. II, nos. 7 & 11; vol. IV, no. 8; vol. VI, nos. 4 & 7
Teall, Gardner: vol. II, no. 12; vol. IV, nos. 3, 6, 7
Thanet, Octave: vol. V, no. 6
Thompson, Charles Miner: vol. I, no. 2
Thompson, John Stuart: vol. IV, no. 10; vol. V, no. 7
Thompson, Maurice: vol. II, no. 12; vol. III, no. 10; vol. IV, no. 9; vol. V, no. 4; vol. VI,
    nos. 4, 7, 12; vol. VII, nos. 7 & 10; vol. VIII, no. 8
Thompson, Vance: vol. VII, no. 11
Thomson, John Stuart: vol. IV, no. 6; vol. VII, no. 12
Triggs, O. L.: vol. VII, no. 7
Turner, G. K.: vol. IV, no. 9; vol. VI, no. 5

Valloton, F.: vol. II, no. 3; vol. III, nos. 1 & 7; vol. V, no. 1; vol. VI, no. 9
Verlaine, Paul: vol. I, nos. 4 & 9

Wagner, Rob: vol. V, no. 10
Wallace, Elizabeth: vol. II, no. 10
Walsh, Thomas: vol. VII, no. 11; vol. VIII, nos. 3 & 11
Warren, Donald: vol. I, no. 10
Waterbury, Jennie Bullard: vol. VI, no. 4
Watson, Dawson: vol. II, nos. 3 & 5; vol. III, no. 10; vol. V, no. 8
Watson, J. B. Marriott: vol. III, nos. 4, 8, 12
Watson, William: vol. VII, no. 6
Waugh, Arthur: vol. III, no. 7
Way, W. Irving: vol. VIII, no. 7
Weed, Raphael A.: vol. III, no. 4
Wellford, Clarence: vol. VIII, no. 3
Wells, Carolyn: vol. V, no. 8; vol. VII, no. 1; vol. VIII, nos. 3 & 8
Wells, H. G.: vol. IV, no. 7
Wetherald, Ethelwyn: vol. V, nos. 1 & 4
Wharton, Anne Hollingsworth: vol. VIII, no. 7
White, Eugene R.: vol. V, no. 3; vol. VI, no. 8; vol. VIII, no. 10
White, Stewart E.: vol. VIII, no. 12
Wiggin, Kate Douglas: vol. VI, no. 8
Wilcox, Ella Wheeler: vol. V, nos. 2 & 7; vol. IX, no. 4
Wildman, L.D.: vol. IV, no. 6
Williams, H. M.: vol. V, no. 11
Witte, Beatrice: vol. VII, no. 2

Woodberry, George Edward: vol. VI, no. 12; vol. VII, no. 3; vol. VIII, no. 2; vol. IX, nos. 1, 2, 3, 4
Wright, Jean: vol. III, no. 5
Wratislaw, Theodore: vol. II, no. 7; vol. III, no. 5
Wyatt, Edith F.: vol. VII, no. 12; vol. VIII, no. 2

Yeats, S. Levett: vol. IV, nos. 2 & 3
Yeats, William Butler: vol. V, no. 2

Zangwill, Israel: vol. II, no. 2; vol. III, nos. 5 & 9; vol. IV, nos. 1 & 5; vol. VI, no. 6; vol. VIII, no. 2; vol. IX, no. 3

Notes

Chapter 1

1. Max Nordau, *Degeneration* (New York: D. Appleton & Co., 1895) pp. 300, 1, 300.

2. This idea was fostered by Arthur Symons in his pioneering apologia, *The Symbolist Movement in Literature* (London: William Heineman, 1899), when he identified the practitioners of this movement as allied with those writers who have "always fought on behalf of a 'transcendental' art in which we should recognize much of what is most essential in the doctrine of Symbolism." (p. v.) Numerous studies have followed, outlining the Romantic background of Symbolism. See, for instance, A.G. Lehmann, *The Symbolist Aesthetic in France, 1885–1895* (Oxford: *Basil Blackwell*, 1950); and Joseph Chiari, *Symbolisme from Poe to Mallarmé* (London: Rockliff, 1956).

3. The word "animate" is used with some deliberateness to capsulize twentieth-century judgments on literary practitioners of nineteenth-century ideals. This critical tradition, as articulated in such well-known studies as George Santayana's "The Genteel Tradition in American Philosophy," 1911 (now available in Douglas L. Wilson, ed., *The Genteel Tradition* [Cambridge: Harvard University Press, 1967]); Van Wyck Brooks, "America's Coming of Age," 1915 [available in Claire Sprague, ed., *Van Wyck Brooks: The Early Years* [New York: Harper & Row, 1968]); and D.H. Lawrence, *Studies in Classic American Literature* (New York: The Viking Press, 1923, 1971), has continued to shape our appraisals of contemporary literature. See, for instance, Marshall Van Deusen's history of twentieth-century literary criticism in "Movements in Literary Criticism," *American Literature Since 1900*, ed., Marcus Cunliffe, (London: Barrie & Jenkins, 1975), pp. 184–213.

4. Henry Adams, *The Education of Henry Adams* (New York: The Modern Library, 1931 [1918]), p. 457.

5. Grant C. Knight, *The Critical Period in American Literature* (Chapel Hill: University of North Carolina Press, 1951), p. 4.

6. Henry Steele Commager, *The American Mind: An Interpretation of American Thought and Character Since the 1880's* (New Haven: Yale University Press, 1950), pp. 41–54; John Higham, "The Reorientation of American Culture in the 1890's," *The Origins of Modern Consciousness*, ed., John Weiss (Detroit: Wayne State University Press, 1965), pp. 24–48, see particularly p. 40.

7. *The Chap-Book*, vol. I, no. 2 (June 1, 1894), p. 45; vol. VI, no. 1 (November 15, 1896), p. xiii.

8. Earnest Calkins, "Chronicle on the Chap-book," *The Colophon*; Part Ten, 1932, n-p.

9. Frank L. Mott, *A History of American Magazines*, 1885–1905, vol. IV (Cambridge: Harvard University Press, 1957), p. 450.

10. Gelett Burgess, *Epilark*, Book II, no. 25 (May 1, 1897), n-p.

11. Hamlin Garland, *Crumbling Idols* (Chicago and Cambridge: Stone & Kimball, 1894), p. 150.

12. As quoted by Algernon Tassin, *The Magazine in America* (New York: Dodd, Mead and Co., 1916), p. 342.

13. Larzer Ziff, *The American 1890s* (New York: Viking Press, 1966), pp. 131–32.

14. Percival Pollard, *Their Day in Court* (London: Johnson Reprint Corp., 1969 [1909]), p. 375.

15. *The Chap-Book*, vol. IX, no. 5 (July 15, 1898), n-p.

16. See particularly: Mott, *A History of American Magazines*, pp. 386–87; Tassin, *The Magazine in America*, p. 356; Frederick J. Hoffman, et al., *The Little Magazine* (Princeton: Princeton University Press, 1946), p. 235; Ziff, *The American 1890s*, p. 134; and Henry May, *The End of American Innocence: A Study of the First Years of Our Own Time 1913–1917* (New York: Alfred A. Knopf, 1959), p. 103. See also *The Chap-Book*'s disavowal of responsibility in parenting little magazines that did not measure up to their critical standards, vol. II, no. 11 (April 15, 1895), pp. 446–47.

17. As quoted in *The Chap-Book*, vol. VII, No. 10 (October 1, 1897), p. 369.

18. Herbert [S. Stone] to [Melville E.] Ned [Stone], 10 December 1896, Personal Correspondence, Book III, Stone & Kimball Collection, The Newberry Library.

19. Herbert [S. Stone] to [Melville E.] Ned [Stone], 20 March 1897, Personal Correspondence, Book III, S & K Coll., Newberry.

20. See: Herbert to Ned, 10 December 1896, Personal Correspondence, Book III; Herbert to Ned, 9 April 1898, and Herbert to Father [Melville E. Stone], 11 April 1898, Personal Correspondence, Book IV, S & K Coll., Newberry.

21. Henry Blake Fuller, "The Upward Movement in Chicago," *The Atlantic Monthly*, vol. LXXX, no. CCCCLXXX (October 1897), p. 545.

22. Earnest Calkins, "Chronicle on the Chap-book," n-p.

23. Pollard, *Their Day in Court*, p. 376.

24. Sidney Kramer, *A History of Stone & Kimball and Herbert S. Stone & Co., 1893–1905* (Chicago: Norman W. Forgue, 1940), pp. 45–46, 50–52, 53.

25. Jack Patnode, "English and American Literary Relations in the 1890s," Unpublished Doctoral Dissertation: Univ. of Minnesota, 1968; pp. 161–62.

26. Unfortunately, the available facts are limited, as the business records of both Stone & Kimball and Herbert S. Stone & Co. did not survive their dissolutions. The facts upon which the estimates of the business operations of both companies were based have been gleaned from Herbert Stone's personal correspondence and an incomplete file of business correspondence, both found in the Stone & Kimball Collection, Newberry.

27. Herbert to Ned, 10 October 1896, Personal Correspondence, Book III, S & K Coll., Newberry.

28. Herbert to Dear Ones [family], [Spring: 1894; Pencilled identification on the document reads "1895: Spring], Personal Correspondence, Book III, S & K Coll., Newberry.

29. Herbert to Ned, 10 December 1896.

30. See: Herbert to Ned, 10 December 1896; 17 February 1897; and 20 March 1897, Personal Correspondence, Book III, S & K Coll., Newberry.

31. Herbert to Ned, 13 April 1897, Personal Correspondence, Book III, S & K Coll., Newberry.

32. See Herbert's correspondence with the family, January–February 1893, particularly: Herbert to "My dear Ones," [February 1893, letterhead: "La Conférence Française de l'Université Harvard"]; and [Herbert] to Ned, [incomplete; pencilled identification reads May 1893, another fragment marked "page 13" is likely part of the same letter, and both should be dated February (2–6?), 1893], Personal Correspondence, Book II, S & K Collection, Newberry.

33. The Harvard Crimson Minutes, vol. III (1892–   ), May 4, 1894, p. 62; May 23, 1894, p. 65; June 5, 1894, p. 66; Harvard University Archives.

34. Herbert to "Dear Ones" [family], 20 August 1894, Personal Correspondence, Book III, S & K Coll., Newberry.

35. Herbert to Mother & Sister, 13 June 1895, Personal Correspondence, Book III, S & K Coll., Newberry.

36. Herbert to Father, 11 July 1895; and Herbert to "My dearest Ones" [family], 26 July 1895; Personal Correspondence, Book III, S & K Coll., Newberry.

37. Herbert to Ned, 4 April 1896, Personal Correspondence, Book III, S & K Coll., Newberry.

38. As quoted in Kramer, *Stone & Kimball*, pp. 88–89.

39. Ellen Glasgow to Herbert S. Stone, August 15, 1897, Authors' Correspondence File, Box D–G, S & K Coll., #849, Newberry.

40. See: Katherine Bates to "Editor of 'The Chap-Book' ", February 21, 1895, Authors' Correspondence File, Box A–Be, S & K Coll., #86, Newberry. "Some three weeks ago I wrote to you asking if I was entitled to any pay for an unsolicited story published by you several months ago. I have received no reply and I hardly think I am unreasonable in expecting one. As I stated then I had received no notice of the acceptance of the story, in fact one or two letters in regard to it were totally ignored. . . ."

41. Herbert to Ned, 24 May 1898, Personal Correspondence, Book IV, S & K Coll., Newberry.

42. While Sidney Kramer maintains that circulation fell off during the period of its enlarged size (*Stone & Kimball*, p. 53), there are no figures to substantiate this claim.

43. Herbert to Ned, 15 June [1898], Personal Correspondence, Book IV, S & K Coll., Newberry.

44. Herbert to "Dearest ones" [family], 2 November [1899], Personal Correspondence, Book V, S & K Coll., Newberry.

45. See Sidney Kramer, *Stone & Kimball* (pages 124–37), for an account of the last years of Stone's publishing business, 1900–1905.

46. Henry May, *The End of American Innocence*, pp. 103, 198.

47. Gilman Ostrander, *American Civilization in the First Machine Age: 1890–1940* (New York: Harper & Row, 1970), p. 174.

48. Larzer Ziff, *The American 1890s*, pp. 134–38.

49. George Bornstein, ed., *Romantic and Modern: Revaluations of Literary Tradition* (Pittsburgh: University of Pittsburgh Press, 1977), p. ix.

50. "Notes," *The Chap-Book*, vol. III, no. 12 (November 1, 1895), p. 509.

Chapter 2

1. Charles Eliot Norton, "Harvard University in 1890," *Harper's New Monthly Magazine*, September 1890, p. 582; reprinted in "Harvard," *Four American Universities* (New York: Harper & Brothers, 1895), p. 4.

2. Herbert Stuart Stone to "My Darling Parents, Sister and Relations," August 13, [1890], Personal Correspondence, Book I, Stone & Kimball Collection, The Newberry Library.

3. HSS to "My Darling Mother, Brother, and Sister," September 25, [1890], Personal Correspondence, Book I, S & K Coll., Newberry.

4. Norton, "Harvard University in 1890," p. 591.

5. "Harvard University," p. 582.

6. "Harvard University," p. 582.

7. Melville E. Stone, *Fifty Years a Journalist* (New York: Doubleday, Page & Co., 1921).

8. *The Daily Crimson*, vol. XVIII, no. 16 (October 13, 1890), p. 3.

9. Charles William Eliot to Edward C. Towne, August 1, 1895, as quoted by Henry James, *Charles W. Eliot: President of Harvard University 1869–1909*, Vol. II (Boston & New York: Houghton, Mifflin Co., 1930), p. 88.

10. Samuel Eliot Morison, *The Development of Harvard University 1869–1929* (Cambridge: Harvard University Press, 1930), p. xv.

11. Morison, *Harvard University*, pp. 154–55.

12. William Guild Howard, Lecture Notes, Norton's Fine Arts 4: Lecture #34, February 16, 1892, n.p., Harvard University Archives.

13. Howard, Fine Arts 4: Lecture #34, February 16, 1892; and Lecture #42, March 15, 1892, n.p., Harvard University Archives.

14. Howard, Fine Arts 4: Lecture #62, May 10, 1892, n.p., Harvard University Archives.

15. Norton lectured: "A thought to reinvigorate Gothic architecture for our purposes is as vain as to reinvigorate Greek. Each age has its peculiar needs & possibilities. It is a sign of weariness & not of true culture to desire to live in any age but one's own."

Howard, Fine Arts 4: Lecture #34, February 16, 1892, n.p., Harvard University Archives.

16. Ralph Adams Cram, *My Life in Architecture* (Boston: Little, Brown & Co., 1936; Kraus Reprint Co., New York, 1969), p. 13.

17. Ibid., p. 19.

18. Ibid., pp. 60, 72.

19. Ibid., pp. 57, 59.

20. Herbert Stuart Stone, Class of 1894, 1st Class Report, Secretary's Copy, Harvard University Archives.

21. Young Men's Christian Association of Harvard, Membership Register 1886–1902, "Class of 1894," pp. 1, 86–7, Harvard University Archives.

22. Hannibal Ingalls Kimball, Class of 1894, 1st Class Report, Secretary's Copy, Harvard University Archives.

23. HSS to "My Dear Ones" [family], October 4, [1892], Personal Correspondence, Book I, S & K Coll., Newberry.

24. *The Daily Crimson*, vol. XVII, no. 26, October 24, 1890, p. 1; no. 30, October 29, 1890, p. 2.

25. Cram, *My Life*, pp. 14–16.

26. Charles R. Nutter, "Notes in English 7, 1892–93," n.p., Harvard University Archives.

27. Charles R. Nutter, "English 9 Notes & Papers, 1891–92," n.p., Harvard University Archives.

28. Lewis E. Gates, *Three Studies in Literature* (New York: The Macmillan Co., 1899), pp. 122, 108.

29. Gates, *Three Studies in Literature*, p. 111.

30. Ibid., p. 70.

31. Daniel Gregory Mason, ed., *Some Letters of William Vaughn Moody* (Boston & New York: Houghton, Mifflin Co., 1913), p. 15.

32. *The Harvard Monthly* will be used extensively in this chapter to document what Harvard students and faculty were thinking. This seems appropriate for two reasons. First, many of their authors were later contributors to *The Chap-Book*, and Stone would have been quite familiar with their writings in the *Monthly*. Second, the *Monthly* itself was recognized in 1910 on its twenty-fifth anniversary of publication, as being "a record, for the quarter of a century, of the workings of the undergraduate mind about the college." H.T. P[arker], "The Harvard Monthly," *Transcript*, May 7, 1910; Harvard Monthly "Clippings, Notices, etc.," Harvard University Archives.

33. Robert Morss Lovett, "Cardinal Newman: II," *The Harvard Monthly*, vol. XV, no. 4, January 1893, pp. 141, 143.

34. Lovett, "Cardinal Newman: II," p. 146.

35. Norman Hapgood, "Mr. Mallock and the Positivists," *The Harvard Monthly*, vol. XI, no. 2, November 1890, pp. 69, 60.

36. P.H. Savage, *The Harvard Monthly*, vol. XIII, no. 2, November 1891, p. 79.

37. Robert W. Herrick, "The Laboratory Method in the Study of English," *The Harvard Monthly*, vol. XVI, no. 4, June 1893, pp. 138, 145.

38. *The Daily Crimson*, vol. XVIII, no. 7, October 2, 1890, p. 1; no. 9, October 4, 1890, p. 2; no. 14, October 10, 1890, p. 2; no. 15, October 11, 1890, p. 1; no. 9, October 4, 1890, p. 1.

39. *The Daily Crimson*, vol. XVIII, no. 18, October 15, 1890, p. 1.

40. Josiah Royce, *The Spirit of Modern Philosophy* (Boston & New York: Houghton, Mifflin & Co., 1892), pp. 35–36.

41. Ibid., p. 17.

42. Ibid., pp. 124–25.

43. Ibid., p. 137.

44. Ibid., p. 17.

45. Ibid., p. 137.

46. Howard, Fine Arts 4: Lecture #3, October 17, 1891, n.p., Harvard University Archives.

47. Howard, Fine Arts 4: Lecture #4, October 20, 1891, n.p., Harvard University Archives.

48. George R. Noyes, Fine Arts 3: Lecture II, October 4, 1892, n.p., Harvard University Archives.

49. Noyes, Fine Arts 3: Lecture II, October 4, 1892, Harvard.

50. Noyes, F.A. 3: October 27, 1892, Harvard.

51. Noyes, F.A. 3: December 8, 1892, Harvard.

52. Noyes, F.A. 3: October 4, 1892, Harvard.

53. Howard, F.A. 4: Lecture #2, October 15, 1891, Harvard.

54. Howard, F.A. 4: Lecture #3, October 17, 1891, Harvard.

55. Howard, F.A. 4: Lecture #3, October 17, 1891, Harvard.

56. Noyes, F.A. 3: Lecture V, October 11, 1892, Harvard.

57. Noyes, F.A. 3: Lecture V, October 11, 1892, Harvard.

58. Royce, *The Spirit of Modern Philosophy*, pp. 128, 129–30. See also: Josiah Royce, "How Beliefs Are Made," (1882) in *Fugitive Essays* (Cambridge: Harvard University Press, 1920), pp. 345–77, particularly pp. 361–62.

59. George Santayana, "What is a Philistine?" *The Harvard Monthly*, vol. XIV, no. 3, May 1892, pp. 93, 96, 97.

60. Ibid., p. 97.

61. Ibid., pp. 98–99.

62. John Cummings, "Imaginative," *The Harvard Monthly*, vol. XIV, no. 2, April 1892, pp. 73, 75–76.

63. Paul R. Frothingham, "The Place of Mysticism in Modern Life," *The Harvard Monthly*, vol. XIII, no. 2, November 1891, pp. 47–8.

64. John Rathbone Oliver, "Maurice Maetterlink," *The Harvard Monthly*, vol. XVI, no. 3, May 1893, pp. 129, 117.

65. Henry Copley Greene, "French Prose Symbolism," *The Harvard Monthly*, vol. XVIII, no. 3, May 1894, pp. 107, 116, 11, 119, 120.

66. Howard, Fine Arts 4: Lecture #1, October 8, 1891, n.p., Harvard University Archives.

67. George R. Noyes, Fine Arts 3: Lecture Notes vol. II, February 23, 1893, n.p., Harvard University Archives.

68. "The Month," *The Harvard Monthly*, vol. XVI, no. 1, March 1893, p. 40.

69. While Cram does not specifically date this attempt, he calls it his first magazine venture, which would place it prior to his involvement with *The Knight Errant*, April 1892.

70. Cram, *My Life in Architecture*, p. 54.

71. Louise Imogen Guiney, Charles Eliot Norton, Bertram Grosvenor Goodhue, Ralph Adams Cram, Agnes Lee, Brander Matthews and Bliss Carman.

72. Cram, *My Life*, pp. 86–7, 85.

73. Louise Imogen Guiney to Herbert E. Clarke, as quoted in Louise Imogen Guiney, *Letters* (New York: Harper & Brothers, 1926), p. 31.

74. Cram, *My Life*, pp. 85–86, 88.

75. "Notes," *The Chap-Book*, vol. I, no. 7, August 15, 1895, pp. 173–74.

76. HSS to "My Dear Ones" [family], December 15, [1891], Personal Correspondence, Book I, S & K Coll., Newberry.

77. HSS to "My Dear Ones," n.d. [late winter, 1892], Personal Correspondence, Book I; HSS to "My Dear Ones," January 19, [1892], Personal Correspondence, Book I; HSS to "My dear Parents & Sister," December 16, 1891, Personal Correspondence, Book I; S & K Coll., Newberry.

78. HSS to Ned [Melville E. Stone], [Spring 1892], Personal Correspondence, Book I, S & K Coll., Newberry.

79. HSS to Ned, n.d. [ca. March 1892], Personal Correspondence, Book I, S & K Coll., Newberry.

80. Noyes, Fine Arts 3: Lecture Notes, vol. II, March 4, 1893, n.p., Harvard University Archives.

81. HSS to "My dearest Ones," January 3, 1893, Personal Correspondence, Book II, S & K Coll., Newberry.

82. HSS to "My dear Ones," January 29, 1893, Personal Correspondence, Book II, S & K Coll., Newberry.

83. HSS to "My dear Ones," January 28, [1894], Personal Correspondence, Book III, S & K Coll., Newberry.

84. HSS to "My dear Father," "The fifteenth day" [February 1894], Personal Correspondence, Book III, S & K Coll., Newberry.

85. HSS to "My dear Ones," n.d. [spring 1894], Personal Correspondence, Book III, S & K Coll., Newberry; quoted by Sidney Kramer, *A History of Stone & Kimball and Herbert S. Stone & Co., 1893–1905* (Chicago: University of Chicago Press, 1940), p. 25.

86. See Chap-Book Posters, S & K Coll., Newberry.

87. Toulouse-Lautrec's poster was issued in June 1896. See Chapter 1 for a discussion of *The Chap-Book's* critical reception.

Chapter 3

1. Carman's signed contributions appeared in twenty-six of *The Chap-Book's* one hundred issues. Henry James ran second to Carman, appearing in fifteen separate issues, with, however, only one short story and a serialized novel. Louise Imogen Guiney, who frequently contributed anonymous "Notes," (See Guiney folder, Box D-G, Stone & Kimball Collection, The Newberry Library), had signed contributions in fourteen separate issues. See Appendix for a list of contributors and the issues in which their contributions appeared.

2. James Cappon, *Bliss Carman: And the Literary Currents and Influences of his Times* (New York & Montreal: Louis Carrier & Alan Isles, Inc., 1930), p. 205. Cappon places special emphasis on the "spiritual traditions of New England Puritanism" which Carman inherited, and on the literary tradition of Emerson's and Thoreau's transcendentalism in which he was instructed.

3. Bliss Carman, "Contemporaries—V. Mr. Charles G.D. Roberts," *The Chap-Book*, vol. II, no. 4 (January 1, 1895), pp. 169–70.

4. Bliss Carman, "Mr. Charles G.D. Roberts," pp. 170–71.

5. Bliss Carman, *The Kinship of Nature* (Boston: L.C. Page & Co., 1903), pp. viii, vi–vii.

6. James Cappon, *Bliss Carman*, pp. 9–10.

7. Bliss Carman, "Mr. Francis Thompson's Poetry," *The Chap-Book*, vol. I, no. 1 (May 15, 1894), p. 6; See above p. 43. See also, Bliss Carman, *The Kinship of Nature*, pp. 3–5.

8. Bliss Carman, *The Kinship of Nature*, pp. 149, 148.

9. Ibid., pp. 186–87.

10. Ibid., p. 38.

11. Ibid., pp. 93–94.

12. As quoted by Peter McArthur, "On Having Known a Poet," *Atlantic Monthly*, May 1906, vol. 97, p. 712; identified by James Cappon, *Bliss Carman*, p. 26. McArthur quoted the poet, caught in what he called a "Coleridgean mood," at length: "I often wish," he once exclaimed, "that I could rid the world of the tyranny of facts. What are facts but compromises? A fact merely marks the point where we have agreed to let investigation cease. Investigate further, and your fact disappears. Under the scrutiny of thought all facts are alike, from the atom to the universe,—merely compromises or splendid guesses,—and they dissolve, even as

The cloud-capped towers, the gorgeous palaces,
The solemn temples, the great globe itself,
Yea, all which it inherit, shall dissolve.

And it is only after facts have dissolved and vanished into the mystery of things that the poetic soul can begin to recreate, and devise forms of beauty. The soul that is trammeled with facts is a hopeless prisoner within petty limits, and for it great achievement is impossible."

13. Bliss Carman, *The Kinship of Nature*, pp. 87–88, 84–85, 88.

14. Ibid., p. 138.

15. Charles G.D. Roberts, "The Unsleeping," *The Chap-Book*, vol. I, no. 1 (May 15, 1894), p. 3.

16. Bliss Carman, "Mr. Charles G.D. Roberts," *The Chap-Book*, vol. II, no. 4 (January 1, 1895), p. 169.

17. Bliss Carman, "Mr. Francis Thompson's Poetry," *The Chap-Book*, vol. I, no. 1 (May 15, 1894), pp. 5–8.

18. Bliss Carman, "Mr. Francis Thompson's Poetry," pp. 6, 6–7.

19. Ibid., p. 7.

20. Bliss Carman, *The Kinship of Nature*, pp. 150-51.

21. Herbert Stone's marked copy of the first issue off the press attributes this essay to Guiney. See Stone & Kimball Collection, The Newberry Library.

22. [Louise Imogen Guiney,] "A Bitter Complaint of the Ungentle Reader," *The Chap-Book*, vol. I, no. 1 (May 15, 1894), p. 9.

23. Carman and Guiney, as noted earlier, both had been previously associated with *The Knight Errant*. Stone, Carman and Guiney were all acquaintances of Louise Chandler Moulton and often gathered at her afternoons "at home" in Boston. See also Guiney's letters of introduction for Carman to Herbert E. Clarke (22 April 1896) and Clement Shorter (23 April 1896) in which she describes Carman as "an old colleague and great friend of mine," Louise Imogen Guiney, *Letters* (New York: Harper & Bros., 1926), pp. 103–4, 104–5.

24. [Louise Imogen Guiney,] "A Bitter Complaint," pp. 9–10.

25. Ibid., p. 11.

26. Bliss Carman, "Mr. Charles G.D. Roberts," p. 169.

27. The most important *Chap-Book* contribution detailing a child's acquisition of knowledge was Henry James's *What Maisie Knew*, which appeared serially from January 15, 1897 through August 1, 1897. See above Chapter 4, pp. 79–83.

28. See Herbert S. Stone's marked copy of vol. I, no. 1 in The Stone & Kimball Collection, The Newberry Library.

29. "Notes," *The Chap-Book*, vol. I, no. 1 (May 15, 1894), p. 18.

30. Mr. T.B. Meteyard, "Titlepage for 'The Ebb Tide,' " *The Chap-Book*, vol. I, no. 1 (May 15, 1894), p. 4.

31. [Herbert S. Stone,] "Mr. Beardsley—After Himself," *The Chap-Book*, vol. I, no. 1 (May 15, 1894), p. 17. See: "Illustrations from Old Chap-books," *The Chap-Book*, volumes IV and V, discussed above, Chapter 5, pp. 91–92.

32. While the text of the magazine amply demonstrated its desire to publicize the works of known romantics, so does its advertisements. For instance, in this first issue: Little, Brown & Co. featured an ad for forty-eight volumes of *The Romances of Alexander Dumas;* Houghton, Mifflin & Co. drew attention to the poetry of William Wetmore Story and Thomas William Parson; Copeland and Day marketed the works of Carman, John Davidson, Katherine Tynan Hinkson, Richard Le Gallienne and John Bannister Tabb; and Stone & Kimball promoted their titles by Stevenson, Carman, Louise Chandler Moulton, and featured a new ten-volume set of the complete writings of Poe, edited by Edmund Clarence Stedman and George Woodberry, and illustrated by Aubrey Beardsley. *The Chap-Book*, vol. I, no. 1 (May 15, 1894), pp. 23, 24, 2, 20–21.

33. Clinton Scollard, "The Walk," *The Chap-Book*, vol. I, no. 8 (September 1, 1894), p. 183.

34. Archibald Lampman, "Inter Vias," *The Chap-Book*, vol. II, no. 5 (January 15, 1895), pp. 207–08.

35. Theodore Wratislaw, "Ave Maris Stella," *The Chap-Book*, vol. III, no. 5 (July 15, 1895), p. 171.

36. Stephen Crane, "Verses," *The Chap-Book*, vol. IV, no. 8 (March 1, 1896), p. 372.

37. John Bannister Tabb, "A Rubric," *The Chap-Book*, vol. V, no. 12 (November 1, 1896), p. 529.

38. George Woodberry, "In Love's Confessional," *The Chap-Book*, vol. VI, no. 12 (May 1, 1897), p. 465.

39. Carman was especially prone to this weakness, and attributed it to at least one of his colleagues, much to her dissatisfaction. See the discussion of Carman's analysis of Louise Imogen Guiney in Chapter 5, p. 99.

40. Ruth McEnery Stuart and Albert Bigelow Paine, "God's Music," *The Chap-Book*, vol. VI, no. 10 (April 1, 1897), p. 395.

41. Maria Louise Pool, "Me 'N' Maje," *The Chap-Book*, vol.I, no. 1 (May 15, 1894), pp. 12–16.

42. Animal stories were enjoying great popularity in the decade that saw the first publication of Anna Sewell's best seller *Black Beauty. The Chap-Book,* principally through publication of Maria Louise Pool's dog stories, such as "Boss," *The Chap-Book*, vol. III, no. 12 (November 1, 1895), pp. 475–81, participated in this vogue, and in the process called attention to the romantic belief that creatures of nature, in these cases dogs, were capable of life-sacrificing acts of love.

43. John Burroughs, "Sympathetic Criticism," *The Chap-Book*, vol. IX, no. 4 (July 1, 1898), p. 111.

44. Ibid., pp. 111–12.

45. Ibid., p. 112.

46. On the average, one out of every two *Chap-Books* contained a contribution that in some way dealt with a theme involving love and death.

47. Wallace de Groot Rice, "The Lesson," *The Chap-Book*, vol. VII, no. 2 (June 1, 1897), p. 50.

48. Unsigned, "The Crowned Poet of the Academy," *The Chap-Book*, vol. VIII, no. 10 (April 1, 1898), p. 410.

49. As quoted by H.H. Boyesen, "Ibsen's New Play," *The Chap-Book*, vol. II, no. 6 (February 1, 1895), p. 251.

50. John Davidson, "A Ballad of an Artist's Wife," *The Chap-Book*, vol. III, no. 2 (October 15, 1895), pp. 423–29; see particularly pp. 427, 424, 423, 427.

51. See a later discussion of Garland and realism as set forth in *Crumbling Idols*, above, "Chapter 4: Facts and Fancies—The Fusion of Realistic Literature," pp. 70–71.

52. Hamlin Garland, "Wagner," *The Chap-Book*, vol. III, no. 10 (October 1, 1895), pp. 379–80.

53. John Davidson, "A New Ballad of Tannhaeuser," *The Chap-Book*, vol. V, no. 4 (July 1, 1896), pp. 180–87; see particularly pp. 185–86.

54. Gilbert Parker, "Tales of the Voshti Hills—I: The Golden Pipes," *The Chap-Book*, vol. II, no. 10 (April 1, 1895), pp. 399–400.

55. Gilbert Parker, "The Golden Pipes," pp. 402–4.

Chapter 4

1. See, for instance, Claude Bragdon's poster, "The Carriage," 1896, Stone & Kimball Collection, The Newberry Library. See, also, the title page for the index to *The Chap-Book*, vol. I (1894).

2. Walker Kennedy, "The Passion Flower of Magdala," *The Chap-Book*, vol. I, no. 11 (October 15, 1894), pp. 276, 277, 279.

3. Ibid., pp. 286, 288, 289.

4. Ibid., p. 291.

5. Ibid., p. 310.

6. Ibid., pp. 315, 318.

7. Ibid., pp. 318, 319.

8. Accounts of the life of Mary Magdalene ranged from total fabrications, such as Rev. Thomas S. Preston, *The Life of St. Mary Magdalene* (New York: P. O'Shea, 1861); to devotional commentary on the scriptures, such as Fr. Pius Cavanagh, O.P., *Gleanings for Saints and Sinner about St. Mary Magdalen* (London: The Catholic Truth Society, 1888); to fictional biography based on scripture, such as Edgar Saltus, *Mary Magdalen* (New York: Brentano's [1891], 1925). Saltus's very orthodox interpretation of the life of Mary Magdalene is particularly interesting as it comes from the pen of one of America's few "decadent" writers. Very little historical facts are known of the life of Mary, even today, and in the 1890s she did not even receive standard encyclopedic references.

9. H.S.S., "The Story of Jesus Christ," *The Chap-Book*, vol. VIII, no. 6 (February 1, 1898), pp. 249–50.

10. Text illustration of a gothic cathedral, *The Chap-Book*, vol. I, no. 2 (June 1, 1894), p. 37. Eugene Grasset, "The Rosary," *The Chap-Book*, vol. I, no. 4 (July 1, 1894), p. 85. Bertram Grosvenor Goodhue, "The Knight Errant," *The Chap-Book*, vol. I, no. 7 (August 15, 1894), p. 173. See also: Will H. Bradley, "The Dolorous Knight," *The Chap-Book*, vol. II, no. 8 (March 1, 1895), p. 342; griffins and unicorns to accompany "Notes," *The Chap-Book*, vol. II, no. 10 (April 1, 1895), pp. 416–19. And Frank Hazenplug's "St. Hieronymus," *The Chap-Book*, vol. IV, no. 9 (March 15, 1896), n.p.; "St. Sebastian," *The Chap-Book*, vol. IV, no. 12 (May 1, 1896), p. 594; and unidentified illustrations to accompany W. B. Yeats, "S. Patrick and the Pedants," *The Chap-Book*, vol. V, no. 2 (June 1, 1896), p. 50. There are also numerous other full-page illustrations and border designs reminiscent of this time period. See, for instance: Frank Hazenplug's illustrations to accompany John Davidson, "A Ballad of An Artist's Wife," *The Chap-Book*, vol. III, no. 11 (October 15, 1895), pp. 423–29; J. E. Southall, "The Departure of Blue Beard," *The Chap-Book*, vol. III, no. 11 (October 15, 1895), p. 441; Andhre des Gachons, "Illustration for a Poem by Jean Lorrain," *The Chap-Book*, vol. IV, no. 7 (February 15, 1896), p. 350; and Frank Hazenplug's illustrations for "From the Passion Play of Arnoul Greban, 15th Century," *The Chap-Book*, vol. VI, no. 3 (December 15, 1896), pp. 109–14. Original drawings cease as *Chap-Book* illustrations when it enlarged its format with the issue of January 15, 1897, vol. VI, no. 5.

11. "Notes," *The Chap-Book*, vol. III, no. 9 (September 15, 1895), p. 352.

12. Frank Hazenplug, "St. Hieronymus," *The Chap-Book*, vol. IV, no. 9 (March 15, 1896), n.p.

13. Ralph Adams Cram, "The Ride of the Clans," *The Chap-Book*, vol. I, no. 6 (August 1, 1894), pp. 139–40; Herbert Small, "A Legitimist Kalendar," *The Chap-Book*, vol. I, no. 6 (August 1, 1894), pp. 140–43.

14. Guiney's poem, "On The Fly-Leaf of Clarendon's History Of The Rebellion," led off the third number of volume three, *The Chap-Book*, vol. III, no. 3 (June 15, 1895), p. 91. In this same issue, the "Notes" took account of a Jacobite celebration in England held by the White Rose Society, and called for some American activity. The "Note" reads, in part: "If it be salutary for the soul to love a lost and hopeless cause, may we not look for something on this side? The Stuart Restoration is no more a lovely and belated dream here than there. Those who read Mr. Walter Blackburne Harte's 'Meditations in Motley' know what of aspiration towards an ideal, of hatred of the drab monotony of our daily lives, may be read into the folly of the little Boston band of enthusiasts. Are there no others who will forget the present for a day and drink 'The King, may he come to his own again'? The season for midsummer madness is not far away." *The Chap-Book*, vol. III, no. 3, p. 109. As Guiney had contributed all of the "Notes" in vol. III, no. 1 (May 15, 1895), and all of the "Notes" in every other issue of vol. II preceding this volume, it is very likely that these "Notes" in vol. III, no. 3 were hers as well. They not only reflect her interests, they also resemble her style. See: Guiney's manuscript drafts, Guiney folder, Box D–G, Stone & Kimball Collection, The Newberry Library.

15. Thomas Hardy, "The Duke's Reappearance," *The Chap-Book*, vol. VI, no. 3 (December 15, 1896), pp. 97–107.

16. See above, Chapter 2, pp. 32–33.

17. "Notes," *The Chap-Book*, vol. I, no. 7 (August 15, 1894), p. 174.

18. Jeannette Barbour Perry, "The Romantic Essay," *The Chap-Book*, vol. VIII, no. 1 (November 15, 1897), p. 15.

19. Presumably referring to the students of Herbert Baxter Adams and other monograph writers trained in the Germanic mode of scientific history.

20. Unsigned review, "Louis XV and His Court," *The Chap-Book*, vol. VIII, no. 1 (November 15, 1897), p. 25.

21. Dorothea Moore, "The Workers," *The Chap-Book*, vol. VIII, no. 4 (January 1, 1898), pp. 178-79.

22. Bliss Carman, "Mr. Gilbert Parker," *The Chap-Book*, vol. I, no. 12 (November 1, 1894), p. 342.

23. Bliss Carman, "Mr. William Sharp's Poems," *The Chap-Book*, vol. I, no. 9 (September 15, 1894), p. 221.

24. "Notes," *The Chap-Book*, vol. VII, no. 2 (June 1, 1897), p. 46.

25. J.L. Steffens, "Schloma, The Daughter of Schmuhl," *The Chap-Book*, vol. V, no. 3 (June 15, 1896), pp. 128, 132.

26. I. Zangwill, "Romeo and Juliet and Other Love Stories," *The Chap-Book*, vol. IV, no. 1 (November 15, 1895) pp. 16, 18.

27. Arthur Morrison, "What is a Realist?" *The Chap-Book*, vol. VI, no. 8 (March 1, 1897), p. 323.

28. The classic interpretation of Garland's estrangement from the Eastern literary establishment may be found in Vernon L. Parrington, *The Beginnings of Critical Realism in America: 1860–1920* (New York: Harcourt, Brace & World, 1930, 1958), pp. 292–93.

29. Hamlin Garland to Melville E. Stone, Sr., March 5, 1893, #821, "Laid in book box 1–1000," Stone & Kimball Collection, The Newberry Library.

30. Herbert [Stuart Stone] to My dearest Ones, March 9, [1893], Personal Book II, Stone & Kimball Collection, The Newberry Library.

31. Hamlin Garland, *Roadside Meetings* (New York: The Macmillan Company, 1930), p. 276.

32. Hamlin Garland, *Crumbling Idols: Twelve Essays on Art Dealing Chiefly with Literature, Painting, and the Drama* (Chicago and Cambridge: Stone & Kimball, 1894). Available in facsimile edition (Gainesville, Fla.: Scholars' Facsimiles & Reprints, 1952).

33. Ibid., p. 22.

34. Ibid., p. 21.

35. Ibid., pp. 26–27, 52, 34, 35.

36. Ibid., pp. 28, 29.

37. Hamlin Garland, "The Cry of the Artist," *The Chap-Book*, vol. IV, no. 1 (November 15, 1895), pp. 7–8.

38. Hamlin Garland, *Roadside Meetings,* pp. 277–78.

39. Hamlin Garland, "The Land of the Straddle-Bug," *The Chap-Book,* vol. II, no. 1 (November 15, 1894), pp. 5–11; vol. II, no. 2 (December 1, 1894), pp. 73–76; vol. II, no. 3 (December 15, 1894), pp. 134–42; vol. II, no. 4 (January 1, 1895), pp. 182–89; vol. II, no. 5 (January 15, 1895), pp. 223–29; vol. II, no. 6 (February 1, 1895), pp. 261–71; vol. II, no. 7 (February 15, 1895), pp. 304–19.

40. Hamlin Garland, "The Land of the Straddle-Bug," *The Chap-Book,* vol. II, no 1 (November 15, 1894), pp. 6, 9.

41. Hamlin Garland, "The Land of the Straddle-Bug," *The Chap-Book*, vol. II, no. 2 (December 1, 1894), pp. 74–75. These feelings were not merely those of Blanche and her husband; the other settlers felt them as well. See, for instance: vol. II, no. 3 (December 15, 1894), pp. 138.

42. Hamlin Garland, "The Land of the Straddle-Bug," *The Chap-Book,* vol. II, no. 3 (December 15, 1894), pp. 138–39.

43. Ibid., p. 142.

44. Hamlin Garland, "The Land of the Straddle-Bug." *The Chap-Book,* vol. II, no. 5 (January 15, 1895), pp. 224, 229.

45. Hamlin Garland, "The Land of the Straddle-Bug," *The Chap-Book,* vol. II, no. 7 (February 15, 1895), pp. 305, 304.

46. Ibid., pp. 305, 308.

47. Ibid., pp. 305, 313–14, 314.

48. Ibid., p. 316.

49. See particularly the chapter "Impressionism" in Hamlin Garland, *Crumbling Idols,* pp. 121–41; especially pp. 122, 124, 133.

50. Herbert Stone's correspondence from England with the office of Herbert S. Stone & Co. in Chicago during the month of May 1898 details the financial dilemmas that Stone, his magazine and his publishing company were facing. He repeatedly urged that their English authors be paid first, with checks from Chicago, and paid James himself out of the money he had with him to finance his trip. See: Herbert [Stuart Stone] to Ned [Melville E. Stone, Jr.], 28 May 1898, Personal Book IV, The Stone & Kimball Collection, The Newberry Library. By paying James, he not only was willing to keep his American creditors waiting, but ended up being stranded in England with not enough money to return home. See letters of Herbert [Stuart Stone] to Ned [Melville E. Stone, Jr.], 28 June 1898, 9 July [1898], and Herbert [Stuart Stone] to Mother, 9 July [1898], Personal Book IV, The Stone & Kimball Collection, The Newberry Library.

51. See above: Chapter 3, note 1, page 138. The serialized literary staples of James and Garland helped carry over twenty percent of *The Chap-Book*'s total issues.

52. Preface to the 1908 edition of Henry James, *What Maisie Knew* (New York: Charles Scribner's Sons, 1908), p. xiii.

53. Henry James, "The Way It Came," *The Chap-Book,* vol. IV, no. 12 (May 1, 1896), pp. 562–93.

54. Henry James, "The Way It Came," pp. 565, 569, 570.

55. Ibid., p. 579.

56. Ibid, p. 584, and again p. 586.

57. Ibid., pp. 592, 593.

58. Ibid., p. 590.

59. Henry James, "What Maisie Knew," *The Chap-Book,* vol. VI, no. 5 (January 15, 1897), pp. 214–19; vol. VI, no. 6 (February 1, 1897), pp. 253–60; vol. VI, no. 7 (February 15, 1897), pp. 289–95; vol. VI, no. 8 (March 1, 1897), pp. 326–31; vol. VI, no. 9 (March 15, 1897), pp. 361–67; vol. VI, no. 10 (April 1, 1897), pp. 395–401; vol. VI, no. 11 (April 15, 1897), pp. 428–34; vol. VI, no. 12 (May 1, 1897), pp. 478–85; vol. VII, no. 1 (May 15, 1897), pp. 16–25; vol. VII, no. 2 (June 1, 1897), pp. 57–62; vol. VII, no. 3 (June 15, 1897) pp. 90–97; vol. VII, no. 4 (July 1, 1897), pp. 125–31; vol. VII, no. 5 (July 15, 1897) pp. 162–68; vol. VII, no. 6 (August 1, 1897), pp. 198–209.

60. Henry James, "What Maisie Knew," *The Chap-Book,* vol. VI, no. 5 (January 15, 1897), p. 215.

61. Ibid., p. 217.

62. "What Maisie Knew," *The Chap-Book,* vol. VII, no. 1 (May 15, 1897), p. 23.

63. See particularly the beginning of Chapter XIX when Maisie is with her father, "What Maisie Knew," *The Chap-Book,* vol. VI, no. 12 (May 1, 1897), p. 481; and again in the beginning of Chapter XXIX, "What Maisie Knew," *The Chap-Book,* vol. VII, no. 5 (July 15, 1897), p. 165.

64. "What Maisie Knew," *The Chap-Book,* vol. VII, no. 6 (August 1, 1897), p. 204.

65. "What Maisie Knew," *The Chap-Book,* vol. VI, no. 5 (January 15, 1897), pp. 214, 216; vol. VI, no. 6 (February 1, 1897), p. 254; vol. VI, no. 9 (March 15, 1897), p. 367; vol. VI, no. 10 (April 1, 1897), p. 400.

66. "What Maisie Knew," *The Chap-Book,* vol. VI, no. 7 (February 15, 1897), p. 292; vol. VI, no. 12 (May 1, 1897), p. 483 and again vol. VII, no. 1 (May 15, 1897), p. 23; vol. VI, no. 7 (February 15, 1897), p. 292.

67. "What Maisie Knew," *The Chap-Book,* vol. VI, no. 8 (March 1, 1897), pp. 326, 327, 328; vol. VI, no. 10 (April 1, 1897), pp. 398, 399; vol. VII, no. 2 (June 1, 1897), pp. 57, 58.

68. See the last chapter, "What Maisie Knew," *The Chap-Book,* vol. VII, no. 6 (August 1, 1897), p. 208.

69. "What Maisie Knew," *The Chap-Book,* vol. VI, no. 11 (April 15, 1897), p. 430.

70. These references are not numerous either, however. See Mrs. Wix's in "What Maisie Knew," *The Chap-Book,* vol. VI, no. 6 (February 1, 1897), p. 259. Sir Claude, Maisie's stepfather, addresses her once as belonging to her parents, i.e. Miss Farange, in "What Maisie Knew," *The Chap-Book,* vol. VII, no. 1 (May 15, 1897), p. 17; once as "Maisie boy," in "What Maisie Knew," *The Chap-Book,* vol. VII, no. 3 (June 15, 1897), p. 93; and once as Maisie when he says good-bye, in "What Maisie Knew," *The Chap-Book,* vol. VII, no. 6 (August 1, 1897), p. 209. Maisie is referred to by name more often than she is addressed, but these references are also few, being far exceeded by the number of times she is referred to by sobriquets.

71. "What Maisie Knew," *The Chap-Book,* vol. VI, no. 6 (February 1, 1897), p. 256.

72. "What Maisie Knew," *The Chap-Book,* vol. VII, no. 1 (May 15, 1897), p. 24.

73. "What Maisie Knew," *The Chap-Book,* vol. VI, no. 8 (March 1, 1897), p. 330.

74. "What Maisie Knew," *The Chap-Book,* vol. VI, no. 9 (March 15, 1897), p. 361.

75. See, for instance, when she is guided by a look of her governess, Miss Overmore, "What Maisie Knew," *The Chap-Book,* vol. VI, no. 5 (January 15, 1897), pp. 216–17; and when she relates how she knew her father liked Miss Overmore, "What Maisie Knew," *The Chap-Book,* vol. VI, no. 5 (January 15, 1897), p. 219.

76. "What Maisie Knew," *The Chap-Book,* vol. VI, no. 6 (February 1, 1897), p. 254.

77. Ibid., p. 253.

78. "What Maisie Knew," *The Chap-Book,* vol. VII, no. 3 (June 15, 1897), p. 92.

79. As Maisie noted, Mrs. Wix was "nobody," see "What Maisie Knew," *The Chap-Book,* vol. VII, no. 5 (July 15, 1897), p. 165; and Maisie's reference to the fact that she felt she had lost everything, "What Maisie Knew," *The Chap-Book,* vol. VII, no. 6 (August 1, 1897), p. 206.

80. Leon Edel, *Henry James: The Treacherous Years 1895–1901* (Philadelphia, New York: J.B. Lippincott Co., 1969), p. 14.

81. Review of *What Maisie Knew* from *The London Chronicle,* as quoted by *The Chap-Book,* vol. VII, no. 11 (October 15, 1897), p. 378.

82. F.O. Matthiessen and Kenneth B. Murdock, eds., *The Notebooks of Henry James* (New York: Oxford University Press, 1947), p. 263.

83. Leon Edel, *Henry James: The Treacherous Years,* p. 114.

Chapter 5

1. Paul Verlaine, "Moonlight," trans. Gertrude Hall, *The Chap-Book*, vol. I, no. 4 (July 1, 1894), p. 79.

2. Anatole France, "Paul Verlaine: A Propos of his Book, 'My Hospitals,' " trans. M. G. M., *The Chap-Book,* vol. I, no. 4 (July 1, 1894), pp. 80, 81, 81, 84.

3. Ibid., p. 83.

4. Ibid.

5. Ibid., p. 84.

6. Eugene Grasset, "The Rosary: Design for a Stained-Glass Window, Reproduced from 'La Plume,' " *The Chap-Book,* vol. I, no. 4 (July 1, 1894), p. 85.

7. William Gaunt, *The Aesthetic Adventure* (New York: Schocken Books, 1967), p. 125.

8. "Notes," *The Chap-Book,* vol. I, no. 10 (October 1, 1894), p. 264.

9. "Notes," *The Chap-Book,* vol. V, no. 7 (August 15, 1896), p. 336.

10. Paul Verlaine, "Epigrammes," *The Chap-Book,* vol. I, no. 9 (September 15, 1894), p. 211.

11. Mrs. Reginald de Koven, "Verlaine:—A Feminine Appreciation," *The Chap-Book,* vol. IV, no. 6 (February 1, 1896), p. 285.

12. Ibid., pp. 285–89.

13. "The World Turned Upside Down," *The Chap-Book,* vol. IV, no. 7 (February 15, 1896), p. 325.

14. See: "Illustrations From Old Chap-Books," *The Chap-Book,* vol. IV, no. 4 (January 1, 1896), p. 193; vol. IV, no. 7 (February 15, 1896), p. 325; vol. IV, no. 11 (April 15, 1896), pp. 538, 539; vol. V, no. 1 (May 15, 1896), p. 41; vol. V, no. 2 (June 1, 1896), pp. 76, 77; vol. V, no. 4 (July 1, 1896), p. 175; vol. V, no. 5 (July 15, 1896), p. 225; vol. V, no. 6 (August 1, 1896), p. 285; vol. V, no. 8 (September 1, 1896), p. 377.

15. See, for instance: "Riddle: From 'The True Trial of Understanding; or, Wit Newly Reviv'd. Being a Book of Riddles adorned with a variety of Pictures.' " *The Chap-Book,* vol. IV, no. 11 (April 15, 1896), p. 538.

16. Georges Pissaro, "In the Garden," *The Chap-Book,* vol. III, no. 9 (September 15, 1895), p. 350; "Notes," *The Chap-Book,* vol. III, no. 12 (November 1, 1895), p. 509.

17. W. B. Yeats, "S. Patrick and the Pedants," *The Chap-Book,* vol. V, no. 2 (June 1, 1896), pp. 50–55.

18. For a quite literal representation of an enchantment which occurs to a man while he hangs suspended between life and death, the material world and the spiritual, see John Regnault's short story, "The Soul of the Rogue," *The Chap-Book,* vol. VIII, no. 10 (April 1, 1898), pp. 403–5. A rogue attempts to commit suicide by hanging himself from the ceiling, but only succeeds in suspending himself twelve inches above the floor in a painful yet conscious state. "The somber, the familiar, the prosaic scene grew extremely fantastic; the outlines gleamed, and all the colors that danced before his eyes quivered and vanished by flashes." (p. 403) Before his eyes there appears a dwarf, the mirror of his inner life, who was released during the rogue's unsuccessful fall. He had been locked up in his body before: "I was then sitting on the blind side of you; I had my tragic mask on, and my mantle about me. Come, look at me now and note me well!—an opportunity of the kind is rare. Behold, I am the very flower of all enigmas, immortal and modest, and seldom visible, the most real of breathing phantasms, the vital mirror of your inner graces,—your roguish soul dancing here at liberty while my dear lord dangles." (p. 405) He, through the aid of magic, shows the rogue both the evil and delights of his life. After having done so, he leaps back onto the breast of the rogue. As the rogue writhes in pain, seemingly absorbing the fantastical creature back into his body, the rope snaps and the long-suspended rogue falls to the floor. The enchantment has disappeared.

19. Unsigned review of "The Secret Rose" by W. B. Yeats, *The Chap-Book*, vol. VIII, no. 7 (February 15, 1898), p. 290.

20. "Notes," *The Chap-Book,* vol. IV, no. 1 (November 15, 1895), p. 31.

21. Gouveneur Morris, "A Chapter from Alice in Wonderland Lately Recovered," *The Chap-Book,* vol. IX, no. 4 (July 1, 1898), pp. 113–15.

22. "Notes," *The Chap-Book,* vol. II, no. 5 (January 15, 1895), pp. 231–32.

23. Ella Wheeler Wilcox, "Illusion," *The Chap-Book,* vol. V, no. 2 (June 1, 1896), p. 49.

24. See, for instance, J. Robert Barth's recent study, *The Symbolic Imagination: Coleridge and the Romantic Tradition* (Princeton: Princeton University Press, 1977), particularly re: Coleridge, pp. 3–4; and Carlyle, p. 117. A. G. Lehman in *The Symbolist Aesthetic in France, 1885–1895 (Oxford: Basil Blackwell, 1950), p. 258* also discusses Carlyle's definition of symbolism in *Sartor Resartus*. Joseph Chiari, *Symbolisme from Poe to Mallarmé: The Growth of a Myth* (London: Rockliff, 1956), p. 46 also traces the symbolists' indebtedness to the romantic law of "correspondances" in nature.

25. See Louise Imogen Guiney's handwritten manuscript for these notes in a folder labeled "Guiney: Unidentified Notes, vol. II no. 8" # 892, Box D–G, Stone & Kimball Collection, The Newberry Library.

26. "Notes," *The Chap-Book*, vol. I, no. 6 (August 1, 1894), pp. 144–45.

27. Bliss Carman, "Longfellow Through Modern Eyes," *The Chap-Book*, vol. VIII, no. 10 (April 1, 1898), p. 400.

28. Bliss Carman, "Contemporaries—IV. Louise Imogen Guiney," *The Chap-Book*, vol. II, no. 1 (November 15, 1894), pp. 33, 34.

29. Louise Imogen Guiney to Rev. W. H. Van Allen, 11 September 1896 as quoted in Louise Imogen Guiney, *Letters* (New York: Harper & Bros., 1926), p. 134.

30. Richard Hovey, *The Plays of Maurice Maeterlinck* (Chicago: Stone & Kimball, 1894), p. 3.

31. Richard Hovey, *The Plays of Maurice Maeterlinck*, pp. 4–5.

32. Ibid., p. 9.

33. Ibid., pp. 5–7.

34. Ibid., p. 11.

35. Bliss Carman, "Contemporaries—V. Mr. Charles G. D. Roberts," *The Chap-Book*, vol. II, no. 4 (January 1, 1895), p. 166.

36. Charles G. D. Roberts, "Origins," *The Chap-Book*, vol. II, no. 4 (January 1, 1895), pp. 172–73.

37. L. Hereward, "Rondel," *The Chap-Book*, vol. II, no. 2 (December 1, 1894), p. 55.

38. See Chapter 3: The Romantic Vision: A Familiar Perspective," pp. 56–58.

39. Arthur Symons, *The Symbolist Movement* (London: William Heineman, 1899), p. 10.

40. Arthur Symons, *The Symbolist Movement*, p. 9.

41. James G. Nelson, *The Early Nineties: A View from the Bodley Head* (Cambridge: Harvard University Press, 1971), pp. 215–16.

42. William Watson, "The Captive's Dream," *The Chap-Book*, vol. VII, no. 5 (July 15, 1897), p. 159.

43. William Watson, "The Captive's Dream," p. 159.

44. William Carman Roberts, "To Lilith," *The Chap-Book*, vol. VII, no. 9 (September 15, 1897), p. 322.

45. Edmund Wilson, *Axel's Castle: A Study in the Imaginative Literature of 1870–1930* (New York: Charles Scribner's Sons, 1931), see particularly pp. 259–65.

46. "Notes," *The Chap-Book,* vol. I, no. 12 (November 1, 1894), p. 358.

47. Edmund Wilson, *Axel's Castle,* p. 283.

48. Stéphane Mallarmé, "Arthur Rimbaud," *The Chap-Book,* vol. V, no. 1 (May 15, 1896), p. 12.

49. Ibid., p. 15.

50. Ibid., p. 11.

51. Jack Patnode, "English and American Literary Relations in the 1890's," (Unpublished dissertation: University of Minnesota, 1968), p. 198.

52. Stéphane Mallarmé, "Arthur Rimbaud," p. 11.

53. Percival Pollard, "The Dream of an Agreement," *The Chap-Book,* vol. I, no. 7 (August 15, 1894), pp. 168, 170.

54. Unsigned review, "A Justification of Faith," *The Chap-Book,* vol. IX, no. 1 (May 15, 1898), p. 29.

55. Ibid., p. 29.

56. Ibid.

Chapter 6

1. See a lengthy discussion of the positions of intellectual "insurgents" and "custodians" of nineteenth-century culture in Henry May, *The End of American Innocence: A Study of the First Years of Our Own Time 1913–1917* (New York: Alfred A. Knopf, 1959).

2. Closing statement of *The Chap-Book,* vol. IX, no. 5 (July 15, 1898), n.p.

3. See a discussion of the scholarship regarding the 1890s and *The Chap-Book,* above in "Chapter 1: Misconceptions of a Mind and a Magazine," particularly pp. 1–8.

4. In a recent analysis of the current status of American intellectual history, Paul Conkin has raised serious questions regarding the kind of sweeping generalizations that have led to intellectual categorizations of this sort. Speaking of the 1950s, he confessed: "We indulged sweeping and loosely unifying labels, such as enlightenment, romanticism, naturalism, and irrationalism, or labels I now just as carefully repudiate." [Paul K. Conkin, "Intellectual History: Past, Present, and Future," *The Future of History,* ed. Charles F. Delzell (Nashville: Vanderbilt University Press, 1977), p. 122.] He applauds the trend toward more specialized studies that explode the myths of earlier generalizations as evidence of intellectual history's intellectual maturity. It may be important to concede, however, that such maturity might not have been gained without those initial generalizations to establish a framework for more specialized study. See also Paul K. Conkin, "Afterword," *New Directions in American Intellectual History,* eds. John Higham & Paul K. Conkin (Baltimore: The Johns Hopkins University Press, 1979).

5. See above, "Chapter 2: A Harvard Education, 1890–1894," pp. 15-17. See also Howard Mumford Jones, *The Age of Energy: Varieties of American Experience 1865–1915* (New

York: The Viking Press, 1970), pp. 223–34, commenting on the profession of publishing as part of "The Genteel Tradition" and mentioning *The Chap-Book* by name.

6. Official record of Herbert Stuart Stone, Class of 1894, Harvard University. Copy available in The Stone & Kimball Collection, The Newberry Library.

7. Interpretations following this line of thought can be traced back to Vernon Parrington's *Main Currents in American Thought: The Beginnings of Critical Realism in America* (New York: Harcourt, Brace & World, Inc., 1930, 1958) and continued in important studies by some of intellectual history's most respected scholars. Parrington wrote: "Between 1870 and 1900 the broad movement of thought passed through two sharply differentiating and contradictory phases: The extension of the philosophy of the Enlightenment, and the final rejection of the Enlightenment in consequence of a more rigid application of the law of causality in the light of a mechanistic universe." The first phase was one of optimism based on ideas of human perfectability, and a belief in science. The second phase began in the 1890s: "And then in the nineties the clouds drew over the brilliant Victorian skies. With the substitution of physics for biology came a more somber mood that was to put away the genial romanticism of Victorian evolution, substitute a mechanistic conception for the earlier teleological progress, and reshape its philosophy in harmony with a deterministic pessimism that denied purpose or plan in the changing universe of matter." (pp. 190–91)

   Merle Curti in his *The Growth of American Thought* (New York: Harper & Row, 1943, 1951) likewise picked up the theme of science: "The most striking fact in the intellectual history of the last third of the nineteenth century was the blow to the historic doctrine of supernaturalism by new developments in the biological and physical sciences." (p. 531) Science and its philosophic allies are always pictured as the combatants in the arena in which intellectual growth is taking place. And always they are fighting off the reactionary restraints of intellectually stagnant conservatives who maintain beliefs in nonmaterial or nonrational phenomena. Dominating intellectual history, this interpretive theme can be seen in the scholarship noted earlier (Chapter 1) regarding the 1890s and America's literary choices.

   Not until Howard Mumford Jones's *The Age of Energy* (1971) was there any serious attempt made to see these "genteel" idealistic intellectuals in a more positive light. This critical myopia, in Jones's estimate, was the result of a historical vision which, for instance, saw "the history of the arts from 1865 to 1915 principally as a battle between an emergent and admirable modernity and a senescent and deplorable romanticism." (p. 242)

8. It is disheartening to note, in light of Paul Conkin's assertion that specialized studies (the products of carefully defined methodological inquiry and in-depth investigation) mark a new era of maturity for intellectual history, that a 1971 study of late nineteenth-century religious beliefs could continue to propagate old myths of the period's "spiritual crisis" by reverting to impressionistic methods sloppier than those about which Conkin complained. Paul A. Carter's *The Spiritual Crisis of the Gilded Age* (DeKalb: Northern Illinois University Press, 1971) claims as its purpose the banishment of stereotypes through revelation of the complexities of religious thought. Unfortunately, his complexities become the mere assemblage of contradictory expressions of thought, taken largely without reference to their contexts, which mainly substantiate the old stereotype that there was indeed a spiritual crisis. See also: D. H. Meyer, "American Intellectuals and the Victorian Crisis of Faith," *American Quarterly*, vol. XXVII, no. 5 (December 1975), pp. 586–603.

9. William James, *The Varieties of Religious Experience: A Study in Human Nature*. The subtitle continues: "Being the Gifford Lectures on Natural Religion Delivered at Edinburgh in 1901–1902." Available in paperback (New York: The New American Library, 1958). See particularly Lecture III: "The Reality of the Unseen."

10. Perhaps one of the most interesting examples of a similar aesthetic reverence for the efficacy of spiritual communion in modern society came from the pen of George Bernard Shaw. In the January 1896 issue of England's "decadent" literary journal *The Savoy,* successor in notoriety to *The Yellow Book,* Shaw published an essay entitled "On Going to Church" in which he explained how art made him a "church-goer" after twenty years of professed atheism. Recalling the "genteel suburban Irish Protestant church" in which as a young boy he was forced to endure interminable hours of what never was for him worship, Shaw concluded: "I am sure, from other early experiences of mine, that if I had been turned loose in a real church, and allowed to wander and stare about, or hear noble music there instead of that most accursed Te Deum of Jackson's and a senseless droning of the Old Hundredth, I should never have seized the opportunity of a great evangelical revival, which occurred when I was still in my teens, to begin my literary career with a letter to the Press which was duly printed), announcing with inflexible materialistic logic, and to the extreme horror of my respectable connections, that I was an atheist." A "real church" was a work of real art, a place where services "were decently and intelligently conducted by genuine mystics to whom the Mass was no mere rite or miracle, but a real communion." Unfortunately in Shaw's estimate, there were too many priests in too many churches disturbing the worship of the truly religious. If Shaw in his adolescence had used materialistic logic to disclaim the existence of God, it had come as a result of religion's attempt to make him believe in the materialisation of miracles and the intellectual truth of doctrines. Both materialisations stood in the way of genuine spiritual communion, and he recommended leaving them outside the church door. See particularly pp. 25–28.

11. Louis Sullivan, "Emotional Architecture as Compared with Intellectual: A Study in Subjective and Objective," *Kindergarten Chats and Other Writings* (New York: George Wittenborn, Inc., 1947, 1968), p. 194. On Sullivan, see also: Sherman Paul, *Louis Sullivan: An Architect in American Thought* (Englewood Cliffs, N.J.: Prentice-Hall, Inc., 1962) and his analysis of Sullivan's transformation of transcendental idealism into idealistic pragmatism.

12. Louis Sullivan, "Emotional Architecture as Compared with Intellectual," p. 194.

13. Ibid., pp. 194, 195.

14. Ibid., p. 194.

15. Ibid.

16. Ibid., pp. 194–95.

17. See, for instance, Ann Devoore, "Ballade of the Fields," *The Chap-Book,* vol. V, no. 11 (October 15, 1896), p. 488; or Louise Imogen Guiney, "Monochrome," *The Chap-Book,* vol. V, no. 8 (September 1, 1896), p. 343.

18. See the discussion of Carman above (Chapter 3, p. 41) quoting *The Kinship of Nature,* pp. 84–88.

19. A case that illustrates both points is Charles G. D. Roberts's verses in the very first *Chap-Book*. Recall from the discussion of the poem, above Chapter 3 pp. 42–43, that Roberts is unequivocal in detailing the spirit as the motive force behind all physical

reality, and equally unequivocal in forecasting the destruction of this physical reality. But he waits until the last two lines of the poem to correct the impression that all he is talking about is the impersonal presence of mind within matter. Only in the last two lines does the most attentive reader realize that the subject of the entire poem has been the poet's imagination acting as a synthesizing agent. Artistic perception, effecting the fusion of dust and dreams, creates a new reality that is more than mere matter and will outlast it. The subtlety of Roberts's synthesis suggests the tentativeness of most of the efforts of *The Chap-Book*'s romantics to compromise their idealism with a meaningful dose of reality. Recall Gilbert Parker's short story, "Tales of the Voshti Hills—I: The Golden Pipes," discussed above at the end of Chapter 3, pp. 56–58, as another example.

20. Hamlin Garland, *Crumbling Idols* (Chicago and Cambridge: Stone & Kimball, 1894), p. 22. See Chapter 4: "Facts and Fancies—The Fusion of Realistic Literature," p. 70.

21. Charles Feidelson, Jr., *Symbolism and American Literature* (Chicago: The University of Chicago Press, 1953, 1970), pp. 77–118; see particularly pp. 84–90.

22. F. O. Matthiessen, *American Renaissance: Art and Expression in the Age of Emerson and Whitman* (London: Oxford University Press, 1941, 1968): See particularly "Chapter VII: Allegory and Symbolism," pp. 242–315; and Chapter VIII, Section 3, "From Hawthorne to James to Eliot," pp. 351–68.

23. For Eliot's early background, see: F. O. Matthiessen, *The Achievement of T. S. Eliot: An Essay on the Nature of Poetry* (London: Oxford University Press, 1958, 1976), particularly his intellectual debts as laid out in "Tradition and the Individual Talent," pp. 3–33; Russell Kirk, *Eliot and His Age: T. S. Eliot's Moral Imagination in the Twentieth Century* (New York: Random House, 1971), pp. 22–50; and Stephen Spender, *Eliot* (Glasgow: William Collins Sons & Co., Ltd., 1975), pp. 22–35.

24. Stone complained in his correspondence with his family during the spring of 1898 that the war would have a depressing effect on his publishing efforts, and disliked the attention *The Chap-Book* paid to military and political affairs in an attempt to give the readership what they wanted. See Herbert [Stuart Stone] to Ned [Melville Stone, Jr.], 16 April 1898, 29 April 1898, 28 May 1898, Personal Correspondence, Book IV, Stone & Kimball Collection, The Newberry Library.
    Herbert Stone went down with the Lusitania, May 7, 1915.

25. See Matthiessen, *The Achievement of T. S. Eliot;* a sampling of Eliot criticism in Hugh Kenner, *T. S. Eliot: A Collection of Critical Essays* (Englewood Cliffs, N.J.: Prentice-Hall, Inc., 1962); and John D. Margolis, *T. S. Eliot's Intellectual Development 1922–1939* (Chicago: The University of Chicago Press, 1922).

26. Irving Babbitt, "What is Humanism?" *Literature and the American College* (Boston & New York: Houghton Mifflin Co., 1908), pp. 28, 29. On New Humanism see also Norman Foerster, ed., *Humanism and America: Essays on the Outlook of Modern Civilization* (New York: Farrar and Rinehart, Inc., 1930). For critiques of New Humanism see C. Hartley Grattan, *The Critique of Humanism* (New York: Bower and Warren, Inc., 1930.

27. See above, Chapter 1, for a more detailed account of *The Chap-Book*'s failure as a commercial venture, and its critical reception at the time of its publication and in subsequent scholarship.

Bibliography

I. Manuscript Collections

Cercle Français. Clippings, etc., 1888–1897. Cambridge, Massachusetts: Harvard University Archives.

Harvard Crimson. Clippings, etc., 1873–1903. Cambridge, Massachusetts: Harvard University Archives.

Harvard Crimson Minutes, The. Vol. II (1888–1892) & vol. III (1892-). Cambridge, Massachusetts: Harvard University Archives.

Harvard Monthly. Clippings, Notices, etc. Cambridge, Massachusetts: Harvard University Archives.

Howard, William Guild. Lecture Notes, Norton's Fine Arts 4, 1891–1892. Cambridge, Massachusetts: Harvard University Archives.

Kimball, H. I., Biographical File. Cambridge, Massachusetts: Harvard University Archives.

Kimball, Hannibal Ingalls. Class of 1894; Secretary's Records. Cambridge, Massachusetts: Harvard University Archives.

Noyes, George R. Fine Arts 3 Lecture Notes; 1892–93. Cambridge, Massachusetts: Harvard University Archives.

Nutter, Charles R. English 7 Notes, 1892–93. Cambridge, Massachusetts: Harvard University Archives.

_____. English 9 Notes & Papers, 1891–92. Cambridge, Massachusetts: Harvard University Archives.

Rhodes, Harrison Garfield. Biographical File. Cambridge, Massachusetts: Harvard University Archives.

Stone, Herbert S. Biographical File. Cambridge, Massachusetts: Harvard University Archives.

Stone, Herbert Stuart. Class of 1894; Secretary's Records. Cambridge, Massachusetts: Harvard University Archives.

Stone & Kimball Collection, The. Chicago, Illinois: The Newberry Library.

Young Men's Christian Association of Harvard. Membership Register, 1886–1902. Cambridge, Massachusetts: Harvard University Archives.

II. Journals

The Chap-Book. Vol. I, no. 1 (May 15, 1894)–vol. IX, no. 4 (July 1, 1898). Chicago: Stone & Kimball; Herbert S. Stone & Co..

The Daily Crimson. Vol. XVII & vol. XVIII (1890). Cambridge, Massachusetts: Harvard University.

The Harvard Monthly. Vol. XI (1890)–vol. XVIII (1894). Cambridge, Massachusetts: Harvard University.

The Harvard University Catalogue. (1890–1891)–(1893–1894). Cambridge, Massachusetts: Harvard University.

The Lark. Vol. I, no. 1 (May 1, 1895)–Book II, no. 25 (May 1, 1897). San Francisco: William Doxey.

III. Articles

Babbitt, Irving. "What is Humanism?" *Literature and the American College.* Boston & New York: Houghton Mifflin Co., 1908.

Calkins, Earnest. "Chronicle on the Chap-book." *The Colophon.* Part Ten. New York: The Colophon Ltd., 1932.

Fuller, Henry Blake. "The Upward Movement in Chicago." *The Atlantic Monthly.* LXXX (1897).

McArthur, Peter. "On Having Known a Poet." *The Atlantic Monthly* XCVII (1906).

Norton, Charles Eliot. "Harvard University in 1890." *Four American Universities.* New York: Harper & Brothers, 1895.

Shaw, George Bernard. "On Going to Church." *The Savoy* I (1896).

Sullivan, Louis. "Emotional Architecture as Compared with Intellectual: A Study in Subjective and Objective." *Kindergarten Chats and Other Writings.* New York: George Wittenborn, Inc., 1968.

IV. Books

Adams, Henry. *The Education of Henry Adams.* New York: The Modern Library, 1931.

Carman, Bliss. *The Kinship of Nature.* Boston: L. C. Page & Co., 1903.

Cavanagh, Fr. Pius. *Gleanings for Saints and Sinner about St. Mary Magdalen.* London: The Catholic Truth Society, 1888.

Cram, Ralph Adams. *My Life in Architecture.* Boston: Little, Brown & Co., 1936. Reprint. New York: Kraus Reprint Co., 1969.

Flandrau, Charles Macomb. *Harvard Episodes.* Boston: Copeland and Day, 1897.

Garland, Hamlin. *Crumbling Idols.* Chicago and Cambridge: Stone & Kimball, 1894.

————. *Roadside Meetings.* New York: The Macmillan Co., 1930.

Gates, Lewis. *Three Studies in Literature.* New York: The Macmillan Co., 1899.

Guiney, Louise Imogen. *Letters.* New York: Harper & Brothers, 1926.

The Harvard Crimson, 1873–1906 Cambridge, Mass.: The Harvard Crimson, 1906.

Hovey, Richard. *The Plays of Maurice Maeterlinck.* Chicago: Stone & Kimball, 1894.

James, Henry. *What Maisie Knew.* New York: Charles Scribner's Sons, 1908.

James, William. *The Varieties of Religious Experience: A Study in Human Nature.* New York: The New American Library, 1958.

Mason, Daniel Gregory, ed. *Some Letters of William Vaughn Moody.* Boston & New York: Houghton Mifflin Co., 1913.

Matthiessen, F. O. and Murdick, Kenneth B., eds. *The Notebooks of Henry James.* New York: Oxford University Press, 1947.

Nordau, Max. *Degeneration.* New York: D. Appleton & Co., 1895.

Pollard, Percival. *Their Day in Court.* London: Johnson Reprint Corp., 1969.

Preston, Rev. Thomas S. *The Life of St. Mary Magdalene.* New York: P. O'Shea, 1861.

Royce, Josiah. *Fugitive Essays.* Cambridge: Harvard University Press, 1920.

_____ . *The Spirit of Modern Philosophy*. Boston & New York: Houghton Mifflin & Co., 1892.

Saltus, Edgar. *Mary Magdalene*. New York: Brentano's, 1925.

Santayana, George. *Sonnets and Other Verses*. Cambridge & Chicago: Stone & Kimball, 1894.

Stone, Melville E. *Fifty Years a Journalist*. New York: Doubleday, Page & Co., 1921.

Symons, Arthur. *The Symbolist Movement in Literature*. London: William Heineman, 1899.

V. Sources of Background Information

Balakian, Anna. *The Symbolist Movement: A Critical Appraisal*. New York: Random House, 1967.

Barth, J. Robert. *The Symbolic Imagination: Coleridge and the Romantic Tradition*. Princeton: Princeton University Press, 1977.

Beer, Thomas. *The Mauve Decade: American Life at the End of the Nineteenth Century*. New York: Alfred A. Knopf, 1926.

Bornstein, George, ed. *Romantic and Modern: Revaluations of Literary Tradition*. Pittsburgh: University of Pittsburgh Press, 1977.

Cappon, James. *Bliss Carman: And the Literary Currents and Influences of his Times*. New York & Montreal: Louis Carrier & Alan Isles, Inc., 1930.

Carter, A. E. *Paul Verlaine*. New York: Twayne Publishers, Inc., 1971.

Carter, Paul A. *The Spiritual Crisis of the Gilded Age*. DeKalb: Northern Illinois University Press, 1971.

Chiari, Joseph. *Symbolisme from Poe to Mallarmé*. London: Rockliff, 1956.

Commager, Henry Steele. *The American Mind: An Interpretation of American Thought and Character Since the 1880s*. New Haven: Yale University Press, 1950.

Conkin, Paul and Higham, John, eds. *New Directions in American Intellectual History*. Baltimore: The Johns Hopkins University Press, 1979.

Cornell, Kenneth. *The Symbolist Movement*. New Haven: Yale University Press, 1951.

Cunliffe, Marcus, ed. *American Literature Since 1900*. London: Barrie & Jenkins, 1975.

Curti, Merle. *The Growth of American Thought*. New York: Harper & Row, 1951.

Delzell, Charles F., ed. *The Future of History*. Nashville: Vanderbilt University Press, 1977.

Duffey, Bernard. *The Chicago Renaissance in American Letters: A Critical History*. East Lansing: Michigan State College Press, 1954.

Duncan, Hugh Dalziel. *Culture and Democracy: The Struggle for Form in Society and Architecture in the Middle West during the Life and Times of Louis H. Sullivan*. Totowa, N.J.: The Bedminster Press, 1965.

_____ . *The Rise of Chicago as a Literary Center from 1885 to 1920: A Sociological Essay in American Culture*. Totowa, N.J.: The Bedminster Press, 1964.

Edel, Leon. *Henry James: The Treacherous Years 1895–1901*. Philadelphia, New York: J. B. Lippincott Co., 1969.

Feidelson, Charles Jr. *Symbolism and American Literature*. Chicago: The University of Chicago Press, 1970.

Foerster, Norman, ed. *Humanism and America: Essays on the Outlook of Modern Civilization*. New York: Farrar and Rinehart, Inc., 1930.

Gaunt, William. *The Aesthetic Adventure*. New York: Schocken Books, 1967.

Grattan, C. Hartley. *The Critique of Humanism*. New York: Bower and Warren, Inc., 1930.

Hoffman, Frederick J., et al. *The Little Magazine*. Princeton: Princeton University Press, 1946.

Jackson, Holbrooke. *The Eighteen Nineties: A Review of Art and Ideas at the Close of the Nineteenth Century*. New York: Alfred A. Knopf, 1922.

James, Henry. *Charles W. Eliot: President of Harvard University 1868–1909.* Vol. II. Boston & New York: Houghton Mifflin Co., 1930.

Jones, Howard Mumford. *The Age of Energy: Varieties of American Experience 1865–1915.* New York: The Viking Press, 1970.

Joost, Nicholas. *The Dial, 1912–1920: Years of Transition.* Barre, Mass.: Barre Publishers, 1967.

Kenner, Hugh. *T. S. Eliot: A Collection of Critical Essays.* Englewood Cliffs, Prentice-Hall, Inc., 1962.

Kirk, Russell. *Eliot and His Age: T. S. Eliot's Moral Imagination in the Twentieth Century.* New York: Random House, 1971.

Knight, Grant C. *The Critical Period in American Literature.* Chapel Hill: University of North Carolina Press, 1951.

Kramer, Dale. *Chicago Renaissance: The Literary Life in the Midwest 1900–1930.* New York: Appleton-Century, 1966.

Kramer, Sidney. *A History of Stone & Kimball and Herbert S. Stone & Co., 1893–1905.* Chicago: Norman W. Forgue, 1940.

Lawrence, D. H. *Studies in Classic American Literature.* New York: The Viking Press, 1971.

LeGallienne, Richard. *The Romantic '90s.* New York: Doubleday, Page & Co., 1926.

Lehmann, A. G. *The Symbolist Aesthetic in France, 1885–1895.* Oxford: Basil Blackwell, 1950.

Margolis, John D. *T. S. Eliot's Intellectual Development 1922–1939.* Chicago: The University of Chicago Press, 1922.

Martin, Jay. *Harvests of Change: American Literature 1865–1914.* Englewood Cliffs: Prentice-Hall, Inc., 1967.

Matthiessen, F. O. *The Achievement of T. S. Eliot: An Essay on the Nature of Poetry.* London: Oxford University Press, 1976.

————. *American Renaissance: Art and Expression in the Age of Emerson and Whitman.* London: Oxford University Press, 1968.

May, Henry. *The End of American Innocence: A Study of the First Years of Our Own Time 1913–1917.* New York: Alfred A. Knopf, 1959.

Meyer, D. H. "American Intellectuals and the Victorian Crisis of Faith." *American Quarterly* XXVII (1975).

Mix, Katherine. *A Study in Yellow.* Lawrence: University of Kansas Press, 1960.

Morison, Samuel Eliot. *The Development of Harvard University 1869–1929.* Cambridge: Harvard University Press, 1930.

Mott, Frank L. *A History of American Magazines, 1885–1905.* Vol. IV. Cambridge: Harvard University Press, 1957.

Nelson, James G. *The Early Nineties: A View from the Bodley Head.* Cambridge: Harvard University Press, 1971.

Ostrander, Gilman. *American Civilization in the First Machine Age 1890–1940.* New York: Harper & Row, 1970.

Parrington, Vernon L. *The Beginnings of Critical Realism in America: 1860–1920.* New York: Harcourt, Brace & World, 1958.

Parry, Albert. *Garrets and Pretenders: A History of Bohemianism in America.* New York: Covici-Friede Publishers, 1933.

Patnode, Jack. "English and American Literary Relations in the 1890s." Doctoral dissertation, University of Minnesota, 1968.

Pattee, Fred Lewis. *The New American Literature, 1890–1930.* New York & London: The Century Co., 1930.

Paul, Sherman. *Louis Sullivan: An Architect in American Thought.* Englewood Cliffs: Prentice-Hall, Inc., 1962.

Persons, Stow. *American Minds: A History of Ideas.* New York: Holt, Rinehart and Winston, 1958.

Piper, H. W. *The Active Universe: Pantheism and the Concept of Imagination in the English Romantic Poets.* London: The Athlone Press, 1962.

Schenk, H. G. *The Mind of the European Romantics: An Essay in Cultural History.* London: Constable, 1966.

Spencer, Robin. *The Aesthetic Movement: Theory and Practice.* New York: E. P. Dutton & Co., 1972.

Spender, Stephen. *Eliot.* Glasgow: William Collins Sons & Co., Ltd., 1975.

Sprague, Claire, ed. *Van Wyck Brooks: The Early Years.* New York: Harper & Row, 1968.

Tassin, Algernon. *The Magazine in America.* New York: Dodd, Mead and Co., 1916.

Turner, Susan J. *A History of the Freeman: Literary Landmark of the Early Twenties.* New York & London: Columbia University Press, 1963.

Urban, Wilbur. *Language and Reality.* New York: Macmillan, 1939.

Vanderbilt, Kermit. *Charles Eliot Norton: Apostle of Culture in a Democracy.* Cambridge: The Belknap Press, 1959.

Wasserstrom, William. *The Time of the Dial.* Syracuse: Syracuse University Press, 1963.

Weiss, John, ed. *The Origins of Modern Consciousness.* Detroit: Wayne State University Press, 1965.

Whiting, Lilian. *Louise Chandler Moulton: Poet and Friend.* Boston: Little, Brown & Co., 1910.

Wilson, Douglas L., ed. *The Genteel Tradition.* Cambridge, Mass.: Harvard University Press, 1967.

Wilson, Edmund. *Axel's Castle: A Study in the Imaginative Literature of 1870–1930.* New York: Charles Scribner's Sons, 1931.

Ziff, Larzer. *The American 1890s.* New York: Viking Press, 1966.

Index